GOURMET TRAILS

TRAILS

AUSTRALIA & NEW ZEALAND

INTRODUCTION

Our senses play an important role when we travel and taste is the sense that can elevate our travel experience to another level. It has the power to evoke nostalgic travel memories decades after the moment is gone - whether it's sipping on a dry white wine as the sun dips into the sea, dining on a bold invention at the hottest restaurant, inhaling the aroma of freshly roasted single-origin coffee beans or slurping back a juicy oyster plucked from the sea before your eyes.

This book takes you on a tour of 40 of Australia and New Zealand's best epicurean regions, with itineraries featuring experiences from cocktail bars tucked down laneways in cosmopolitan cities to generations-old wineries in rural beauty. This book showcases why Australia and New Zealand are considered such heavyweights on the global gourmet scene. Surrounded by water, fresh seafood is at the fore; nutrient-rich soil paves the way for vibrant produce; creative chefs continue to reinvent what Australian and NZ cuisine is, and indigenous ingredients are taking centre stage on plates.

With an abundance of hip restaurants, food markets, olive groves, bushtucker tours, craft-beer breweries and vineyards, Australia and New Zealand is a trans-Tasman tapestry of gourmet spots just waiting to give your tastebuds a trip.

CONTENTS

NEW ZEALAND

WESTERN AUSTRALIA

↓

NORTH ISLAND

↓

SOUTH ISLAND

↓

PLEASE NOTE*

At the time of going to print, a few venues were being affected by the 2020 coronavirus situation. Where there might be doubt over a venue's continued trading we have added an asterisk to its name. Always check whether such a business is open before visiting it.

AUSTRALIA & NEW ZEALAND

N

Timor
Sea

07

DARWIN

Gulf of
Carpentaria

9

Coral
Sea

NORTHERN
TERRITORY

QUEENSLAND

Shark
Bay

WESTERN
AUSTRALIA

11

10   04

BRISBANE

08   02

SOUTH
AUSTRALIA

06

29

NEW SOUTH
WALES

03

PERTH
Geographe
Bay

12   13

22

01

SYDNEY

25

05

28

ADELAIDE

20

24

CANBERRA   ACT

14

23

27

Great
Australian
Bight

MELBOURNE

VICTORIA

INDIAN
OCEAN

21

26

Tasman
Sea

17   15

19

TASMANIA

HOBART

18   16

NORTHLAND **(33)**

WHANGAREI

AUCKLAND **(35)**

AUCKLAND **(32)**

HAMILTON **TAURANGA**
WAIKATO BAY OF
PLENTY

NORTH GISBORNE
ISLAND **GISBORNE**

**NEW
PLYMOUTH** **(31)** HAWKE'S
TARANAKI BAY

Tasman **WANGANUI** **HASTINGS**
Sea
MANAWATU-
WANGANUI

TASMAN **(30)** **(34)**
NELSON **(38)**
(40) WELLINGTON

MARLBOROUGH

GREYMOUTH **(39)**
WEST
COAST **(37)**

SOUTH CANTERBURY **CHRISTCHURCH**
ISLAND

SOUTH
PACIFIC
OCEAN

OTAGO

(36)
SOUTHLAND **DUNEDIN**

INVERCARGILL

AUSTRALIA

GET THERE
Canberra's airport is a
close taxi ride into the
city with train and bus
connections to Sydney.

Ø1

CANBERRA

WATSON
DOWNER
LYNEHAM
DICKSON
O'CONNOR
AINSLIE
Canberra
Nature
Park
Black
Mountain
Nature
Reserve
TURNER **06** BRADDON
03 **04**
CIVIC
ACTON **07** REID
CAMPBELL
Lake Burley Griffin
Lake Burley Griffin
Canberra
Airport
YARRALUMLA
BARTON
FORREST **05** KINGSTON
GRIFFITH
FYSHWICK

01 **02**

[ACT]

A SLICE OF AUSTRALIA'S CAPITAL

*Australia's capital swims in coffee culture
and winning wineries, not to mention
the restaurant scene that caters to the
nation's biggest pork-barrellers.*

For years Canberra has been a mysterious secret on the Australian dining scene – a hatted eatery here, a quirky dish there (don't even mention the faddish freakshake from 2015 – indulgent milkshakes overloaded with dessert sauces, cakes, doughnuts etc) – but now the city is stepping out of the shadows to challenge Australia's best. All the ingredients for great cuisine are in and around this micro city: a cosmopolitan embassy culture, a wealth of local produce sourced from around the region and some well-paid, well-fed diners with adventurous palates.

The city's baristas have been getting gongs for their locally roasted coffee for the last decade, although this owes much to an outdoor cafe culture that stretches back to Garema Place's first coffee shops in the 1960s. Then there are the wildcard wineries, many founded by former CSIRO soil scientists who

knew which grapes would thrive in the region and have produced tipples to suit everyone's taste. Many restaurants pride themselves on sourcing locally so you'll find truffles, local meats and seafood from the South Coast feature prominently on menus.

A few years back, Braddon became the hot destination and even though some decry it as past its prime, you can still find a great dining scene in the suburb just north of Civic. The cultural and political precinct is just south of Lake Burley Griffin around suburbs like Parkes where you can explore (or avoid depending on your political disenchantment) Parliament House and other cultural spots. Cafes in government departments love a pun – Treasury has, for example, Coffers Cafe – and are serviceable but rarely worthy of a visit. Instead take this trail through the heart of Canberra: Braddon, Civic and the inner south if you're adventurous.

01 CAPITAL REGION FARMERS' MARKET

Want to know where the chefs are shopping? With over 100 stallholders this weekly market sources produce from across the region from Bredbo black garlic to fresh seafood from the South Coast. It's a great window into the area surrounding the Capital Territory without the hassle of a day trip. Stalls have to be local so you will spot up-and-coming wineries, apple orchards, honey from local hives and all kinds of seasonal fare. Stallholders are growers, farmers, makers and bakers themselves so you can get the inside word on seasonality, cooking advice and ethical growing. It makes for a buzzy breakfast venue with fresh bagels or pastries and local coffee.
Exhibition Park in Canberra (EPIC); 0400 852 227; www. capitalregionfarmersmarket.com. au; 7.30-11.30am Sat

02 MOUNT MAJURA VINEYARD

This rare winery within the ACT borders makes for an easy visit just behind Mount Majura yet a world away from the city. The open cellar door really lets you into the winery including self-guided tours to wander the vines, which is especially fascinating during harvest or pruning. Mount Majura pioneered tempranillo so the Spanish varietals are worth quaffing here, though they do crisp rieslings and solid reds. If you can spare half an hour the seated tasting takes you through the range and can be paired with antipasto including the kangaroo prosciutto and cheeses.
88 Lime Kiln Rd, Majura; 02-6262 3070; www.mountmajura.com.au; 10am-5pm daily

03 BENTSPOKE

Bending the rules of brewing has always been the way for head brewer Richard Watkins and co-owner Tracy Margrain at their microbrewery. Formerly of local favourite The Wig and Pen, Watkins has created 18 beers and ciders from hefty stouts to the drinkable IPA Crankshaft to kooky experiments like the gose that brews with mango and passionfruit.

© Courtesy of Mount Majura Vineyard; Lazy Su; Lazy Su

01 Balloons over Lake Burley Griffin in central Canberra

02 Cool-climate grapes at Mount Majura

03 Asian flavours at Lazy Su

04 Lazy Su's interior

'We are Canberra born and brewed and love to bend the rules of beer, always with Australia's best water fresh from the ACT.'

Felicity Wybrew, Bentspoke

Their tear-off cans are a local bottleshop staple but visiting the Braddon brewery is a treat for its bicycle-themed furnishings (yes that's a bike chain light fitting) and the changing brews on tap. Pub grub here is a cut above, including deep-fried cauliflower bites and hoki tacos.
38 Mort St, Braddon (entry via Elouera St); 02-6257 5220; www.bentspokebrewing.com.au; 11am-midnight

04 LAZY SU

Lazy Su restaurant draws together pan-Asian influences from its co-owners Jared Calnan, Ben Ilic, Andrew Duong and Shaoyi Kuek. They bring in a mix of influences from K-pop to hip hop that make for the Asian kitsch decor complementing the light menu that's perfect for a late night dinner that slides into a splash of Japanese whisky or Korean *makgeolli* (a milky alcoholic brew made from unrefined fermented rice). The menu takes on the same culture sampling like bao-gers that wrap a tasty slab of pork belly between a brioche bun with pickled cucumber and hoi sin. Bigger bites include the Su_shimi platter replete with cuts of Atlantic salmon, yellowfin tuna and hiramasa kingfish. Take a big group for the Miso Hungry banquet or the vegan option.
9 Lonsdale St, Braddon; 02-5105 3812; www.lazy-su.com.au; 5-11pm Mon, from noon Tue-Thu & Sun, to 1am Fri & Sat

they favour single origins from Papua New Guinea though you can find South American beans, too. Their artwork shows off the city's orange ACTION bus stops and you can lounge in the retro-styled upstairs area for hours before grabbing a takeaway bag.
7 Lonsdale St, Braddon; 02-6108 3661; www.lonsdalestreetroasters. com; 6.30am-4pm Mon-Fri, from 8am Sat & Sun

07 BAR ROCHFORD

With a slew of awards (Gourmet Traveller's Bar of the Year 2017 and 2018, plus a Good Food Guide hat) this classic Canberra wine bar (with food) shows off the capital's old-school architecture with the modernist touches of the Melbourne building brought to the fore in simple lines and some archive photography.

The wine list is a tour of some of Australia's best wineries with a few internationals and some key locals that lean towards the playful and biodynamic. Book ahead for dinner and you might be treated to Moonlight Flat oysters or mains such as the tender kangaroo pepped up with macadamia and blackberry. They play vinyl until late so tapas-style dishes will stretch your evening out perfectly.
65 London Circuit; 02-6230 6222; www.barrochford.com; 5pm-late Tue-Thu, 3pm-1am Fri, from 5pm Sat

05 MUSE

The East Hotel's restaurant, Muse, is a bookish hideaway that has a reputation for a Mod Oz menu. A popular brunch spot, their menu runs from a dukkah poached eggs with roasted heirloom tomatoes to a generous full English breakfast, including slabs of locally sourced bacon and black pudding. Guests can also book a group for their bottomless brunch that dips into the Australian winelist. Their very browsable bookshop hosts literary events throughout the year.
69 Canberra Ave, Kingston; 02-6178 0024; www.musecanberra. com.au; Mon-Fri 6:30am-4pm, Sat-Sun 7am-4pm

06 LONSDALE STREET ROASTERS (LSR)

LSR is a pioneer of Canberra's coffee roasting scene and a survivor from when Braddon was just car yards and outdoor activity shops. The suburb might be a touch over-styled these days, as apartment buildings dwarf this little shop on the southern end, but don't be fooled by modest appearances – this is the coffee that conquered Canberra.

Taste their original Smith and Evans – a smooth blend named for the owners – to get started and work your way up to their Johnny Cash with a dark potency that echoes the Man in Black himself. In a nod to our nearest neighbour,

WHERE TO STAY

EAST HOTEL

One of the capital's best boutique hotels, East excels at studios that include espresso machines and kitchenettes to satisfy DIY gourmands. Larger one- and two-bedroom suites are roomy for larger groups or families. From the modish lobby (grab free lollies for a snack) there is a choice of three restaurants, including Muse.
www.easthotel.com.au

LITTLE NATIONAL

Designed with Zen minimalism in mind, suites at this compact spot are ideal for a weekender and are well placed for exploring the inner south cultural precinct and around Parliament House.
www.littlenationalhotel.com.au

WHAT TO DO

NATIONAL GALLERY OF AUSTRALIA (NGA)

The NGA is a treasure trove of art including the Aboriginal Memorial, Dali's Lobster Telephone and a triptych of Francis

Bacon. The sculpture garden makes a good picnic spot.
www.nga.gov.au

NATIONAL PORTRAIT GALLERY (NPG)

Also in the cultural precinct of Parkes, the NPG is a playful gallery space that flaunts the nation's portraits including Howard Arkley's bright portrait of musician Nick Cave, and the distinctive

image of actor Deborah Mailman by Evert Ploeg.
www.portrait.gov.au

CELEBRATIONS

MULTICULTURAL FESTIVAL

Better known as the Multi Culti, this is Canberra's celebration of its many nationalities, cultures and, more importantly, their cuisines with stalls that take over most of Civic.

www.multicultural festival.com.au

CANBERRA DISTRICT WINE WEEK

Canberra's wineries extend into Murrumbateman so over 10 days (there are too many wines for just a week) you can explore the further afield wineries with tours and tastings during April's harvest.
www.canberrawines. com.au

GET THERE
The village of Bangalow roughly marks the centre of the Byron Bay hinterland. It's a half-hour drive north of Ballina–Byron Gateway Airport, and 45 minutes' drive south of Gold Coast Airport.

01

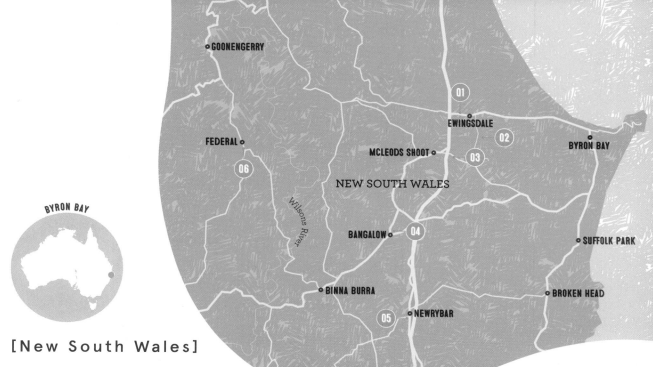

Map labels: GOONENGERRY, 01, EWINGSDALE, 02, BYRON BAY, FEDERAL, MCLEODS SHOOT, 03, 06, NEW SOUTH WALES, SUFFOLK PARK, BANGALOW, 04, Wilsons River, BINNA BURRA, BROKEN HEAD, 05, NEWRYBAR

BYRON BAY

[New South Wales]

A MEANDER AROUND BYRON BAY & THE HINTERLAND

Byron Bay is renowned for its surf beaches and buzzing cafe scene, but the rolling green hills that rise up behind the coast are home to even more foodie delights

Blessed with a temperate subtropical climate, fertile soil, and plentiful produce from land and sea, Byron was made for good eating. But while its traditional owners, the Arakwal people, have been feasting on its bounty for 20,000 years, it was only relatively recently that the culinary potential of this ancient meeting place, where other tribes of the Bundjalung Nation would travel to spear and trap fish during the mullet runs, began to attract serious outside investment and talent.

Sea-changing chefs and artisan producers, whose paddock-to-plate ambitions have outgrown their cramped city restaurants and rooftop beehives, are now flocking in, alongside visitors willing to put their money where their mouths are. But while Byron now attracts a much more varied crowd than the barefoot hippies that put it on the map in the early 1970s, its traditional green leanings largely dictate its culinary offerings, particularly in the Byron Bay hinterland, where much of the produce served in farm-style restaurants is organically grown or reared on-site, or at least ultra-locally. Vegetarians, vegans, and those with food intolerances are also well catered for.

Roughly encompassing the cluster of inland villages located up to an hour's drive west of Byron's town centre, the Byron Bay hinterland can easily be explored in a weekend, though most visitors will discover that there are enough foodie offerings to warrant a repeat visit. Better yet, many of the top stops are within 15 minutes' drive of town, making a taxi a worthwhile option for those keen to sample the region's renowned local libations while you're at it.

01 THREE BLUE DUCKS

Byron locals licked their lips when the chef collective behind Sydney's renowned Three Blue Ducks restaurant opened a Byron outpost in 2015. Set on a community farm just north of town known simply as The Farm, the rustic-style restaurant sprawls across a shady terrace, with pigs, cattle and horses roaming in the paddocks beyond (kids love the farm tours held four times weekly). Open for breakfast, lunch and dinner every day of the week, the Ducks' creative but accessible menu showcases produce from ethical local growers in dishes ranging from farmer's bruschetta, summer veggies, cashew cream, and herbs on toast for brekkie to heartier meals such as Brooklet Springs twice-cooked chicken with tomato, cucumber, corn, barley and chermoula. The family-friendly spot also has a dedicated kids' menu, and a playground for tots to tire themselves out on while parents sip on organic kombucha or perhaps a glass of local wine.

11 Ewingsdale Rd, Ewingsdale; 02-6684 7795; www.threeblueducks. com/byron; 7am-10pm daily

02 FIG TREE RESTAURANT

Just five minutes' drive south of The Farm, the Byron hinterland's stalwart fine diner has been a local favourite since Heather and Charly Devlin opened the farmhouse restaurant in 1981. Named for the giant fig tree on the grounds under which the couple were married (the venue remains a popular wedding destination), the restaurant now run by the couple's son Che is a degustation-only affair, with seven-course dinners featuring local, seasonal produce (much of it grown in the family's garden and orchard) in creative dishes such as Ballina octopus with sunflower and padron pepper to a flavour-bursting rosella, plum and passionfruit dessert. Currently being rebuilt after a devastating fire in 2019 – which cruelly engulfed the restaurant just months after a major renovation – the Fig Tree is expected to reopen in the second half of 2020.

4 Sunrise Ln, Ewingsdale; 02-6684 7273; www.figtreerestaurant.com.au

'The Brook family sources many of Brookie's Byron Dry Gin's native botanicals from the family's regenerated sub-tropical rainforest.'

Zoe Armstrong, Cape Byron Distillery

03 CAPE BYRON DISTILLERY

Not far from the Fig Tree, Cape Byron Distillery offers one of the most unique cellar door experiences in Australia. In the 30-odd years since purchasing the former rundown dairy farm that the distillery now sits on, the Brook family has painstakingly reforested the land with over 35,000 subtropical rainforest trees. Of the 25 botanicals in Brookie's Byron Dry Gin, 17 are sourced locally, many from the onsite rainforest. Held every Friday, Saturday and Sunday, tours take visitors into the rainforest to see, smell and touch the native rainforest botanicals used in the distillery's award-winning Brookie's Byron Dry Gin before heading into the distillery for tastings of its products, which also includes a delicious macadamia liqueur (Mac. By Brookie's). If you're lucky, you might even get a chance to sample the whisky its distillers recently put to barrel.
80 St Helena Rd, McLeods Shoot; 02-6684 7961; www. capebyrondistillery.com

04 WOODS

Sister-cafe to popular Byron hangout Folk, Woods is difficult to beat for an Insta-worthy brunch stop in Bangalow, the largest of the hinterland villages. Housed in a whitewashed weatherboard shack in a sunny arts precinct tucked behind the main drag, its all-day plant-based menu spans everything from organic buckwheat banana hotcakes

with housemade labne, fruit, raw Bundjalung honey, maple, mint and crushed nuts, to nourishing bowls packed with spiced biodynamic brown rice, quinoa, almonds, raisins, cumin-roasted pumpkin, hummus, kohlrabi, kale, sprout and apple slaw, tahini and house kraut. In keeping with its conscious vibe, Woods also brews a superb cup of coffee with beans from ethically minded Sydney roaster Single O, and doesn't charge extra for having it with your fave organic milk, from Barambah dairy to house coconut.
Arts Precinct, Station St, Bangalow; www.instagram.com/ woodsbangalow; 7.30am-2pm Sun-Fri, to 2.30pm Sat

05 HARVEST NEWRYBAR

Set in a gorgeous Queenslander-styled building with a generous deck shaded by a jacaranda tree, Harvest is the Byron hinterland's top destination restaurant. Here,

Head Chef Alastair Waddell works closely with forager and wild food researcher Peter Hardwick to create an ever-changing menu of contemporary Australian dishes featuring native ingredients even most Australians aren't familiar with. Diners are helpfully provided with a native ingredient booklet to help identify the unusual flavours. Next door, the Harvest Deli proffers tasty baked goods from Harvest's 116-year-old wood-fired oven, great coffee, and gourmet pantry supplies, including Hardwick's range of vinegars made from everything from foraged pandanus nuts to kelp. An on-site herb and vegetable garden, solar panels, green waste compost and grey water facilities also support the restaurant's sustainability ethos.
18-22 Old Pacific Hwy, Newrybar; 02-6687 2644; harvestnewrybar. com.au; noon-3pm Mon & Tue, noon-3pm & 6-10pm Wed-Fri, 8am-10pm Sat, 8am-3pm Sun

06 DOMA

If it wasn't for the cars parked along the main drag at weekends, you could blink and miss the village of Federal. The owners of those cars are at Doma. Run by chefs Takayuki Kuramoto and Takashi Yaguchi, the casual Japanese-fusion bistro serves up some of the finest sushi outside Tokyo; grab a box to go or snag a table in the garden and order the roll of the day – or a heartier meal such as the tempura prawn salad with homemade pesto – and be sure to keep one eye on the roaming chickens. Doma serves breakfast (go on, order the Japanese hash brown), lunch and dinner. With many Byronites making the one-hour drive here, expect queues. A few doors down, Moonshine Coffee Roasters brews a pick-me-up while you wait.
3-6 Albert St, Federal; 02-6688-4711 www.domaandqudocafe.com; 7.30am-2.30pm Mon-Fri, to 3pm Sat & Sun

WHERE TO STAY
BYRON VIEW FARM
Watch the sun rise over Cape Byron from the wraparound balcony of this gorgeous little cottage that sleeps just two. Within stumbling distance from Cape Byron Distillery, it's the perfect romantic escape nestled between Byron and Bangalow.
www.byronviewfarm. com.au

BANGALOW GUEST HOUSE
An elegant heritage property tucked off Bangalow's main street, just a short stroll from restaurants and shops, Bangalow Guest House offers a choice of four beautifully appointed rooms in the main house, and three sweet cottages designed in the same early 1900s style.
99 Byron St, Bangalow 02-6687 1317; bangalow guesthouse.com.au

WHAT TO DO
JILLY WINES
If you're not already a fan

of minimal-intervention wines, let winemaker Jared Dixon of Jilly Wines in Clunes, around 30 minutes' drive southwest of Byron, school you in how delicious they can be. The renowned small-batch winemaking company hosts cellar door tours by appointment.
www.jillywines.com.au

NIGHTCAP NATIONAL PARK
Beyond the hinterland lies this lush national park forming part of the Unesco-listed Gondwana Rainforests of Australia. Highlights include the Minyon Falls lookout, from where you can take a two-hour round-trip hike to the base of the spectacular falls, and Protestors Falls, an easier one-hour return walk from the car park.
www.nationalparks.nsw. gov.au

CELEBRATIONS
A TASTE OF NORTHERN NEW SOUTH WALES
Farmers, producers, chefs and foodies converge at the Bangalow Showgrounds on the first Saturday in September for the region's premier food festival, with tasting plates, cooking demos and more.
www.samplefoodevents. com

GET THERE
Sydney has direct air connections across Asia, Oceania and the Middle East, and from these places to the rest of the world. Domestic flights link the city with major destinations in Australia, as do buses and trains, which depart from Central Station.

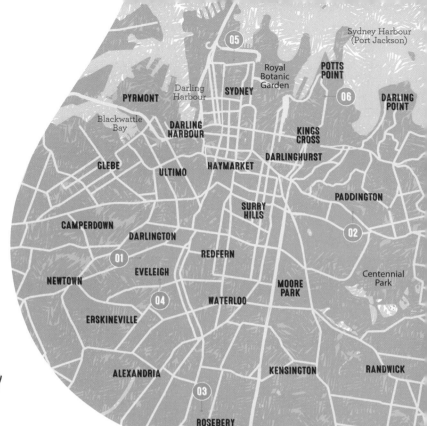

SYDNEY

[New South Wales]

A SELECT SERVING OF SYDNEY

Global flavours, bold experimentation, fresh produce and jaw-dropping views – this is a city that loves to indulge.

Eating in Sydney has never been more exciting. Home to myriad migrant communities, you're never far from a richly authentic international restaurant. And in Sydney's most acclaimed kitchens, this treasure trove of recipes has been raided and reimagined. Global techniques, traditions and ingredients have fuelled both boundary-pushing experimentation and the perfection of centuries-old methods from across the globe.

At the same time, the city has fallen in love with native flavours. Foods such as warrigal greens, Sydney rock oysters, yam daisies, samphire, yabbies, kangaroo, wild currants, native raspberries, saltbush, Murray cod, finger limes, muntries and more are making their way onto menus and you'd be mad not to try them. They share plates with the freshest produce from across Australia, whether it's sticky figs from the Riverland or organic grass-fed beef from Tasmania.

These two elements – a vast library of culinary traditions, and fresh local and native ingredients – have inspired Sydney's dining scene. Here, celebrity chefs – Matt Moran, Neil Perry and Kylie Kwong – don't just cook on TV, they also feed hungry patrons at signature restaurants. They compete with the likes of Tetsuya Wakuda, whose namesake restaurant was once ranked among the top five in the world, and Peter Gilmore who heads Quay and the Opera House's Bennelong – restaurants consistently listed among the nation's finest.

You won't have trouble finding a place to eat in Sydney, but if you're after a special table, or a view of the beach or that stunning harbour, it's well worth booking in advance. It seems like no one in this city eats at home any more. And why should they? Right now, the world is Sydney's oyster – or maybe it's the other way around: Sydney's oysters are absorbing the flavours of the world.

01 Spice Alley hawker market in Sydney suburb Chippendale

02 Archie Rose's rye whisky

03 Still life at Archie Rose

04 Carriageworks cultural precinct hosts a farmers' market

01 CARRIAGEWORKS FARMERS MARKET*

Over 100 regular stallholders gather from across New South Wales to sell their goodies at Sydney's best farmers' market. Here you can chat with the producers of organic chocolate, vegan sausages, boutique wine, ayurvedic tea, wild kombucha, sourdough croissants and hand-rolled tortellini. There's an emphasis on supporting small producers, cutting out the middle man and building community links between the growers in the country and the buyers in the big smoke. Maps of New South Wales above each stall show you where the food has been produced.

Boisterous with dogs and kids and people juggling huge bunches of sunflowers, this is a lovely place to grab a coffee and a pastry to start the weekend. If you're lucky you might also catch a free event, like a chef's demonstration of how to work with seasonal produce. *245 Wilson St. Eveleigh; www. carriageworks.com.au; 8am-1pm Sat*

02 FRED'S

If you love cooking as well as eating, Fred's provides an opportunity to get up close and personal with the preparation process at an acclaimed restaurant. Here there are no walls separating the dining room from the kitchen, and four guest seats are actually at the food-preparation benches. That's right, you nibble delicious dishes while chefs weave their magic on the other side of the bench. If that's not your cup of tea there are plenty of normal tables, but the benches give you a front-row seat on award-winning chef Danielle Alvarez' kitchen.

Her emphasis is on fresh, locally sourced food, with the menu sometimes changing twice a day when new deliveries arrive. The floor staff are happy to discuss your best options, which will no doubt include wood-fired meats or vegetables. Watch them being turned on the open hearth or emerging from the wood-fired oven. *380 Oxford St, Paddington; 02-9114 7331; www.merivale.com/venues/ freds; noon-midnight Tue-Fri & Sun, 8-11am & noon-midnight Sat*

'Create your own gin and whisky in our blending classes.'

Victoria Tulloch, Archie Rose

03 ARCHIE ROSE DISTILLING

The first distillery to open in Sydney in 160 years, Archie Rose launched in 2015 with a young and ambitious team who quickly began impressing judges worldwide. It's taken out gongs for Australia's Best Whisky and Best Australian Gin at London's International Wine & Spirits Competition, as well as World's Best International Contemporary Gin and World's Best International Vodka at the American Distilling Institute Craft Spirits Awards. But Archie Rose is definitely not just a distilling house – the team here has created a hip and hospitable space where they run tours and hold mixology masterclasses, as well as shaking great cocktails for a sophisticated crowd. Behind the gleaming copper bar, surrounded by hand-crafted barrels, chatty staff offer drink recommendations, fix up nibble platters, and dispense Sydney distilling factoids. Like this: Sydney's hot weather means that 8.5% of the batch evaporates each year, compared with only 2% to 3% in Scotland. It all adds to the unique flavour profile.

85 Dunning Ave, Rosebery; 02-8458 2300; www.archierose.com.au; noon-10pm Sun & Mon, to 11.30pm Tue-Sat

04 YERRABINGIN NATIVE ROOFTOP FARM

It's an unlikely spot to connect with nature and the heritage of the land, but up on a rooftop in

05 The interior of
Yellow restaurant

07 The golden
crescent of Bondi
beach

06 Artful vegetarian
cuisine at Yellow

a Redfern industrial park, right in the middle of the city, is Australia's first urban indigenous food farm. With 2000 plants, representing around 20 edible species, the small farm grows native foods to supply a growing demand from chefs throughout Sydney. It also aims to provide a business model and mentoring for other Indigenous communities developing native food businesses.

Kylie Kwong will collaborate with Yerrabingin when she opens her next project, a casual bistro, in the precinct in 2020. Kwong is famous for combining indigenous ingredients with Cantonese cooking traditions and she'll source her native foods from Yerrabingin. You can pop into the farm during weekdays for a picnic, but it's far more engaging to attend one of the many weekly events, like the regular farm tours (12.30pm Friday; AUD15), or workshops such as native cocktail-making or native permaculture.
4th floor, 2 Davy Rd, Eveleigh; www.yerrabingin.com.au; 9am-5pm Mon-Fri

05 AUSTRALIAN WINE CENTRE

The staff here pride themselves on their knowledge of Australian wine and stopping in here is like a short course in antipodean viticulture. With over 1000 wines in stock, they always have iconic producers represented, such as a dozen vintages of the prestigious Penfolds Grange wines and other gems. But the staff's real passion is for smaller producers that are hard to find overseas. There's a good cross-section of Australian wine by region and variety, with a curated selection of whatever is 'telling a good story about Australian wine at the moment'. International shipping can be arranged, and multi-lingual staff members are on hand, too.

42 Pitt St, Circular Quay; 02-9247 2755; www.australianwinecentre. com; 9.30am-8pm Mon-Thu & Sat, to 9pm Fri, 10am-7pm Sun

06 YELLOW

This sunflower-yellow former artists' residence is now a top-notch contemporary vegetarian restaurant. Dishes are prepared with real panache and excellent flavour combinations take your tastebuds on a journey with a beginning, middle and end in each mouthful. The black liquorice bread served here is the stuff of legends, and the tasting menus, which can be vegan, take the Sydney meat-free scene to new levels. Weekend brunch is also a highlight, as is the wine list, which won the Good Food Guide's Wine List of the Year for 2020.
57 Macleay St, Potts Point; 02-9332 2344; www.yellowsydney.com.au; 5-11pm Mon-Fri, 11am-2.30pm & 5-11pm Sat & Sun

© Courtesy of Yellow; Yellow ; © Jonathan Stokes / Lonely Planet

WHERE TO STAY

BONDI BEACH HOUSE

A charming and homey retreat decorated in beachy botanical style with a lazy-Sunday-morning atmosphere. Though only a two-minute walk from the famous beach, you may well be tempted to stay in all day.
www.bondibeachhouse. com.au

OVOLO 1888 DARLING HARBOUR

A converted heritage wool store, with luxury appointments, pops of colour, ironbark-wood beams and harbour views to linger over.
www.ovolohotels.com.au

WHAT TO DO

CARRIAGEWORKS

Carriageworks Market is held on the site of one of Sydney's edgiest art spaces. Located in heritage-listed former railway workshop from the 1880s, the huge building has been sensitively converted to house avant-garde arts. Come in here to see shows (usually free) ranging from VR ayahuasca experiences to exhibitions on contemporary Aboriginal dance.
www.carriageworks.com. au

CATCH A FERRY

Sometimes the simple pleasures are the best and hopping aboard a ferry (from AUD6.12) on Sydney Harbour is a fantastic way to get your Insta moment with the Opera House or Harbour Bridge, or both at once!
www.transportnsw.info

CELEBRATIONS

TASTE OF SYDNEY

Four days of foodie heaven, with top chefs cooking in Centennial Park in mid-March.
www.sydney. tastefestivals.com

GOOD FOOD MONTH

An October-long celebration of food and wine, with dining events, cooking classes and night noodle markets in Hyde Park.
www.goodfoodmonth. com/sydney

GET THERE
The northern fringe of the Tweed Valley is less than 15 minutes south of Gold Coast Airport. The region extends another 20 minutes further south, and around 30 minutes west from the coast.

TWEED VALLEY

[New South Wales]

A TASTE OF THE TWEED VALLEY

In the far northeastern corner of New South Wales, the lush Tweed Valley has emerged as one of Australia's hottest new culinary destinations.

TWEED HEADS

Terranora Broadwater

07

06

04

KINGSCLIFF

TUMBULGUM

Tweed River

Cudgen Creek

05

03

MURWILLUMBAH

BOGANGAR

02

HASTINGS POINT

01

POTTSVILLE BEACH

When renowned Byron Bay chef Steve Snow relocated his famed seafood restaurant Fins to the sleepy seaside town of Kingscliff – nearly an hours' drive north – over a decade ago, many locals thought he was mad. Taking a look around Snow's stomping ground today, however, you get the feeling he was onto something. Spanning roughly 60km (37 miles) from the northern outskirts of Byron Bay up to the small city of Tweed Heads hugging the Queensland border, the picturesque Tweed Valley is now home to some of regional NSW's top culinary pleasures.

It makes sense if you think about it. Nestled between the Pacific Ocean and the rim of an ancient shield volcano that now forms the Tweed Range, the Tweed Valley's fertile soil produces sensational crops that have long supplied the region's produce markets and restaurants. In recent years, a growing number of the region's farms have opened their properties to the public in the form of tours, farmgate boutiques, on-site eateries and even cellar doors, tempting visitors to linger for much longer than the obligatory roadside stop to select a juicy-looking pineapple and drop a few coins into an honesty box.

A steady stream of top chefs have since followed Snow's lead by upping sticks from Byron Bay and beyond to open restaurants and cafes in the small villages dotted along the coastal road that Australia's foodies are now crossing the country to dine at. Throw in a string of pristine, mostly-deserted beaches, tangles of pretty country roads, laidback locals and a handful of wonderful places to stay, and it becomes easier to see how the Tweed Valley has become less of a pitstop, and more of a bona fide destination.

01 PIPIT

Expectations were high when Byron Bay chef Ben Devlin announced he would be departing Cabarita restaurant Paper Daisy to open a fine diner in Pottsville, 7km (4 miles) south. Opened in 2019, Pipit – named for his daughter with partner in life and business Yen Trinh – didn't disappoint. The huge open kitchen is the star of the minimalist, one-hatted restaurant, which redefines the concept of modern Australian cuisine via creative, seasonal dishes spanning mullet roe finger buns with Davidson plum to fragrant bowls of steamed pipis served with potato, macadamia, wing beans and foraged kelp. Accompanied by a superb wine list with an emphasis on drops from coastal regions, it's a meal worth carving out an entire afternoon to savour.
8 Coronation Ave, Pottsville; 0490 380 117; www.pipitrestaurant.com; see website for opening hours

02 PAPER DAISY

Anchoring the Hamptons-meets-the-Mediterranean–styled boutique hotel Halcyon House, the Paper Daisy restaurant is widely credited for putting the Tweed Valley food scene on the map. In early 2019, Head Chef Ben Devlin passed the reins to Jason Barratt, who farewelled Byron Bay's ritzy Rae's on Wategos to put his own spin on the simple yet sophisticated seafood dishes that earned Paper Daisy its chef's hat for 2020. The bright, airy restaurant is can be experienced at a twilight dinner, when the cerulean sea can be glimpsed through the pandanus trees, and the Halcyon Daze cocktails (made with Brookie's Byron Dry Gin, citrus, lemon myrtle syrup, mint and passionfruit foam) slip down a treat.
21 Cypress Cres, Cabarita Beach; 02-6676 1444; www.halcyonhouse. com.au

03 OSTERIA CASUARINA

In 2019, renowned UK-born chef Matt Kemp, who trained at Michelin-starred London restaurant The Square before securing a chef's hat for

Owners Ben and Ursula Watts learned how to perfect French baking in Paris; two years later they opened this sunny riverside cafe, Cubby Bakehouse.

The Byron at Byron resort's restaurant, signed on as executive chef for leading Northern Rivers hospitality group, Perfect Last Bite (PLB). Doubling as a community hub, rustic-chic Osteria is its flagship restaurant. Perfect for a casual Italian-inspired feed at any time of the day, Osteria's sustainability philosophy is evident in everything from the flavour-packed produce from the on-site garden to the organic and biodynamic drops on the wine list. *1 Barclay Dr, Casuarina; 02-6674 9962; www.osteriacasuarina.com. au; 7am-1pm Mon & Tue, to 3pm Wed-Sat*

04 CUBBY BAKEHOUSE

For the crunchiest baguettes and the flakiest croissants this side of the Seine, Cubby Bakehouse has you covered. In 2016 owners Ben and Ursula Watts (the same duo behind popular Gold Coast cafes Paddock and BamBam Bakehouse) travelled to Paris to learn how to perfect the basics of French baking. Two years later, they opened this sunny, riverside cafe and bakery, pumping out arguably the best baked goods in the Tweed. Grab a haul to go or nab a table and stay for brunch, served until 3pm daily. *162 Chinderah Bay Dr, Chinderah 0458 958 852; www. cubbybakehouse.com; 7am-3pm*

05 FARM & CO

It found Insta-fame as the 'sunflower place' for its fields of bright yellow blooms, but since mid-2019 this family farm has also been attracting visitors for its equally photogenic on-site cafe. Open for breakfast and lunch, Farm & Co's short menu is a lesson in how delicious plant-based (and mostly also vegan) food can be, with dishes crafted from farm-fresh produce and other goodies from local suppliers. Wash down your meal with a cold-pressed juice or a caffeine hit from Zephyr Coffee Co based in nearby Kirra.
529 Cudgen Rd, Cudgen; 02-6693 2196; www.farmandco.com.au; 8am-2.30pm

06 HUSK DISTILLERS

It's Australia's only agricole rum distillery (with rums made from homegrown sugar cane juice rather than molasses), but Husk is best known for its delicious Ink Gin, which turns a pretty pink hue when tonic water is added. In mid-2019, the family-run distillery migrated from a crude shed to a beautiful new venue on their Tumbulgum farm, complete with a distillery door open for tours and tastings from Wednesday to Sunday. With incredible views towards Wollumbin-Mt Warning from the front lawn, it's a scenic spot to indulge in a rum or gin cocktail or two, with grazing boards and rum-infused treats on offer for the peckish.
1152 Dulguigan Rd, North Tumbulgum; 02-6675 9149; www. huskdistillers.com

07 POTAGER KITCHEN GARDEN

It would be wise to download an offline map to help find your way to Potager, tucked deep in the green hills rising up behind the Tweed Valley. But once you locate this small, charming restaurant set in a converted farmhouse, where co-owner David Burr welcomes diners like family, you'll be grateful you made the journey. Only open from Friday to Sunday, Potager's Mediterranean-inspired menu showcases homegrown produce alongside proteins from the who's who of local producers, from Fair Game Wild Venison to PKG Seafoods in West Tweed. Save room for dessert.
502 Carool Rd, Carool; 02-5590 7403; www.potager.com.au; noon-4pm & 6-10pm Fri & Sat, noon-4pm Sun

WHERE TO STAY
THE HIDEAWAY
Just steps from Cabarita Beach, this hip low-impact boutique glamping resort opened in 2019 with accommodation in luxuriously furnished bell tents and contemporary ensuite bathrooms and communal lounge areas housed in recycled shipping containers.
www.hideaway-cabaritabeach.com.au

CRYSTAL CREEK RAINFOREST RETREAT
The stunning drive to this boutique retreat tucked up in the foothills of the Tweed Range sets the scene for a romantic stay in one of its 13 luxury cabins surrounded by rainforest. The 102-hectare (252-acre) property is laced with 8km (5 miles) of trails, including a short walk to a magical glow worm cave.
www.ccrr.com.au

WHAT TO DO
TWEED REGIONAL GALLERY AND MARGARET OLLEY ART

CENTRE
In South Murwillumbah, this fantastic gallery houses a recreation of the Paddington, Sydney home studio where the late Margaret Olley – Australia's most celebrated still life painter – created her famous works, filled with over 20,000 items Olley collected over many years as subject matter.
https://artgallery.tweed.nsw.gov.au

TWEED VALLEY WHEY FARMHOUSE CHEESES
If you're passing through Burringbar between Wednesday and Sunday, pick up some handcrafted artisan farmhouse cheeses, butter and yoghurts from this Burringbar cheesemaker, which also serves platters at its on-site cafe.
www.tweedvalley cheeses.com.au

CELEBRATIONS
TWEED ARTISAN FOOD WEEKEND
Launched in 2019, the three-day food fest sees the Tweed Valley's top farms, restaurants and producers curate culinary experiences that showcase ingredients unique to the Tweed region, from gourmet long lunches to cooking classes, and more.
www.destinationtweed.com.au

GET THERE
Driving from Sydney to Kangaroo Valley takes roughly two hours but it's possible to use public transport: board a train to Bomaderry (Nowra) station and take an onward Kennedy's bus. From Canberra, the drive takes 2¼ hours.

FITZROY FALLS

Fitzroy Falls Reservoir

JAMBEROO

KIAMA DOWNS

04

KIAMA

BARRENGARRY

02

KANGAROO VALLEY

Kangaroo River

01

03

05

GERRINGONG

GERROA

BERRY

KANGAROO VALLEY

Tasman Sea

CAMBEWARRA

TAPITALLEE

[New South Wales]

LOCAL LARDER IN KANGAROO VALLEY

Spot roos and swirl chardonnay in Kangaroo Valley. This verdant township in New South Wales is jam-packed with gourmet produce and classic Aussie comfort food.

Kangaroo Valley is two hours' drive southwest of Sydney and it couldn't be more different. Unlike New South Wales' glamorous capital, Kangaroo Valley is green and has something of an English country village feel. Its deep river valley, with spectacular sandstone cliffs, has meadows, farms and forests unfurling in its surrounds. Locals credit the volcanic soil and regular rain with the quality of local dairy, fruit and veggies, and for the output of Kangaroo Valley's award-winning wineries.

The 33km- (20.5 mile) long valley is a tempting destination for lovers of the outdoors. Kayakers and canoeists float along the curves of the Kangaroo River, alighting on riverbanks to listen for lyrebirds. South is the Cambewarra mountain range (complete with a marvellous lookout point), while to the north beauty spots such as Fitzroy Falls beckon to hikers.

These wild landscapes offer a few insights into Kangaroo Valley's past. The original Wodi Wodi people thrived here for some 200,000 years. European settlers who arrived in the 19th century were ill-equipped for the untamed landscape, but gradually founded dairies and moonshine producers, sowing the seeds for Kangaroo Valley's future foodie credentials.

Dedicate a day to a cooking class, fuel some fresh-air rambles with pies and Anzac biscuits, then finish in a classic indoor-outdoor pub. After sleeping it off, visit a winery in a sublime location, tucked among fruit trees and vineyards, and detour to the town of Berry for fresh donuts to guzzle on the drive home.

And the name? No lie, Kangaroo Valley is a fantastic place to spot wildlife. Wombats and roos are easy to encounter towards twilight, with Bendeela Recreation Area a particular hot-spot.

01 Kangaroo Valley residents' association

02 Tropical trees at Yarrawa Estate

03 Wine tasting at Yarrawa Estate

04 The ancient escarpment of Kangaroo Valley

01 FLAVOURS OF THE VALLEY*

'Simple is better,' insists Chef Toni. 'Pick it, cook it, eat it, done.' The culinary philosophy at Flavours of the Valley cookery school places the emphasis on seasonal ingredients prepared without pretension. The setting of these cooking classes is sumptuous: a tasteful wood and corrugated metal atrium adjoining a state-of-the-art kitchen, set in 40.5 hectares (100 acres) of bush.

As a self-described 'tactile cook', Toni's methods are intuitive. Her advice for budding chefs? 'Look, see, feel. Recipes are a guide.' With a combination of technical expertise and encouragement, her classes are suitable for confident cooks and kitchen fumblers alike.

Former high school teacher Toni was inspired by MasterChef to create her own cookery school, later bringing her husband Rob on board to assist in running the business. They offer a smorgasbord of options, such as pasta making, Middle Eastern menus and banquets of vegan produce. The one constant is the eco-consciousness underpinning their shared kitchen. Produce is sourced locally, and some of the herbs and veggies are grown in their own garden. 'We share with the possums and the wombats as well,' laughs Toni. 'We don't mind them having their share, as long as they don't eat it all.'

Naturally there's a feast at the end, where attendees share what they've cooked up. Reserve well ahead for this upscale introduction to Kangaroo Valley's best produce. Afterwards, you might need to walk it off. Fortunately Bendeela Recreation Area is close by, one of the best kangaroo-spotting locations in town.

Wildwood Estate, 407D Bendeela Rd, Kangaroo Valley; 02-4465 2010; www.flavoursofthevalley.com.au

02 KANGAROO VALLEY PIE SHOP

Returning east from Flavours of the Valley to main road Moss Vale, head north until you see a sign heralding the 'world's best pies'. It's no idle boast: seven hot and heavy varieties of pie, from steak and

> **'The secret to making great pies is baking them fresh every day with responsibly sourced, local meat.'**
>
> *Irene Saito, Kangaroo Valley Pie Shop*

mushroom to curried vegetable, are handmade at this small, family run shop. All the fillings are made from scratch on the premises – there isn't an instant gravy in sight.

'The secret to making a great Aussie pie is a combination of things,' explains Irene Saito, co-owner of Kangaroo Valley Pie Shop. 'Our meat is sourced from a great butcher who grows, kills and butchers his own animals, therefore our pies are paddock to plate. We do not pre-make our pies days in advance, they are made and cooked fresh every day. My personal favourite is the beef and red wine.'

The classic Aussie mince pie is most popular, but don't neglect the sweeter side of the menu.

Deep-filled apple pies and Anzac biscuits – buttery oat cookies – are perfect additions to a pie picnic. The tricky part is deciding on a picnic spot: buy an armful of goodies and drive 30 minutes west to Tallowa Dam, or 20 minutes north to Fitzroy Falls, a beauty spot laced with walking trails. *2167 Moss Vale Rd, Kangaroo Valley; 02-4465 1360; www. worldsbestpies.com.au; 9am-3pm Thu-Sun*

03 THE FRIENDLY INN

Return south to the centre of Kangaroo Valley town for a sundowner in one of the region's oldest pubs. The Friendly Inn styles itself as an unfussy watering hole but the food tells a more

05 The popular town of Berry

06 Try your hand at kayaking Kangaroo Valley

interesting story. Soft-shell crab burgers, barbecued octopus salads and Malaysian-style curries grace the changing menu, though Aussie mainstays such as steaks and fish 'n' chips are guaranteed. Take your heavy plate out into the big backyard, let the kids exhaust themselves clambering over the playground, and order another craft beer: life is good!
159 Moss Vale Rd, Kangaroo Valley; 02-4465 1355; www.thefriendlyinn. com.au; 10am-10pm

04 YARRAWA ESTATE

On the second day, follow the winding gravel road northeast from town to Yarrawa Estate, a gorgeously tucked-away winery. Run by self-taught wine specialists Sue and Mark Foster, Yarrawa Estate spreads across a magnificently verdant swathe of land. As well as vineyards, Sue and Mark also cultivate oranges, kumquats and other fruit, plus 100 each of macadamia, walnut and pecan trees (some finding their way into their walnut liquor wine).

For oenophiles hesitating between the bright chambourcin and fresh verdelho varietals, there's an option to taste a few different kinds (at a reasonable AUD5 per person). You won't regret adding a nibble of cheeses and antipasti (an extra AUD5). Contemplate the leafy setting over the appley sweetness of their 'Jasmin Grace', the marvellously mineral verdelho, and a top-notch chardonnay, whose scent almost evokes freshly baked banana bread.
43B Scotts Rd, Kangaroo Valley; 02-4465 1165; www.yarrawaestate. com; 10am-5pm Sat, 12.30-5.30pm Sun, or by appointment

05 FAMOUS BERRY DONUT VAN

Leave Kangaroo Valley by travelling east along the B73 before turning onto the Kangaroo Valley Rd for a gourmet stop in the charming town of Berry. Many a road trip has been improved by pausing at Famous Berry Donut Van, where freshly made donuts are rolled in cinnamon sugar before being hastily eaten, deliciously fluffy and still warm, outside this streetside favourite. Everything is made fresh to order so there's often a bit of a wait – fortunately excellent coffee is served to pass the time. Gobble your donuts (or, even better, donut ice cream sandwich) on site, in view of Berry's lively main street. They're best when they're hot...and it lessens the risk of cinnamon sugar sprinkled throughout your rental car.
73 Queen St, Berry; 02-4464 1968; www.facebook.com/ berrydonutvan; 8am-6pm

WHERE TO STAY

THE LAURELS
A gastronomically inclined B&B that offers restaurant-quality eggs Florentine for breakfast. There are four equally lavish rooms, each one furnished in a classically elegant style, while the dining room almost glitters with polished mahogany and crystal. *www.thelaurelsbnb.com.au*

WHAT TO DO

PIONEER VILLAGE MUSEUM
A portal into the lives of NSW's early European settlers, the Pioneer Village Museum is utterly engaging, thanks to the recorded testimonies and creative soundtracks enlivening the recreated schoolroom and collections of artefacts. *www.kangaroovalley museum.com*

WATER SPORTS
Kangaroo Valley looks even lovelier from the water. Rent a single- or double-seater kayak and paddle along tricky rapids or placid waters, looking out for echidnas and lyrebirds on the banks. Kangaroo Valley Canoes also runs multi-day boat safaris. *www.kangaroovalley canoes.com.au*

CELEBRATIONS

KANGAROO VALLEY CRAFT BEER & BBQ FESTIVAL
A showcase of more than 60 craft beers and ciders, accompanied by a mellow assortment of family friendly activities. What heats things up (literally) is the slow-cook barbecue competitive cook-off: 30 teams compete to prepare the most mouthwatering meat. Book tickets in advance. *www.kvbbq.com.au*

SOUTH COAST FOOD & WINE FESTIVAL
An annual extravaganza of local produce takes place in mid-September at locations including Berry Showgrounds and the farmers market in Nowra, a 20-minute drive southwest. Expect masterclasses in culinary techniques, tastings of oysters, wines and cheeses, and trade secrets from mixologists and patissiers. *www.southcoast foodandwinefestival.com.au*

GET THERE
Ulladulla is roughly three hours by road east of Canberra or south of Sydney. Daily buses link Sydney to Ulladulla (taking longer, at five hours).

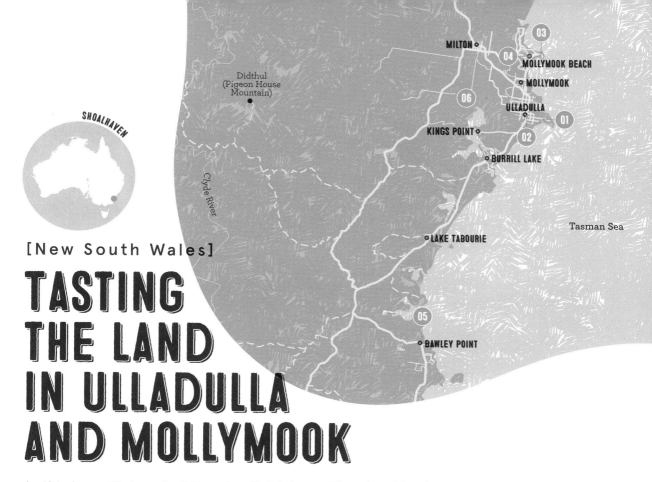

SHOALHAVEN

Didthul
(Pigeon House
Mountain)

Clyde River

MILTON
03
04
MOLLYMOOK BEACH
MOLLYMOOK
06
ULLADULLA
KINGS POINT
01
02
BURRILL LAKE

Tasman Sea

LAKE TABOURIE

05

BAWLEY POINT

[New South Wales]

TASTING THE LAND IN ULLADULLA AND MOLLYMOOK

In this beautiful part of New South Wales, millennia of bush tucker knowledge endures, while modern taste-makers prepare cheeses, wines and seafood with panache.

The Shoalhaven area extends along the coast some 120km (75 miles) south of Sydney and is best known for quiet coves, river cruises, dolphin-spotting and other summery activities. The Shoalhaven offers outstanding local produce, and the neighbouring towns of Ulladulla and Mollymook are ideal for experiencing the bounty of this land. Of the 400,000 bottles filled each year in the Shoalhaven Coast wine region, some of the best are cool-climate varieties from Ulladulla's uplands. Complementing the wine, goat's and sheep's cheeses are crafted by local dairies. And oyster farms still produce their juicy spoils, notably creamy Greenwell Point rock oysters.

Between oyster bars and brilliant brunches, this trail offers opportunities to more deeply understand the land, which is traditionally owned by the Yuin people.

The Yuin people have passed their knowledge of flora and fauna down the generations. The local Aboriginal land council and a private Aboriginal-led tour operator each offer guided walks where visitors can scrunch herbs and pluck fruit from sea cliffs. Learning from Aboriginal guides isn't only a masterclass in foraging, it's an insight into ancient models for sustainable living. Over millennia, Aboriginal people were careful to avoid overeating any particular marine species, leaving signals to neighbouring groups to follow suit – an environmentally sensitive approach that seems light-years ahead of modern fishing methods.

Ulladulla is an excellent base for understanding the region's indigenous food culture. It's adjoined by Mollymook to the north, which has a spread of upscale restaurants, bars and hotels.

01 Mollymook beach

02 Hayden's excellent pieshop

03 Eating at Bannisters

04 Bannisters hotel above Mollymook beach

05 Fish dishes designed by Rick Stein at Bannisters

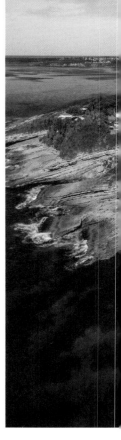

01 COOMEE NULUNGA CULTURAL TRAIL

Walking tours of the Coomee Nulunga Cultural Trail, arranged through Ulladulla Local Aboriginal Land Council, extend a warm welcome – in the Dhurga language, walawaani njindiwan (welcome all, I hope your journey was safe). The trail winds through coastal heathland at Warden Head Reserve, just east of town, where hardy plants cling on against stiff breezes and boardwalks direct walkers towards the electric-blue sea.

Along these 90-minute guided tours, Aboriginal guides point out edible leaves, berries and ancient medicines. Little by little, the bushland begins to resemble a larder and visitors can spot fruits such as Illawarra plums, which resemble tiny purple grapes. After roaming the trail and hearing about the land's history, you'll tell scrub nettles from sea celery with ease.

Other insights also linger. Groups of Aboriginal people have long defined their land using Didthul (Pigeon House Mountain) as a geographical marker. The mountain, shaped like a woman's breast, has symbolic significance for the Yuin people. To continue your education, step inside the council building to see the creations of local Aboriginal artists. The Giriwa Garuwanga Aboriginal Art Gallery is free to enter and you'll often see artists at work. *66 Deering St, Ulladulla; 02-4455 5883; www.facebook.com/ulladullaulalc*

02 HAYDEN'S PIES

Back in Ulladulla, enjoy a satisfying lunch at Hayden's Pies. The pie occupies the highest rung in the Aussie food pantheon. European migrants to Australia brought with them their favourite recipes for this conveniently portable, belly-filling food, and roaming pie-sellers were common in Australian cities in the 19th century. As a working-class food that could be eaten on the hoof, pies were quickly embraced in the towns established by settlers, and they endure as a favourite snack. Throughout the country, pie production remains a point of pride and the best crust in town is essential local knowledge. In Ulladulla, it's all about Hayden's, who are locally famed for their curry

04

05

'Our Provenance chardonnay pairs beautifully with our Croobyar, an Alpine-style cow's milk cheese that is 12 months old'

Libby Cupitt

steak pie and other hot favourites, such as Thai chicken curry, mash and gravy, and pumpkin and feta. Gluten-free pies are also available, so no one need miss out.
2/166 Princes Hwy, Ulladulla; 02-4455 7798; www.haydenspies.com.au; 6am-5pm Mon-Sat, from 7am Sun

03 RICK STEIN AT BANNISTERS

Burn off all that pie by jogging or swimming at long, sandy Mollymook Beach, so you're hungry enough to appreciate the modern seafood at Rick Stein's restaurant later on. The local catch determines the menu, while Asian inflections add piquancy and rich aromas – perhaps their Singapore-style crab, or South

Indian curry of blue-eye trevalla, made tart with tamarind. The fish and chips is glorious, while the fish pie is almost legendary, with prawns, snapper, scallops and a truffled sauce bubbling away beneath the crunchy parmesan topping.
191 Mitchell Pde, Mollymook; 02-4454 7400; www.bannisters.com.au/rick-stein; dinner Mon-Sat, lunch Sat & Sun

04 TALLWOOD EATERY

Once known for its breakfasts, Tallwood is now a must-do for dinner, serving three-course set menus centred around regional produce and locally sourced fruit and veg. As well as mains like red-braised short ribs with kohlrabi kimchee or miso pork skewers, there

Ø6 Gathering fresh
ingredients at Cupitt's

Ø7 Delicious diversions
at Cupitt's

Ø8 Gum trees beneath
Pigeon House Mountain

are vegan options such as cavatelli pasta in a parsley and pine-nut sauce or an almond and rosemary cake. *Shop 2/85 Tallwood Ave; Mollymook; 02-4455 5192 ; www. tallwoodeat.com.au*

05 NURA GUNYU

Drive south to Bawley Point for a guided walk along a spectacular stretch of coast. The leader of Aboriginal-led tour outfit Nura Gunyu, Noel Butler, will reveal leaves and berries to snack on while your group rambles between beaches and forests. Likely nibbles include the red-fleshed Mullumbimby plum, packed with antioxidants, and carpets of spinach-like warrigal greens, which proliferate in sandy grounds. Noel will point out medicines, too, perhaps antimicrobial lemon myrtle leaves. Nature's pantry even has kitchenware, like paperbark that has long been used by Aboriginal people to wrap food before cooking it. *Bawley Point; 0405 646 911 www.facebook.com/nuragunyu*

06 CUPITT'S ESTATE

A sensational finale for a trip to Ulladulla is Cupitt's, a fromagerie, winery and brewery with views of Pigeon House Mountain and Burrill Lake. Its stone creamery dates back to the 1850s and is thought to be the district's oldest building still in commercial use. Today, it turns out buttery Flor Azul cheese, nutty, 12-month-matured Tomme de Chèvre (goat's cheese) and other delectable dairy products.

In tandem, Cupitt's makes highly awarded, old-world-style wines. The options are copious – blossom-scented marsanne, fruity riesling, spicy tempranillo – calling for a full wine tasting. In 2014 Cupitt's opened a brewery, adding hoppy, ales and crisp pilsners to the menu. Their chocolatey stout is enhanced with the addition of cow's whey, a by-product from the dairy. There's a wine or beer match for every dish.

Cupitt's runs events year-round, such as June's Winemaker Dinner, gourmet masterclasses on oysters, organic gardening and more, tours of the cheesemaking facilities, plus charity dinners on public holiday weekends. The turn of autumn (March) is especially compelling for foodies. 'It is a great time to take a Tour and Taste Experience,' explains Libby Cupitt, one member of the family team running Cupitt's, 'because you can see the early processes such as the wine fermentation.' Whatever the season, aim for a Sunday session, when live music wafts across the terrace, amplified by the tinkling of wine glasses raised in toast. *58 Washburton Road, Ulladulla; 02-4455 7888; www.cupitt.com.au; cellar door 10am-5pm, restaurant noon-2pm daily & 6-9pm Thu-Sat*

© Courtesy of Dane Singleton studio / Cupitt's Estate; Cupitt's Estate; © Stephen Dwyer / Alamy Stock Photo

WHERE TO STAY

ULLADULLA GUEST HOUSE

A five-star B&B with the best stocked wine bar we've ever had the privilege to encounter. The pool has a tropical feel, plus there's an elegant lounge, cedar sauna and you can order a massage to your room. *www.guesthouse.com.au*

WHAT TO DO

HIKING

New South Wales' rugged interior offers splendid hikes, notably Didthul (Pigeon House Mountain), which affords sweeping views from the summit. Ulladulla is also a jumping-off point to Murramarang National Park; it's less than an hour's drive to Pretty Beach, one of a string of golden sands inset from tree-shaded walking trails.

CELEBRATIONS

ULLADULLA BLESSING OF THE FLEET FESTIVAL

There's no clearer sign of how seriously the Shoalhaven area takes

its seafood than the Blessing of the Fleet. In a tradition begun by European migrants, a procession of colourful floats is led down the highway with a representation of the patron saint of fishing, St Peter, at the front. For the locals who pile into the streets, and visitors from around,

it's a good excuse for an Easter knees-up, complete with beach games and market stalls selling edibles (with an emphasis on, of course, seafood). *www.blessingofthefleet. info*

FARMERS' MARKETS

There are occasional Sunday markets at

Mollymook Beach, always with fresh-baked goodies, fruit and veg, and kitschy fashions on offer. In Milton, a few kilometres northwest, Saturday markets display regional produce and bric-a-brac around the showground. Expect berry cordials and baked treats galore. *www.ulladulla.info*

GET THERE

Given its remote location, most choose to fly into Darwin, with direct flights offered from both Australia and Asia. If coming by car, be prepared for long distances, with around a 1500km (932 mile) journey separating it from the nearest major town, Alice Springs.

01

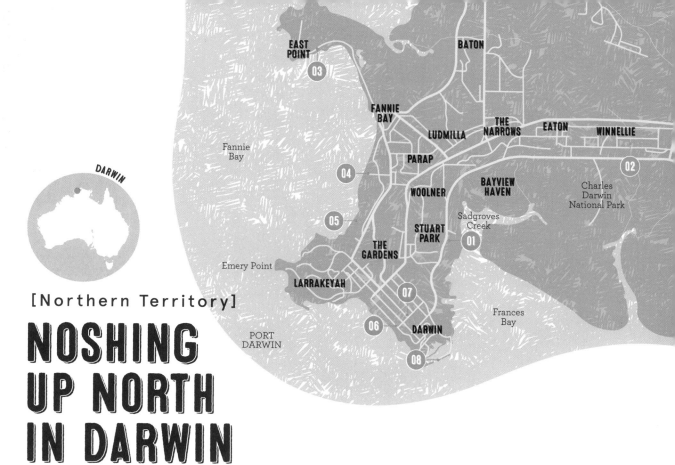

[Northern Territory]

NOSHING UP NORTH IN DARWIN

Keep your cool in Darwin's tropics with icy beer and G&Ts, while digging into evening seafood feasts to a backdrop of swaying palms and pink sunsets.

Representing the Top End, Darwin is the nation's most idiosyncratic capital. The usual NT stereotypes – crocs, outback pubs and beer-swilling locals – are part of its DNA, but Darwin is no longer a provincial outpost. If you like to eat and drink, you'll love Darwin. Come for its al fresco dining scene, where balmy evenings are spent devouring fresh seafood accompanied by blazing sunsets over the Timor Sea. Add in unique food markets, hip breweries, urban cafes and authentic multicultural cuisine, and it's clear Darwin has an appetite for good eating.

In a city where fishing for barra (barramundi) is a way of life, seafood makes up a big part of the diet in Darwin. You'll see barra on the menu anywhere from the local fish and chip store to swanky waterfront restaurants, along with Moreton Bay bugs, lobster and a heap of other fresh catch to savour. Seafood's not the only food source coming out of the ocean: crocodile – the most Territorian cuisine of all – is also regularly featured on menus.

With Indonesia and Malaysia closer to Darwin than any cities on the mainland, Darwin's climate is similar to Southeast Asia, and the same can be said about its food. This is evident when you hit the city's food markets where vendors cook up laksa and rendang, among other spicy Southeast Asian curries and snacks.

This being the tropics, a cold beer is a necessity. Whether cracking open a tinny while fishing or quaffing a cold one at the pub, it's the perfect accompaniment to most things here. Things have moved on from those giant NT lager stubbies – today microbreweries produce speciality beers for city taphouses.

01 A sultry sunset at Mindil beach, Darwin

02 Amazing mouthfuls at Pee Wee's

03 Exotic cocktails at Pee Wee's

04 Pee Wee's superlative setting

05 Time for a cold one at One Mile Brewing

01 FRYING NEMO

When you're the winner of Australia's best fish and chips, you know you're doing something right, and it's a testament to the quality of seafood fried up at Nemos. Located on the wharf, here they specialise in locally caught wild fish from NT barramundi and black tip shark to Spanish mackerel, all battered in your choice of beer, panko crumbs or tempura, or opt for the healthier grilled option. A tempting alternative to battered fish are the Territorian burgers, filled with anything from croc and buffalo to barra. Grab a cold beer or glass of wine to enjoy while looking out to the water
Shop 10, 90 Frances Bay Dr,
Stuart Park; 08-8981 2281; www.
fryingnemo.com.au; 5pm-9pm
daily, 12pm-2pm Fri–Sun

02 ONE MILE BREWING COMPANY

Leading the charge in bringing craft beer to the Top End are these two blokes who brew beautifully styled beers that err on the lighter side to suit these tropical climes. Grab a seat among the industrial graffiti-splashed decor and sample their core beers, which includes a kolsch, red and bright ale, along with a popular pink lady cider and mid-strength ginger beer. All go beautifully with pizza.

Craft beer lovers should also check out Six Tanks (www. facebook.com/sixtanks) in the city, who brew their own ales, that feature among 26 other craft beers on tap here.
8/111 Coonawarra Rd, Winnellie
0429 782 870; www.
onemilebrewery.com.au; 5-8pm
Thu & Fri, noon-7.30pm Sat

03 PEE WEE'S AT THE POINT

Right on the water's edge, Pee Wee's is the place where locals come to treat themselves to a nice meal out. Seafood's an undoubted highlight, with entrees such as reef fish sashimi, tempura soft-shell crab or scallops Rockfeller, and modern Australian mains such as roasted wild barramundi that comes crumbed in native flavours of macadamia

© Courtesy of Pee Wee's at the Point, Pee Wee's at the Point.

'Our beers have been known to remedy 'Mango Madness' and other tropical conditions.'

Stuart Brown and Bardy Bayram, One Mile Brewing Company

nuts and lemon myrtle. Otherwise pop by for an Aperol Spritz to enjoy with oysters and one of Darwin's ethereal sunsets.
Alec Fong Lim Dr, East Point; 08-8981 6868 ; www.peewees.com.au; from 6.30pm

04 DARWIN SKI CLUB

Just the place to enjoy a balmy Darwin arvo, this waterfront bistro is home to the NT waterskiing club. A favourite among locals, it's all about kicking back in the beer garden among the palms with a cold drink to enjoy the sunset while digging into a steak sanga, beer-battered barra or delicious beef red curry. Live music most weekends makes it one of the city's most social spots.

Conacher St, Fannie Bay; 08-8981 6630; www.darwinskiclub.com.au; noon-10pm

06 MINDIL BEACH SUNSET MARKET

During the dry season, foodies will not want to miss out on this twice-weekly market that sets up along the palm-lined foreshore of attractive Mindil Beach. Of the 200 stalls, some 60 are dedicated to food, with local flavours such as barra, croc and kangaroo on offer, among authentic Asian bites such as sate, laksa, Vietnamese rice paper rolls and Thai curries. There's a heap of burgers, Mexican and barbecue stalls to grab a feed while taking a sunset stroll along the promenade

Ø6 Mindil beach draws
a crowd at sundown

Ø7 Boating on Yellow
Water Billabong in
Kakadu National Park

browsing stalls selling handmade jewellery, Aboriginal art and Southeast Asian crafts.
off Gilruth Ave; www.mindil.com. au; 4-9pm Thu & Sun May-Oct

07 ABORIGINAL BUSH TRADERS CAFE

Offering a wonderful opportunity to sample authentic Australian flavours is this not-for-profit organisation (Ironbark Aboriginal Corporation) that's opened a cafe with a menu of bushtucker inspired items. Set within the historic Lyons Cottage, here you can order freshly baked damper with bush jams such as Kakadu plum or wild rosella, or a savoury version of feta spiced with native aniseed and lemon myrtle and bush tomato relish. Otherwise try a sandwich filled with bush-spiced marinated kangaroo and feta, or saltbush dukkah, avocado and feta smash. While you're here you can pick up spices from its shop as well as Aboriginal artworks, jewellery and books.
cnr Esplanade & Knuckey St; 09-8942 4023; www. aboriginalbushtraders.com; 7.30am-3pm Mon-Fri

08 PM EAT & DRINK*

One of Darwin's best spots for contemporary cuisine is this tasteful city bistro that's all about beautifully presented shared plates of dishes made from locally sourced ingredients. Fresh seafood is the standout, with the likes of locally caught grilled cuttlefish, sardines, prawns and whole snapper, along with more casual items of gourmet pizzas and tempura fish burgers. Gastronomes meanwhile may want to opt for one of the degustation 'banquet' menus, paired with wines, to get an idea of what its take on NT modern Australian fare is all about.
cnr Knuckey St & Austin Lane; 08-8941 3925; www.pmeatdrink.com; noon-late Tue-Sat

09 CRUSTACEANS

Take in a tropical sunset over Frances Bay while feasting on a seafood platter with a chilled bottle of white wine at this modern wharf restaurant, which is another fixture on Darwin's culinary scene. Local fresh fish, chargrilled Moreton Bay bugs, mud crabs and lobster are all on the menu, along with crocodile skewers, scotch fillet steaks and Thai Massaman beef curry, which rounds out a very good representation of what Darwin cuisine is all about
Stokes Hill Wharf; 08-8981 8658 www.crustaceans.net.au; 5.30-11pm, last order 8.30pm

WHERE TO STAY
VIBE HOTEL
The contemporary Vibe Hotel on Darwin's vibrant waterfront makes for a reliable and stylish place to stay. It's close to restaurants, cafes, the outdoor cinema and the popular Wave Lagoon waterpark. Rooms are smart without being over the top, fitted with all the mod cons and many that feature views out over the water.
www.vibehotels.com

WHAT TO DO
MUSEUM & ART GALLERY OF THE NORTHERN TERRITORY
Aboriginal culture is an integral component to any visit to the NT, so any opportunity to see quality, original indigenous art shouldn't be missed. The varied collection here features carvings from the Tiwi Islands, dot art from remote desert communities and bark paintings from Arnhem Land. The museum also includes an exhibition on Cyclone Tracy, Indonesian artifacts

and taxidermy of a 5m- (16ft-) long estuary crocodile named Sweetheart!
www.magnt.net.au

KAKADU NATIONAL PARK
Darwin is the gateway town to several Top End national parks, including the Unesco World Heritage–listed Kakadu, Australia's largest national park. Covering 20,000 sq km (7722 sq miles)

Kakadu is known for its timeless landscapes, extensive river systems, abundance of bird and wildlife, and ancient Aboriginal culture and rock art that dates back 60,000 years.
www.parksaustralia.gov.au/kakadu

CELEBRATIONS
BEER CAN REGATTA
A good example of your classic, offbeat, outback humour is this iconic boat race featuring vessels made entirely of beer cans. Held at Mindil Beach, the festival has been going some 50 years, attracting a fun-loving crowd here to enjoy a day of festivities ranging from thong (flip-flop) throwing contests to sandcastle building.
www.beercanregatta.org.au

GET THERE
The region is reached by car from Brisbane, Gold Coast or the Sunshine Coast, taking up to three hours depending on route. Brisbane and Gold Coast both have airports with international and domestic flights. Toow-oomba's airport has flights from Melbourne, Sydney, Darwin and Townsville.

TOOWOOMBA

Map labels: OAKEY, HIGHFIELDS, 07, 08, TOOWOOMBA, GATTON, LAIDLEY, Condamine River, PITTSWORTH, CAMBOOYA, GREENMOUNT, NOBBY, MILLMERRAN, CLIFTON, ALLORA, QUEENSLAND, WARWICK, YANGAN, KILLARNEY, 06, URBENVILLE, 05, NEW SOUTH WALES, 04, STANTHORPE, 03, 02, GLEN ALPIN, 01

[Queensland]

DIG IN AROUND THE DARLING DOWNS AND GRANITE BELT

Delight in the novelty of rugging up in southeast Queensland, where woolly jumpers replace bathing suits to enjoy Mediterranean-style reds and cheese by an open fire.

When people think of southeast Queensland their minds go straight to the beaches of the Gold Coast or perhaps the cultured capital, Brisbane. In-the-know gastronomes, however, will tell you that inland is where it's at. A few hours by car from the coast, the hills and pastoral countryside of the Granite Belt region are home to Queensland's wine country and artisanal food producers, from cheesemakers and chocolatiers to truffle farmers.

To the north of the Darling Downs is the country town of Toowoomba (population 120,000) the 'big smoke' of this fertile farming region. Here you'll find a lively bar and cafe scene to go with gourmet food stores and cosmopolitan dining. It's also famous as the birthplace of the lamington cake, an Aussie icon!

From here the route follows the edge of the Great Dividing Range into cooler climates for vineyards, orchards and olive groves. The Granite Belt is one of Australia's more distinctive wine regions with intimate cellar doors open for tastings of unusual grape varieties such as verdelho, fiano, durif, nebbiolo, saperavi, marsanne and monastrell rosé. Many also have restaurants offering produce-driven menus.

The Granite Belt Bike Trail is a leisurely way to explore the area along a 34km- (21 mile) trail between Stanthorpe and Ballandean. Stock up on local olives, farmhouse triple bries, chutneys, cider and organic produce along the way. Beer lovers will be happy to pause at a number of local breweries, including a few doing brews made using Manuka honey.

01 Darling Downs is farming country

02 Special occasions at Ballandean Estate

03 Full-bodied flavour at Ballandean Estate

04 Picnic Point Lookout in Toowoomba

01 BALLANDEAN ESTATE

In the small town of Ballandean, in the Granite Belt wine country, is Queensland's oldest family owned vineyards, where the Puglisi family have been at it since 1931. Stop in to taste its interesting range, from a fantastic merlot, saperavi or durif to a full-bodied fiano, and try to time your visit for its daily 11am winery tour. Also here is the region's best restaurant, Barrelroom & Larder (www.barrelroomrestaurant. com), offering culinary delights such as slow-cooked roast lamb shoulder and handmade fettuccini with prawns and scallops, among other dishes made using regional produce. Enjoy it among the 150-year-old wine barrels filled with port and muscat. If you call ahead you can order one of their gourmet picnic hampers to feast on among the vineyards. On the first weekend of May they host the Opera in the Vineyard festival with performances by Opera Queensland.
354 Sundown Rd, Ballandean; 07-4684 1226; www.ballandeanestate. com; 9am-5pm

02 JAMWORKS OF GLEN APLIN

A great place to tap into local Granite Belt produce is this cafe-provedore, which makes its own relishes, chutneys, marmalades and jams using quality local ingredients. Most are featured on the menu, from breakfast burritos with house-made smoky beans, chorizo, bacon, avocado, eggs and onion-chilli relish, to gourmet rump steak sandwiches with beetroot relish and tomato sauce. Many local wines and beers are available, and its shop sells award-winning cheeses, locally smoked meats and marinated vegetables, along with their own jams, jellies and chutneys, which you're welcome to taste test
7 Townsend Rd, Glen Aplin; 07-4683 4171; www.jamworks.com.au; 9.30am-4.30pm Fri-Tue

03 BRASS MONKEY BREW HOUSE

Pop by for an arvo session at this family-run nanobrewery just south of Stanthorpe. Its award-winning, small-batch beers are made using local hops, and include an English brown, alcoholic root

04

Sweet tooths will want to make a beeline for the strawberry cheesecake pastry at the Bakers Duck.

and ginger beers, and the usual suspects of pale ales, IPAs and pilsners among other European and American-style ales and ciders. Grab a tasting paddle and order from its beer-friendly menu of homemade bratwurst, pizzas and burgers to enjoy by the fire in the atmospheric, rustic tin shed. *106 Donges Rd, Severnlea; 0488 967 401; www.brassmonkey brewhouseptyltd.com; 10am-6pm Thu-Mon*

04 VARIAS

While Varias is easily Stanthorpe's finest place to dine, this restaurant isn't your everyday arrangement. Located within the Queensland College of Wine Tourism, here student chefs hone their culinary

skills under the supervision of professionals, where the emphasis is on seasonal, regional produce from the Granite Belt used for innovative mains. Order a la carte or with wine-matched set menus, where you can expect the likes of smoked goose sausages, grilled Thai lamb cutlets or slow-cooked sirloin in wine jus. Bookings are recommended. Foodies will also want to take the 10.30am tour (Thursday to Sunday), which involves a cooking demo and tastings of local wines and food. *Queensland College of Wine Tourism, 22 Caves Rd, Stanthorpe; 07-4685 5050; www.varias.com.au; 11am-2pm daily, 11am-2pm & 6-8pm Fri & Sat*

05 All sorts of truffled treats at the Truffle Discovery Centre

06 The magic ingredient

07 Granite Belt vines

05 TRUFFLE DISCOVERY CENTRE

Lovers of truffles won't want to miss out on this discovery centre and farm dedicated to one of the culinary world's most prized ingredients. Here they've planted French Black Perigord truffles, and there's a small interpretive centre where you will learn all about this delicious fungi on informative tours that include tastings of truffle-infused oils – available for purchase at its on-site shop. It's a good spot to stock up on gourmet provisions from the Granite Belt region, including local olives, cheeses, condiments and other homemade artisanal goods.
335 Church Rd, the Summit; www. trufflediscoverycentre.com.au; 10am-3.30pm Wed, Sat & Sun

06 BOIREANN WINES

Lauded by Aussie wine guru James Halliday – who ranked the premium reds here as good as any in Australia – Boireann Wines grow French and Italian grape varieties to produce quality, uncommon, cool-climate wines such as nebbiolo, sangiovese, mourvèdre and tannat. All are available for tasting in its small cellar door, which keeps things blissfully simple – no food; it's all about the wine. It's located on a bucolic property, 13km (8 miles) north of Stanthorpe.
26 Donnellys Castle Rd, the Summit; 07-4683 2194; www. boireannwinery.com.au; 10am-4pm Fri-Mon

07 THE BAKERS DUCK

Revered for its artisan organic sourdough and pastries, the Bakers Duck has become something of a Toowoomba institution. Sweet-tooths will want to make a beeline straight for the strawberry cheesecake pastry, or delectable, sugar-dusted almond croissants, all beautifully paired with top-notch filter coffees by local roaster Ground Up. For lunch, tuck into the likes of pork sausage rolls or bacon quiche, among a salivating-inducing range of savoury options.
124 Campbell St, Toowoomba; 1300 339 592; www.thebakersduck.com. au; 7am-1pm Wed-Sun

08 ZEV'S BISTRO

Toowoomba's acclaimed culinary choice is the hatted Zev's, set in the heart of town and run by owner-chef Kyle Zevenbergen. Here they abide to a locavore philosophy, changing the menu at a whim to what's available on any given day to create innovative modern Australian dishes, best experienced by ordering the chef's tasting menu and matched with local wines.
517 Ruthven St, Toowoomba; 07-4564 8636; www.zevsbistro.com; 5pm-late Tue-Sat

WHERE TO STAY

RIDGEMILL ESTATE

Get right among the vines of the Granite Belt with a night at Ridgemill Estate, offering boutique cabins with timber decks to enjoy views of the countryside and mountains. All have king beds, contemporary art, stylish furnishings and log fires. While you're here, sign up for a guided tasting with the winemaker. *www.ridgemillestate. com/stay*

WHAT TO DO

WINERY TOURS

Given most visitors come to the Granite Belt specifically for the wine, it makes sense to sign up for a boutique tour to get the most out of your time here. Stanthorpe Tours (www.stanthorpetours. com.au) are one of the recommended companies, run by guides Angie and Lachlan, offering a curated experience of the region with a focus on the winemakers and food producers.

Otherwise get on your bike and join Granite Belt Bicycle Tours (www. granitebeltbicycles.com. au), pedalling your way through Queensland wine country on anything from a four-hour to two-day tour, or take a self-guided trip with mapped itineraries and picnic hampers provided.

CELEBRATIONS

APPLE & GRAPE HARVEST FESTIVAL

This biennial harvest festival takes place during even years, with a celebration of the region's food and wine running over a 10-day period from late February to early March. On the last weekend, the festival culminates with a street parade and wine fiesta in Stanthorpe. *www.appleandgrape.org*

GET THERE
Fly into Cairns international
airport then hire a car to
explore the Tablelands region.
Note that public transport is
virtually non-existent.

01

ATHERTON TABLELANDS

[Queensland]

FARM-FRESH FARE ON THE ATHERTON TABLELANDS

A sprawling farming region in Far North Queensland, tucked away in the hills behind Cairns, has long capitalised on some of Australia's most fertile land.

The Atherton Tablelands is the common catchall used to describe the hinterland west of Cairns. Between long blinks, the landscape can change from crunchy bushland strewn with giant termite nests, to dense tropical rainforest, to undulant mountains and valleys, which stand as subtle reminders of an explosive past. Violent volcanoes not only restructured the region's topography tens of thousands of years ago, but also fertilised the land with nutrient-rich soil, subsequently creating one of Australia's most important agricultural areas.

For more than a century, farmers have toiled the Atherton Tablelands' prized plateau, rearing cattle and growing crops such as sugar cane, bananas, avocados, mangoes and maize, along with a supplementary list too long to catalogue neatly in a sentence. This produce naturally lends itself to paddock-to-plate food experiences, which have been embraced by local businesses in a down-to-earth way.

A journey along the Atherton Tablelands' food trail is a trip to the frontline of the region's agricultural heart. It's a chance to get an unadulterated look at life on the land, with farming families proudly opening their gates to the public to share the passion that drives them. No fancy facades, no marketing spin; just real people sharing the fruits, vegetables, tea leaves, spirits and milk of their labour with the kind of warm hospitality that's almost exclusive to country towns.

Cuisine and cordiality aside, the Atherton Tablelands also has some of Australia's most beautiful scenery. You can bathe under rainforest waterfalls, hike through national parks, cycle mountain bike trails and spot native wildlife such as wallabies, sugar gliders, platypus and hundreds of species of birds.

① NERADA TEA ROOMS

In Malanda, rows of waist-high *camellia sinensis* (tea) bushes extend across 360 hectares (890 acres) to form Australia's largest tea plantation. Nerada's verdant crop translates into 1.5 million kg (3.3 million lb) of black tea per year (or 750 million cups) and is produced entirely free of pesticides.

Take a guided tour of the farm to watch harvesters slash the tips of tightly packed hedges and see whirring shed machinery wither, grind and pack the fragrant leaves. Finish in the cafe overlooking the tea fields with a Devonshire or high tea (the house-made scones are divine). Pots of freshly brewed tea are a given, and can be infused with delicate flavours such as lemon myrtle or smooth vanilla oil. Nerada also runs tea-blending classes and hands-on tours that run through an abridged tea production line, complete with mini-machinery.

The Nerada property is also one of the best places to see Lumholtz's tree kangaroos, a rare marsupial unique to the Tablelands. *933 Glen Allyn Road, Malanda; 07-4096 8328; www.neradatea.com. au; 10am–4.30pm*

② MUNGALLI CREEK DAIRY

Following deregulation of Australia's dairy trade in 2000, the Watson family dodged the industry's downward spiral by building an on-site processing facility to make biodynamic products, pre-empting the organic trend and ensuing boom. Now, on 364 hectares (900 acres) of farmland overlooking Mount Bartle Frere, Queensland's highest mountain, Mungalli Creek has positioned itself as one of Australia's leading producers of planet-friendly dairy products.

The cafe on Mungalli Creek's working farm shows off many of the company's products via menu items such as savoury quark cheesecake and smoothies made with organic milk and freshly churned ice cream.

Driving to Mungalli Creek is as much of a highlight as a visit to the dairy itself – the road winds through a landscape of deep valleys and green mountains rolling off into the distance. Mungalli Creek is also ideally positioned near Millaa Millaa's rainforest waterfall circuit,

'Tours of the working dairy are only offered to pre-arranged groups, but there is a farmhouse café called 'Out of the Whey' that can be visited.'

Michelle Bell-Turner, Mungalli Creek Dairy

so pop in for lunch after checking out Ellinjaa, Zillie and Millaa Millaa falls. The latter is one of Australia's most photographed waterfalls. *254 Brooks Road, Millaa Millaa; 07-4097 2232; www. mungallicreekdairy.com.au; 10am–4pm*

03 HISTORIC VILLAGE HERBERTON

The question of what constitutes Australian food is a challenging one, but a few culinary mainstays can be drawn from the country's pioneering days. Notably, damper (dense, wheat-based bread), stew and billy (black) tea became the humble sustenance for miners, loggers and other labourers as they tamed and industrialised Australia's

rugged countryside in the 19th century. Although the antithesis of gourmet, this is authentic Aussie food and it's celebrated at the Herberton Historic Village's outdoor 'Pioneer Camp', run on weekends and during school holidays. Everything is prepared traditionally over a campfire and can be enjoyed with views of the Wild River and meticulously curated outdoor museum.

Across 6.5 hectares (16 acres), more than 50 restored buildings filled with thousands of relics showcase Herberton's early years as a tin mining town. Locals Harry and Ellen Skennar founded the village in the 1970s, but the collector's baton has since passed to Craig and Connie Kimberley,

05 Cheesecake choices at Mungalli Creek Dairy

06 The Mungalli Creek Dairy farmstead

07 Lake Eacham in Crater Lakes National Park

who combine an unbridled passion for the past with sharp business acumen (the Kimberleys having founded retail giant Just Jeans) to create a magical snapshot of a bygone era.

Home-style Aussie food is also served in the former Bakerville Hotel (now the Bakerville Tearooms) – built in the 1890s and transported to the village in three sections from its namesake town.
6 Broadway, Herberton; 07-4096 2002; www. historicvillageherberton.com.au; 9.30am–4pm

04 MT UNCLE DISTILLERY

The spirits at Mt Uncle are as good as you'll get anywhere. In fact, maybe better. The distillery's Iridium rum was named best in the world at the 2019 World Rum Awards in London and its Botanic Australis navy-strength gin was awarded best in class by the Australian Gin Distillers Association, adding to a bag of honours consistently collected since Mt Uncle was established in 2001.

The show is fronted by owner and head distiller, Mark Watkins, who began distilling booze at the back of his parents' farm at age 16. The hobby could have been a slippery slope for a cheeky teenager, but for Watkins, it was the seed of a passion that founded a fruitful career.

Watkins puts his potion-making success down to the use of a copper pot still from Germany (affectionately named Helga), optimal altitude, and native Australian botanicals, such as cinnamon myrtle and strawberry gum – many of which are plucked from Mt Uncle's own garden. The distillery's agave plantation fuels a range of white and aged agave spirits, similar to tequila, and rum is made with sugar syrup from the Arriga mill down the road.

Expertly crafted spirits, inspired by everything from a bushfire to a hangover, can be sipped in Mt Uncle's tasting room, peacefully hidden amongst a banana plantation. Say hi to the resident alpacas and donkeys on your way out of the place.
1819 Chewko Rd, Walkamin; 07-4086 8008; www.mtuncle.com; 10am–4pm

05 GOLDEN DROP WINERY

The Nastasi family began replacing their tobacco crop with mango trees in 1975 after sensing the tobacco industry's terminal downturn. They now own one of Australia's largest mango plantations and, reminiscent of the tropics, have secured an unusual niche market by turning mangoes into wine.

Sample mango-based liqueurs and sparkling, fortified and table wine in the tasting room set amid the bustle of the fruit packing shed. Not a fan of the mango? They make citrus and dragon fruit liqueurs too.
227 Bilwon Rd, Biboohra; 07-4093 2750; www.goldendrop.com.au; 9am–5pm

WHERE TO STAY
ROSE GUMS WILDERNESS RETREAT
Bunk in a treehouse on a 93-hectare (230-acre) property for an immersive rainforest experience. The high-ceilinged villas are naturally air-conditioned by mountain breezes, and timber finishes, log fires and large bathtubs exude romance.
www.rosegums.com.au

BLUE SUMMIT HIDEAWAY
These modern apartments and villas in the quaint village of Yungaburra can sleep anywhere from one to six people. The entrance is on the main road into town and the property backs onto parkland.
www.
bluesummithideaway.
com.au

WHERE TO EAT
OBI'S RESTAURANT
Despite its somewhat confused decor and pub-like atmosphere, this place gets the most important thing right – the food. Co-chefs Clinton Oberhauser and Michael Chitavong trained and worked in hatted restaurants in Melbourne before migrating north, and their culinary finesse pegs Obi's as one of the Tablelands' best dining options.
1/222 Byrnes St, Mareeba; 07-4095 2022; www.obisrestaurant. com; Wed-Sat noon–2pm and 5.30–8.30pm

WHAT TO DO
CRATER LAKES
Two deep volcanic vents filled with rainwater are tucked away in the Crater Lakes National Park, 10km (6.2 miles) apart. Lake Eacham is the top pick for swimming, while Lake Barrine is a favourite for its 80-year-old waterfront teahouse. Both are fringed by rainforest and encircled by a walking track.

Off Gilles Range Rd

GRANITE GORGE NATURE PARK
Climb over giant granite boulders for panoramic views of the tableland and to see an adorable mob of wild but sociable rock wallabies. The park is privately owned and hence has an entrance fee. Camping is available.
www.granitegorge.com. au

GET THERE
Having an international airport, the Gold Coast is easily accessible from across Australia and there are direct flights from New Zealand and Asia. It's located halfway between Brisbane and Byron Bay, so it's well positioned for those embarking on a road trip. Otherwise frequent tourist buses ply the route between each of the towns.

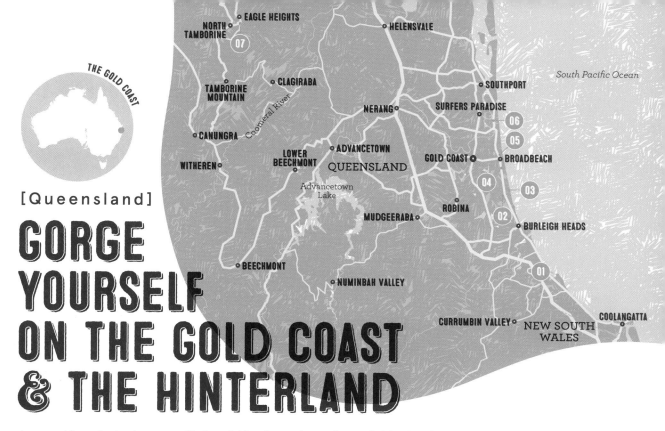

THE GOLD COAST

EAGLE HEIGHTS
NORTH TAMBORINE
07
HELENSVALE
TAMBORINE MOUNTAIN
CLAGIRABA
SOUTHPORT
Coomera River
NERANG
SURFERS PARADISE
06
CANUNGRA
05
WITHEREN
LOWER BEECHMONT
ADVANCETOWN
QUEENSLAND
GOLD COAST
BROADBEACH
Advancetown Lake
04
03
ROBINA
02
MUDGEERABA
BURLEIGH HEADS
01
BEECHMONT
NUMINBAH VALLEY
CURRUMBIN VALLEY
NEW SOUTH WALES
COOLANGATTA
South Pacific Ocean

[Queensland]

GORGE YOURSELF ON THE GOLD COAST & THE HINTERLAND

Leave time in between stints at the beach and poolside to discover the Gold Coast's booming food-and-drink scene, led by a new generation of artisan producers and chefs.

We're not going to pretend you've come to the Gold Coast primarily for its culture and culinary pleasures. Of course you're here for the beach and the surf – and with that long, white sandy coastline, why wouldn't you? But once you're here, you will be pleasantly surprised by just how much of a food destination the Gold Coast has become in recent years, with an epicurean scene that's booming.

Big-city foodies – who've not dared set foot on the Gold Coast – might be inclined to put a line through it as a gourmet destination based on the outdated stereotype that it's nothing but high-rises, tacky beach resorts, fast-food chains and daggy restaurant chains. But news flash! Things have definitely changed here since the 1980s. These days it has fantastic third-wave coffee roasters; some of the country's best microbreweries; hip cafes dedicated to everything sustainable, ethical,

local and organic; and coastal modern Australian restaurants set up by creative chefs doing gastronomic menus loaded with seasonal flavours.

While Surfers Paradise is the most famous destination along the Gold Coast, south from here lies a 52km (32 mile) sprawl of beach towns and neighbourhoods – Mermaid Beach, Burleigh, Curumbin, Miami – where food is really taking off. With a young, passionate new generation at the helm, here you'll find coastal chic cafes and hip bars serving up inventive dishes.

The region also encompasses the subtropical Gold Coast Hinterland. A short drive inland from the beaches will lead you to its cool-temperate rainforests, mountain ranges and national parks full of wildlife. Among the forested townships are lovely rustic cafes, artisanal food producers, winemakers and breweries that make the hinterland an essential detour.

01 The Gold Coast on the horizon

02 Fresh pizza at Miami Marketta

03 Miami Marketta

04 Delicious dishes at Bam Bam Bakehouse

❶ BALTER BREWING COMPANY

While its location in the industrial backstreets can't compete with the beach views of the surf life-saving club bistros around these parts, the beer certainly can. For several years in a row, Balter have been voted Australia's best craft brewery, and a visit to its taproom is a must for beer lovers. Make your way through its fruity, hoppy and flavoursome range, offering a full spectrum of tastes from sessionable and hazy to big and bold. While it's no longer certified independent (it was bought by CUB in 2019), the quality ingredients and style remains unchanged. Local surf legend Mick Fanning is one of the owners and occasionally can be seen pulling beers behind the bar in a space surrounded by production vats. If you're after a feed you'll find food trucks parked out front cooking up tacos, Korean and burgers.
14 Traders Way, Currumbin Waters; 07-5525 6916; www.balter. com.au; 2-8pm Wed-Sun

❷ MIAMI MARKETTA

Catering to coastal hipsters with a hankering for global street food, this abandoned warehouse has been converted into a food and bar precinct. Decked out in fairy lights and with art on the walls, it's an atmospheric spot to wander and decide between the likes of American BBQ, woodfired pizza, homemade pasta, authentic soft-corn tacos or Japanese tempura to woof down on tables scattered about. There are several bars too, shaking up cocktails and serving cold cans of local craft beer.
23 Hillcrest Parade, Miami; 0488 590 599; www.miamimarketta. com; 5pm-late Wed & Fri, 4pm-late Sat

❸ BSKT CAFE

A shining example of the Gold Coast's thriving urban-beachside food scene is this laidback corner cafe just a few steps from Nobby's Beach. Here it's all about healthy, clean eating with a menu of contemporary, organic breakfast and brunch fare to enjoy among industrial-chic environs. There's a heap of choices to keep all diners

Be sure to visit the arty town of Tamborine Mountain, known for its artisanal food producers, including the award-winning Witches Chase cheesemakers.

happy – from vegans and paleos, to everyone in between – with flavours that span the globe.

Try its signature chicken banh mi in a crusty baguette and loaded with fresh chilli, a vegan pad thai made using zucchini noodles, or fresh salmon poke bowl. Good coffee – and all manner of modern health drinks – is available along with an equally appealing yet less healthy choice of locally brewed booze. The fact that it's dog friendly sums up the cruisy disposition of this place.
4 Lavarack Rd, Mermaid Beach; 07-5526 6565; www.facebook. com/BSKTcafe; 6am-1pm

04 BAM BAM BAKEHOUSE

Another Gold Coast gem away from the beach is this elegant, leafy cafe that overlooks a park and caters to in-the-know foodies who've sought out the place from word-of-mouth devotees. Most folk are drawn in by its house-baked cream-filled pastries, buttery croissants and artisanal sourdough, but end up staying to order brunch from its menu featuring omelettes with chilli crab or the crispy Karaage (Japanese fried chicken) burgers. It has its celebrity fans too, including Hollywood A-lister, and local Gold Coast girl, Margot Robbie.
2519 Gold Coast Hwy, Mermaid Beach; 0488 085 802; www. bambambakehouse.com; 6.30am-3pm

05 Street food at
Miami Marketta

06 Explore temperate
rainforest in Lamington
National Park

05 SOCIAL EATING HOUSE & BAR

One of the Gold Coast's best for modern Australian is this hatted, casual fine diner on the ground floor below a contemporary high-rise complex. Shared plates of locally sourced seafood and meats are the focus here, with a hulking 1kg (2lb) slow-cooked lamb, marinated in sheep-milk yoghurt, being the standout. Smaller plates of its house charcuterie, or fried zucchini blossom filled with buffalo ricotta, pinenuts and honey, are the perfect way to kick things off, accompanied by well-made cocktails and a quality wine list. *Shop 137/3 Oracle Bvd, Broadbeach; 07-5504 5210; www. socialeatinghouse.com.au; noon-midnight*

06 PARADOX COFFEE ROASTERS

There's no shortage of coffee places in Surfers, but the challenge is finding a good one. And that's where Paradox steps in with its third-wave approach, sourcing single-origin beans directly from farmers and co-ops across the globe to ensure quality and sustainability. Its beans are roasted on-site at red-brick premises, where knowledgeable baristas prepare filter coffees using V60, Aeropress or Chemex, along with all the usual milk (and non-dairy) concoctions. Food is also a highlight, with an all-day menu of bagels, burgers and big brekkies. *10 Beach Rd, Surfers Paradise; 07-5538 3235; www.paradoxroasters. com; 7am-2pm*

07 WITCHES CHASE CHEESE COMPANY

As lovely as the Gold Coast's beaches are, you don't want to miss out on its rainforest interior, so jump in the car for a day exploring the hinterland national parks, comprising walking trails, superb landscapes and rewarding wildlife viewing. Be sure to visit the arty town of Tamborine Mountain, known for its artisanal food producers, including the award-winning Witches Chase cheesemakers. All its dairy goodness is made on-site, from yoghurt and ice cream to their signature small-batch cheeses. Sample the likes of goat cheese feta, triple cream brie, 'misty mountain' blue, clothbound and aged cheddars, milk curds and the 'Tamembert', their local version of camembert. The attached Fortitude Valley Brewery (www. fortitudebrewing.com.au) also stocks their cheese, so you can pair it with a tasting paddle of IPA, pale, golden, and summer ales. *165/185 Long Rd, Tamborine Mountain; 07-5545 2032; www. witcheschasecheese.com.au; 10am-4pm*

WHERE TO STAY

SONGBIRDS

This classy rainforest retreat just outside Tamborine Mountain is a must for foodies and nature lovers. Its six elegant, light-filled villas are immersed among 21 hectares (51 acres) of lush tranquil forest; each tastefully furnished and featuring a spa, king-size bed and balcony to enjoy the views. Its restaurant is open Thursday to Sunday, offering creative cuisine using produce grown in its kitchen garden and there is an excellent wine list. *www.songbirds.com.au*

WHAT TO DO

LAMINGTON NATIONAL PARK

With a whole coastline of lily-white sandy beaches and theme parks to choose from, there are plenty of things to keep you busy on the Gold Coast, but its hinterland is something that shouldn't be missed. Vast areas of national parks feature sublime rainforest,

magical waterfalls and mountainous scenery. The 206-sq-km (80-sq-mile) Lamington National Park is one of its most beautiful, and most famous for its World Heritage-listed subtropical rainforest, offering plenty of walking trails, birdlife and native animals. *http://parks.des.qld.gov. au/parks/lamington*

CELEBRATIONS

GOLD COAST FOOD AND WINE FESTIVAL

This yearly expo showcases the best of the region's gourmet produce and artisanal food and beverage. There's opportunity to sample Gold Coast cheese, beer and wine, along with interesting cooking demos conducted by well-renowned, local chefs. *www.facebook.com/ goldcoastfoodandwine*

GET THERE

Brisbane Airport, 16km (10 miles) from the city centre, has domestic connections, as well as direct international flights to New Zealand, the Pacific islands, North America and Asia. This trail begins in the West End – best way to access the area from the airport is with the Airtrain to South Brisbane station. For drivers, there's street parking in the area. Brisbane also has buses, taxis, and the CityCat river boats.

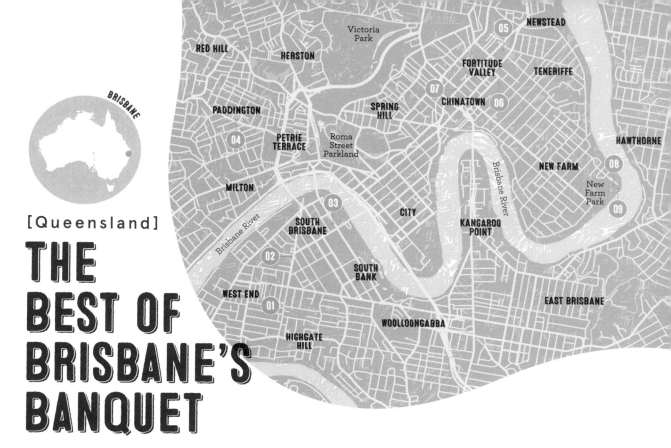

BRISBANE

RED HILL

HERSTON

Victoria
Park

NEWSTEAD

05

PADDINGTON

FORTITUDE
VALLEY

TENERIFFE

04

PETRIE
TERRACE

SPRING
HILL

07

CHINATOWN

06

Roma
Street
Parkland

MILTON

03

Brisbane River

HAWTHORNE

New Farm

08

New
Farm
Park

09

Brisbane River

SOUTH
BRISBANE

CITY

KANGAROO
POINT

02

WEST END

SOUTH
BANK

EAST BRISBANE

01

WOOLLOONGABBA

HIGHGATE
HILL

[Queensland]

THE BEST OF BRISBANE'S BANQUET

Queensland's riverside capital has a host of modern restaurants and cafes that make the most of local produce and aren't afraid to tinker with the classics.

Brisbane takes a lot of people by surprise. This is the city that's supposed to be little more than a country town, a place ironically and lovingly referred to by its residents as 'Brisvegas', with all of Sin City's bright lights and largesse (or not). Food-loving visitors tend not to expect a lot from the Queensland capital, tucked into the state's south-east corner. And then they arrive, however, and find that the place has boomed.

There's plenty to eat in Brisbane these days, plenty that's fresh and local and good, expertly prepared and professionally served. The modern culinary scene here runs the gamut from artisan coffee to inventive cocktails, from authentic takes on world cuisine to wildly creative modern Australian food, from no-frills casual eateries to sumptuous fine-diners. Brisbane's booming scene is attracting chefs from around the country, but it's also nurturing some impressive local talent.

Every neighbourhood here has its own foodie identity, from the cafes of artsy West End to the modern eateries of smart South Brisbane, the upmarket fine-diners in bustling Fortitude Valley to the open-air markets in languid New Farm. If there's a thread that binds these disparate culinary parts it's the use of high-quality regional produce, the likes of bugs from Moreton Bay, scallops from Hervey Bay, and beef from Queensland farms, all of which appear regularly on local menus.

Brisbane's venues do take their cues from other Australian cities – you'll find Melbourne-style wine bars here, and Sydney-style brunch cafes – but they're presented with a style and an attitude all of their own, a friendly, unpretentious manner that's as refreshing to many visiting diners as a cold beer on a warm, tropical afternoon.

01 Brisbane, also known as BrisVegas

02 The city's skyline

03 Eating at Gerard's

04 The interior of Gerard's Bistro

01 MORNING AFTER

Brisbane's West End is one of those classic inner-city suburbs, the kind that used to be a little shady, with pool halls and takeaway joints, but which has morphed into one of the city's most exciting creative hubs, brimming with high-quality restaurants and cafes. One of the purveyors of fine coffee is Morning After, a bright space with white-tiled walls and plenty of natural light, where owners Soula Passaris and her son Yianni are serving up an inventive menu. Don't miss the breakfast carbonara: pappardelle pasta with a 63-degree egg, mushrooms, pancetta and manchego.
Cambridge St, West End; 07-3844 0500; www.morningafter.com.au; 7am-4pm

02 THE GUNSHOP CAFE

A little further down the road in West End, the Gunshop is a suburban stalwart, one of the first cafes to shake the area up, and one that remains extremely popular. That's thanks in no small part to the excellent coffee and brunch options (the potato and feta hashcakes are legendary), but also to the evolving night-time fare. From Wednesdays to Saturdays the cafe does a restaurant-style dinner seating, serving modern Australian cuisine paired with inventive cocktails.
53 Mollison St, West End; 07-3844 2241; www.facebook.com/The. Gunshop.cafe; 7am-9pm Wed-Sat, 7am-3pm Sun-Tue

03 GAUGE

For signs of South Brisbane's artistic cred, head directly to GoMA, the Gallery of Modern Art, an exhibition space that has attracted some of the world's biggest names – Picasso, Warhol, Matisse – since its inception in 2006. And for further proof, turn your attention nearby to Gauge, a local restaurant with a seriously inventive menu. Chefs Cormac Bradfield and Phil Marchant have gradually eased Gauge from a breakfast-friendly cafe into an avant-garde fine-diner, with guests served the likes of beef tartare with XO sauce and capers, 'blood taco' with mushroom and bone marrow duxelles, and 'garlic bread' with brown butter and burnt vanilla.

04

It sounds challenging, but these guys know what they're doing. *77 Grey St, South Brisbane; 07-3638 0431; www.gaugebrisbane. com.au; 5-10.30pm Wed-Fri, 8am-2.30pm, 5-10.30pm Sat, 8am-2.30pm Sun*

04 NGON

Brisbane is a multicultural city with restaurants serving a host of authentic cuisines, from Thai to Sri Lankan, Greek to Lebanese. There's also some excellent Vietnamese food, headed up by Ngon, a casual place in the formerly one-paced Given Terrace area of Paddington. Run by chef Tuan Nguyen, Ngon serves up classics such as hearty bowls of pho, rice-paper rolls and curries, but has also become famous for its breakfast banh mi, a crusty baguette filled with eggs, pate, bacon and pickled vegetables. *233 Given Tce, Paddington; 07-3705 3082; ngonbrisbane.com.au; 11am-2.30pm, 5.30-9pm Tue-Sat, 11am-2.30pm Sun*

05 TARTUFO

The tour now leads to the place it was always heading: Fortitude Valley. This formerly divey neighbourhood has been at the heart of Brisbane's gastronomic scene for decades now, with everything from wine bars to dumpling joints to award-winning fine-diners popping up. 'The Valley' is still a nightlife hub, but mostly people come here to eat, and one of the best venues to do that is Tartufo. Nestled in the fancy Emporium complex, all blushing red banquettes and art-deco trimmings, this is the perfect location for classic Italian fare, and Naples transplant chef Tony Percuoco doesn't disappoint: try mackerel crudo with orange and fennel, linguine with wild mushrooms and truffle, or sous vide lamb with gremolata. *1000 Ann St, Fortitude Valley; 07-3852 1500; www.tartufo.com.au; noon-10pm*

06 GERARD'S BISTRO

Gerard's was always good – but now it's great. Set on bustling James St, amid cafes and wine bars and boutiques, this restaurant was the pioneer of Middle Eastern–inspired

05 Take a boat along
the Brisbane River

06 Post Office Square
in downtown Brisbane

fine-dining in Brisbane, a concept that has been refined by chef Adam Wolfers. The former Sydney resident creates art on a plate, taking Levantine classics and pairing them with Australian ingredients: kangaroo kafta with labne, grilled Wagonga oysters with Baharat butter, and Moreton Bay bugs with tabbouleh and bisque. Take a look around on any night in Gerard's and you'll see a who's who of Brisbane foodies: this is the hottest table in town.
14 James St, Fortitude Valley; 07-3852 3822; gerardsbistro.com.au; noon-3pm & 6pm-midnight Thu-Sun, 6pm-midnight Mon-Wed

07 GREASER

The Valley wasn't always fancy. It used to be all dive bars and dark clubs, music venues and late-night eateries. Greaser is a throwback to those times, a subterranean bar with a retro American fit-out, graffiti for artwork and bare wooden stools.

The menu is wall-to-wall dude food: burgers and fried chicken, hot dogs and jalapeño poppers. The drinks are local microbrews or American craft beers. If you're wondering where Brisbane's cool kids are hanging out late at night, it's here.
259 Brunswick St, Fortitude Valley; 07-3648 9036; www.greaser.com. au; 5pm-midnight Wed, Thu & Sun, 5pm-3am Fri-Sat

08 JAN POWERS FARMERS' MARKET

Jan Power was a pioneer of the Brisbane food scene, a passionate local cook and foodie who dragged the city almost single-handedly into culinary awareness. Her legacy lives on, too, in a series of popular farmers' markets in three locations around the city. The Saturday market at the Powerhouse – a power station turned performance space beside leafy New Farm Park – is the original and the best; the

ideal place to pick up organic, locally grown produce. There are also stalls here selling pastries, pizzas, coffee, dumplings, and more.
119 Lamington St, New Farm; www. janpowersfarmersmarkets.com.au; 6am-noon Sat

09 BAR ALTO

Once the farmers' markets have died down, head inside the Powerhouse to visit another Brisbane institution: Bar Alto, which serves modern Italian food paired with a stunning view of Brisbane River. You come here to eat, of course, to try chef Sajith Vengateri's fried zucchini flowers with peas and ricotta, his risotto with Hervey Bay scallops, or calf's liver with caramelised onions. But you stay for that view, as quintessentially Brisbane, languid and lazy, as you'll find.
119 Lamington St, New Farm; 07-3358 1063; www.baralto.com.au; 9.30am-midnight Tue-Sun

WHERE TO STAY

THE CALILE HOTEL

The Calile is a smart boutique hotel in the James St restaurant precinct, with 50s-style interiors and an Instagram-worthy pool. It's also home to Hellenika, an excellent modern Greek restaurant.
www.thecalilehotel.com

OVOLO THE VALLEY

Another boutique hotel that's walking distance to plenty of the restaurants mentioned in this trail, Ovolo is a colourful, eclectic property with all the mod-cons, plus a rooftop pool and a sauna.
www.ovolohotels.com

WHAT TO DO

SIRROMET WINERY

Tropical Queensland isn't exactly known for its wine. However, Sirromet, a vineyard just outside Brisbane in pretty Mt Cotton, is worth the drive. The company offers wine tastings, dining at Lurleen's, and accommodation on-site.
www.sirromet.com

SOUTH BANK

Brisbane lies between two beach hotspots – the Gold and Sunshine Coasts – but doesn't have a patch of sand to call its own. That is, except at South Bank, which has a manmade beach and lagoon, perfect for cooling off in summer.
www.visitsouthbank.com.au

CITYCAT

Brisbane's river-borne public transport system, the CityCat, is both ferry service and tourist attraction, the perfect way to get around and see the city from the water.
www.brisbane.qld.gov.au

CELEBRATIONS

REGIONAL FLAVOURS FESTIVAL NEW SOUTH WALES

This free two-day festival, held on the banks of the river each July, celebrates local produce and chefs.
www.regionalflavours.com.au

GET THERE
The South Australian capital's airport services nine international destinations directly with onward connection to 300+ locations. Just a 10-minute drive from the city centre, the airport services over 480 weekly domestic flights and is easily accessed from all major Australian cities and many regional centres.

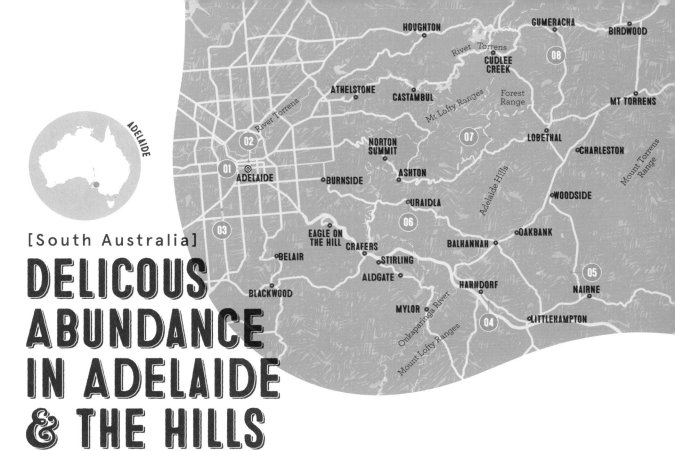

[South Australia]
DELICOUS ABUNDANCE IN ADELAIDE & THE HILLS

This bohemian capital spearheads South Australia's sophisticated small-bar culture while the surrounding foothills offer a patchwork of vines, orchards and farms.

Adelaide and its bordering foothills, known as the Adelaide Hills, are bursting with ingenious and adventurous producers determined to disrupt established norms. South Australia is home to some of the world's most celebrated and awarded independent grocers who collaborate and cooperate with each other and their customers: the boisterous Adelaide Central Market continues to shine as one of the best of its type in the Southern Hemisphere.

Easy-to-navigate Adelaide is arguably Australia's cultural hub and home to the much-lauded Adelaide Festival, Adelaide Fringe Festival and WOMADelaide, which crowd the capital's events calendar in March. In recent years, a small-bar culture has rejuvenated the city's former 'red-light' zones. Gin-thusiasts can rejoice, the proliferation of locally distilled gins has seen Adelaide referred to as 'Australia's Gin Capital';

not bad for a city that's a gateway to the country's highest yielding wine regions.

The patchwork of boutique producers in the surrounding leafy Adelaide Hills exemplifies the region's diversity. First-class wineries rub shoulders with cute berry farms, ambitious microdistilleries, clever cheesemongers and reinvented country pubs. At the heart of each is a focus on showcasing the region's best sustainably sourced ingredients. From sampling fragrant small batch gins in an old 1940's coldstore at Gumeracha's Applewood Distillery to handpicking juicy strawberries at Beerenberg Farm, the Adelaide Hills producers clearly care for their surrounds where the focus of the experience is on consumer education. Rustic charm, delightful characters and a respect for the material's source all await visitors to this perfect little patch of the planet.

01 ADELAIDE CENTRAL MARKET

This market has been a thriving food hub of South Australia's capital for over 150 years, with stallholders jostling for attention. Cases of seafood, caught off the wild South Australian coast, sit opposite stands devoted to the fragrant honey and gin of Kangaroo Island and condiments from the Barossa Valley. The undercover market, one of the largest in the Southern Hemisphere, is the ultimate showcase of the state's produce network. Start the day with a freshly-ground coffee.
44-60 Gouger St, Adelaide; 08-8203 7494; www. adelaidecentralmarket.com.au; 7am-5.30pm Tue, 9am-5.30pm Wed, 9am-7pm Thu, Sat 7am-3pm

02 CLEVER LITTLE TAILOR

The 'West End' of Adelaide's CBD has become a haven for small bars and niche dining. Tucked away on Peel St, near the Adelaide Central Market, is Clever Little Tailor one of the state's best little drinking joints. Oozing design cred the bar's rustic charm, enhanced by the exposed brickwork, sets the tone. The cocktail list is loaded with concoctions, specialising in locally produced gins and vodkas from the likes of Red Hen and 23rd Street Distillery. If gin's not your thing then check the wine list for a carefully tailored selection of the state's best drops.
19 Peel Street, Adelaide; www. cleverlittletailor.com.au; 4pm- midnight Mon-Thu, to 2am Fri & Sat

03 PATIO COFFEE ROASTERS

Tamp like a boss they promise and tamp you will. Located on busy South Road, Patio Coffee Roasters is not only a roaster/ cafe but also a training school offering caffeine fiends an opportunity to join a 'home barista' or 'home roasting' course. These short one- or two-day courses allow attendees to optimise their home technique, helping punters make the most out of their machines. Whether it's beans, a brew (hot or cold) or education that you're after, Patio's passionate coffee professionals have you covered.
678 South Road, Glandore; 08-8463 1651; www.patiocoffee.com.au

01 South Australia's
first vines were planted
in Adelaide in 1836

02 An edible selection
at Lot 100

03 Garry Sweeney, Mt
Lofty Ranges' owner
and winemaker

04 Lot 100's vineyards

04 BEERENBERG FARM

Producing some of Australia's best jams, chutneys and condiments, Beerenberg Farm is an Adelaide Hills institution whose history dates back 200 years. Translating to 'Berry Hill' in German and located on the outskirts of the outrageously kitsch town of Hahndorf, the farm has been owned by the same family for six generations. During the summer guests are invited to take part in the Taste of Beerenberg; a 90-minute tasting, grazing, storytelling and strawberry-picking experience. From November to April, weather depending, the strawberry field is open for the foraging of the fruit. *2106 Mount Barker Road, Hahndorf; 08-8388 7272; www.beerenberg. com.au; shop 9am-5pm daily*

05 LOT 100

This collective of businesses has become the darling of the Adelaide culinary trail; essentially a cellar door experience that's been completely reinvented to cater for a modern audience. Adelaide Hills Distillery, Mismatch Brewing, the Hills Cider Company, Vinteloper, Ashton Valley Fresh Juices and the Lot 100 restaurant all cohabit under the one roof offering meandering views of the Hay Valley.

The 'better liquid, better nourishment' philosophy of the venture permeates through the entire experience. The casually stylish restaurant delivers an unpretentious and old-school Italian-style menu not afraid to offer a few surprises such as Coorong mullet and Goolwa pipis alongside simple pizzas and a mind-blowing baked gnocchi. The vast bar offers five different beverage flights –the pick being Shannon's selection from the Adelaide Hills Distillery offering a sample of, amongst others, its famous Green Ant Gin. *68 Chambers Road, Hay Valley; 08-7077 2888; www.lot100.com.au; 11am-5pm Thurs-Sun*

06 URAIDLA HOTEL

The perfect example of an Aussie pub reinvented. Utilising some of South Australia's most lush produce-growing areas this unashamedly quirky Adelaide Hills landmark is leading the way

05 Tasting time at Applewood Distillery

06 Applewood Distillery

07 Good times at Crush wine festival

for Aussie pubs with a mantra of 'reduce, re-use, refuse and recycle'. The menu is broad and thoughtful and the servings beyond generous, think Port Lincoln sardines with currants and capers or a local lamb rump topped with a pistachio salsa. All of the ingredients are sourced directly from produce grown on-site or via ethically sustainable suppliers from within South Australia. Their soil-to-soul philosophy, the killer wine list and the recently opened bakery, cafe and brewery make the Uraidla Hotel the perfect place for a long lunch in the Hills. *154 Greenhill Rd, Uraidla; 08-8390 0500; www.uraidlahotel.com. au; noon-2.30pm & 5.30-8.30pm Thu-Sat, noon-2.30pm & 5.30-8pm Sun-Wed*

07 MT LOFTY RANGES WINES

Located on a typical winding Adelaide Hills road Mount Lofty Vineyard is the quintessential Hills winery. The dramatically steep and picturesque vineyard, located on a former apple orchard, the charming barn-door-style cellar door and the award-winning restaurant combine to make for the perfect wining and dining experience. Although classified as a cool-climate vineyard, it's surprising to see a robust shiraz on offer alongside a deliciously crisp *méthode traditionnelle* sparkling. Bookings for lunch are essential with every table offering panoramic views of the vineyard where, if you're lucky, you may spot an echidna wandering under the vines. *166 Harris Rd, Lenswood; 08-8389 8339; www.mtloftyrangesvineyard. com.au; 11am-5pm*

08 APPLEWOOD DISTILLERY / UNICO ZELO WINERY

A former fruit coldstore, erected in the 1940s on the outskirts of sleepy Hills town Gumeracha, is now the artfully restored dual home of micro-distiller Applewood Distillery and Unico Zelo winery. With distillery tours offered twice daily visitors can meet the iconic Kath & Kim, two of Applewood's recently installed stills, while also being introduced to ancient wine practices such as amphora vessels. Applewood's generous gin flights not only contain their signature gin and Native Australian Okar, a spin on Campari, but surprise visitors with the inclusion of samples of their seasonal small-batch offerings. *24 Victoria St, Gumeracha; 08-8389 1250; www. applewooddistillery.com.au; 11am-4pm Mon-Thu, to 6pm Fri-Sun*

WHERE TO STAY
MAYFAIR HOTEL
Centrally located on bustling King William St, the chic Mayfair Hotel is the perfect base to explore Adelaide's laneways and small-bar scene and only a short walk from the Adelaide Central Market.
www.mayfairhotel.com.au

WHAT TO DO
NATIONAL WINE CENTRE OF AUSTRALIA
Nestled in Adelaide's picturesque Botanic Gardens sits a massive wine-barrel-shaped building where visitors can explore Australia's relatively young wine history and sample its spoils.
nationalwinecentre.com.au

CELEBRATIONS
CRUSH FESTIVAL
Taking place annually in late January the Crush Festival celebrates the Adelaide Hills wine community with a weekend of wine, regionally sourced food, song and dance. You'll

need a designated driver for this one!
www.crushfestival.com.au

TASTING AUSTRALIA
One of the world's most exciting and unique food festivals Tasting Australia takes place in Adelaide across late March and early April annually. The 10-day festival is an indulgence fest where

long lunches, culinary masterclasses and the best eating and drinking experiences await.
www.tastingaustralia.com.au

WOMADELAIDE
Make sure you've packed the sunscreen for this iconic outdoor festival that takes place in Botanic Park on the outskirts of Adelaide's

CBD at the end of the hot Aussie summer. Eclectic, electric and not-to-be-missed this four-day festival takes place during Adelaide's 'Mad March', which includes the much-lauded Adelaide Festival and accompanying Adelaide Fringe Festival. Be warned – book well in advance.
www.womadelaide.com.au

GET THERE
Clare Valley is a 120km,
90-minute drive north
from Adelaide. Yorke Pen-
insula Coaches runs from
Adelaide to Clare ($46; 2½
hours) every other day.

CLARE VALLEY

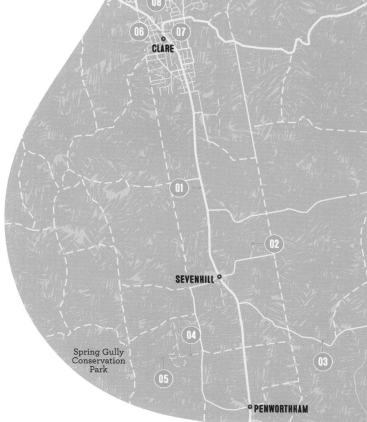

[South Australia]

CYCLING THROUGH THE CLARE VALLEY

Glide past sweet-smelling eucalypts to visit cellar doors in historic stone buildings, while enjoying local, seasonal dining.

You're a long way from the rain-soaked Emerald Isle's County Clare, after which explorers named this region in the mid-1800s. Here you'll find bright open skies, stands of large gumtrees, and rolling brown hills now covered in wheat and vines.

A cluster of towns in the valley – Clare, Mintaro, Sevenhill, Auburn and Burra –date from the 1840s, many built to service copper mines. Today beautiful, historic buildings and colonial street fronts house cafes, restaurants and accommodation, as well as servicing agricultural industries that survive into the twenty-first century despite the region's proximity to desert country.

Pre-book hire bikes or a guided tour, and cycle between cellar doors on the Riesling Trail, one of the region's top gourmet activities. The rail trail passes a number of wineries: detours along rolling back roads will take you to others.

Cellar doors give ample opportunity to taste and purchase wines, meet local vignerons, and learn about contemporary, environmentally friendly viticultural practices as the Australian wine industry prepares for climate changes. The Clare Valley also has its own craft beer scene, with tastings an option at Clare Valley Brewing Co.

A new generation of high-skilled chefs in the region is producing seasonal menus that are matched with the Clare Valley's award-winning wines. Many vineyards have excellent restaurants, so plan your excursions around meals (Skillogalee also does breakfast). Clare, the town, has the most diverse restaurant options, but there are many excellent choices, including a few characterful country pubs in the region.

Produce is often local, and freshly foraged native ingredients are starting to show up on restaurant menus. If you're keen to try indigenous ingredients, head to Bush Devine Cafe at Paulett Wines.

01 SHUT THE GATE

Up a little gravel driveway through some big black gates, this friendly little cellar door in a weatherboard farmhouse has made a few 'Best New Wineries' lists. Taste some of the small batch single source wines (the tempranillo is a hit) in the modest tasting room, or buy a bottle and enjoy it outside.
8453 Main North Rd, Clare; 08-8843 4114; www.shutthegate.com. au; 10am-4.30pm daily

02 SEVENHILL CELLARS

Established by The Society of Jesus (aka the Jesuits) in 1851 originally to produce sacramental wine – which it still ships today – this is the oldest winery in the Clare Valley. Today it's a must visit not only for its excellent cellar door, but to see the beautiful 1866 St Aloysius Church nearby on the same site. Mass is held here on Saturdays at 6pm. The church is made with local stone and local Mintaro slate floors in the Gothic Revival style.

Before or after enjoying a tasting session of the diverse portfolio of wines, visitors are encouraged to tour the museum, underground cellar, and the grounds on a mapped walking tour. To learn more about the significant historic and spiritual sites here, guided tours are conducted at 11am from Monday to Friday.
23 Trevarrick Rd, Sevenhill; 08-8843 5900; www.sevenhill.com.au; 10am-5pm

03 PAULETT WINES & BUSH DEVINE CAFE

High on the hill, not far from Sevenhill in the Polish Hill River sub-region (known for lime-, slate- and mineral-rich soils), Paulett boasts excellent views with its dry-grown whites: six varieties of riesling, plus semillon and chardonnay. But it's the 'bush food' garden – indigenous Australian ingredients such as saltbush, pepperleaf, fingerlimes and davidson plums – that steals the limelight. Share a platter of meats, cheese, chutneys and condiments with a bottle, or dine on main courses such as smoked kangaroo, gnocchi, or caramelised pork belly.
752 Jolly Way, Polish Hill River 08-8843 4328; www.paulettwines. com.au; 10am-5pm

'At sunset we take a bottle and some glasses up to the top of the hill and watch the sun set over the dry sheep and wheat country to the west.'

Dave Palmer, Skillogalee

04 SKILLOGALEE

You'll feel like you've stopped in on friends or family at this excellent winery, known in Australia for its spicy shiraz, fabulous food and zesty rieslings. But if you're planning to make a meal of it, book ahead to enjoy a long, lazy afternoon either inside the stone cottage by the open fire in winter, or out on the shaded verandah any time of the year.

Tables continue outside under the shade of a large old tree overlooking the vines and eucalypts beyond. The home-cooked meals are paired with wines and range from pan-seared trout to Angus eye fillet with unfussy side dishes. Treat a visit as you would dining with family – don't expect to get in and out in under an hour. Wondering about the unusual Celtic sounding name? It comes from a local legend that says the mid-1800s explorer John Horrocks survived here on 'skilly' – a tea made of grass and seeds. *23 Trevarrick Rd, Sevenhill; 08-8843 4311; www.skillogalee.com. au; 7.30am-5pm daily*

05 CLARE VALLEY BREWING CO

Beyond the Clare Valley wine scene, the Clare Valley Brewing Co has a tasting room with Jeanneret Wines overlooking the rolling grassy hills and stands of eucalypts behind Sevenhill. You can work your way through a tasting paddle of their four core brews: a summer ale,

06 Rustic Umbria

07 Handmade pasta at Umbria

08 Live music at the Clare Valley Gourmet Weekend

stout, IPA, and red ale. Order a chilled jug of your preference and head out to the deck to drink in the vistas. If you don't have time to linger, purchase some takeaways in colourfully designed cans.
22 Jeanneret Rd, Sevenhill; 08-8843 4308; www.cvbc.beer; 10am-5pm Mon-Sat, noon-5pm Sun

06 MR MICK CELLAR DOOR & KITCHEN

Right on the Riesling Trail in Clare's township, Mr Mick's cellar door, restaurant and gallery is a picturesque pitstop. The menu ranges from tapas-style sharing plates to a multi-course degustation menu with a couple of children's options, too. Tables are spread on the lawn (a rarity in these parts), or in cooler months get cosy inside the restored stone and corrugated-

iron building. The wines here are consistent and relatively inexpensive with a range of styles made from Clare Valley grapes.
7 Dominic Street, Clare; 08-8842 2555; www.mrmick.com.au; 11am-7pm daily

07 UMBRIA

Umbria looks like a high-end Italian restaurant has been lifted from one of Australia's cities and dropped into the bucolic Clare Valley. The exposed stonework and moody lighting might suggest high-end prices, but this cosy trattoria delivers rustic homemade pastas and pizzas, using local ingredients such as free-range Clare Valley eggs, plus a few meat-focused mains that won't break the bank. A children's menu is also available on request.

308b Main North Road, Clare; 08-8812 1718; www.umbriarestaurant. com.au; Tue-Sat lunch & dinner

08 KNAPPSTEIN

You can't miss the large stone and corrugated-iron winery buildings in Clare's centre selling bottles from this brand's nearby vineyards. Knappstein has built a reputation on taking a minimal-intervention approach to winemaking, paying special attention to sustainable practices and cutting environmental impact. The shiraz and riesling steal the show, but it also makes a mighty fine semillon-sauvignon blanc blend, and a cabernet sauvignon that has been dry-grown since 1974.
2 Pioneer Ave, Clare; 08-8841 2100; www.knappstein.com.au; 9am-5pm Mon-Fri, 11am-4pm Sat & Sun

WHERE TO STAY

MILL APARTMENTS
Six high-spec apartments with private decks overlook the bushland and the slender Hutt River behind Clare's quiet main thoroughfare.
www.themill.apartments

LOFT AT COBBLER'S REST
In a beautiful stone building on the main street, this compact apartment is tastefully decorated in colonial heritage style, and sleeps four. Provedore provisions are included.
www.theloftclarevalley.com.au

WHAT TO DO

THE RIESLING TRAIL
Hire bicycles (there are a couple of places in the town of Clare) and follow a disused railway line that's now an easy-gradient trail between Auburn and Barinia for 33km of wines, wheels and wildlife. It's a two-hour dash end-to-end, but make a day of it: there are three looped detours and extensions

to explore, and dozens of cellar doors to tempt you along the way.
www.rieslingtrail.com.au

MARTINDALE HALL
This 1880 Georgian-style sandstone mansion, just south of Mintaro, was built for young pastoralist Edmund Bowman Jnr, who subsequently partied away the family fortune.

Today the historic 32-room manor features original furnishings, a magnificent blackwood staircase, a locally made billiard table, and an opulent smoking room.
www.martindalehall-mintaro.com.au

CELEBRATIONS

CLARE VALLEY GOURMET WEEKEND
Held in May, this is South Australia's longest-running food and wine festival, which celebrates local wine and produce, and features degustation dinners.
www.clarevalley.com.au

GET THERE

Due to its size the Fleurieu Peninsula region is best explored via car. A 40-minute drive south from Adelaide's CBD and you'll be in the township of McLaren Vale, which is the perfect starting point to explore the region. The McLaren Vale wine region offers a hop-on, hop-off bus service departing daily from the centre of Adelaide (see www.trailhopper.com.au). Adelaide's International Airport is conveniently positioned a mere 10 minutes from the city centre with daily domestic services from all Australian capital cities.

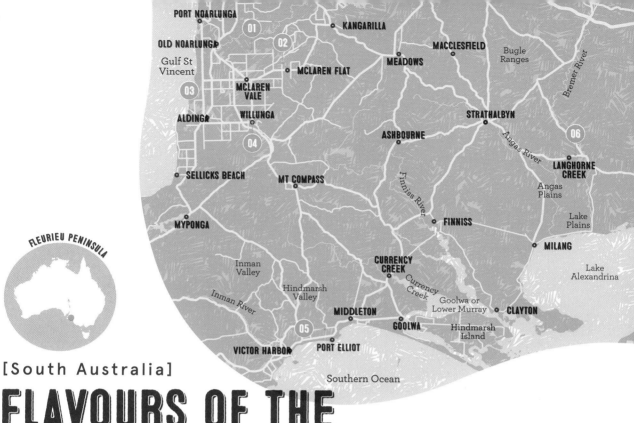

PORT NOARLUNGA
01
OLD NOARLUNGA
02
Gulf St
Vincent
KANGARILLA
MACCLESFIELD
Bugle
Ranges
MCLAREN FLAT
MEADOWS
Bremer River
MCLAREN
VALE
03
STRATHALBYN
WILLUNGA
ALDINGA
ASHBOURNE
Angas River
06
04
LANGHORNE
CREEK
SELLICKS BEACH
MT COMPASS
Angas
Plains
Finniss River
Lake
Plains
MYPONGA
FINNISS
MILANG
Inman
Valley
CURRENCY
CREEK
Lake
Alexandrina
Hindmarsh
Valley
Inman River
Currency
Creek
Goolwa or
Lower Murray
CLAYTON
MIDDLETON
GOOLWA
Hindmarsh
Island
05
VICTOR HARBOR
PORT ELLIOT
Southern Ocean

FLEURIEU PENINSULA

[South Australia]

FLAVOURS OF THE FLEURIEU PENINSULA

The laid-back vibe and old world charm of the Fleurieu Peninsula disguises a progressive produce region devoid of pretension and packing a solid culinary punch.

A 45-minute drive south from South Australia's bohemian capital, the Fleurieu Peninsula is surrounded by some of the state's most gorgeous coastline. A network of early settler towns and sleepy coastal communities combine to create a welcoming, down-to-earth atmosphere. Blessed with a Mediterranean climate, this is a place where the vines trickle down foothills to a blue sea. Boasting four distinct wine regions, from the sophistication of McLaren Vale to the charms of Langhorne Creek, the Fleurieu's wineries are among Australia's very best. With southern European varietals recently infiltrating cellar door tastings, the standard shiraz, for which the region is renowned, now partners with the likes of fiano, montepulciano and negroamaro.

The ragged coastline of the peninsula's north is an aquatic playground – from scuba diving and sea-kayaking to jetty-fishing – lined with white sand beaches that give way to sheltered coves. Seafood is king here and menus are laden with locally caught delights, teamed with craft brews or crisp white wines from nearby producers and all prepared with herbs and vegetables from the verdant hills of the peninsula.

Further south lie the sleepy surf towns of Port Elliot and Middleton. Gorgeous sandstone pioneer cottages and sharp looking modern-day shacks dot the coastline; a favourite for holidaymakers. In recent years a flurry of cute cafes, quality country pubs, brilliant bakeries and boutique coffee roasters have all heard the calling and found their home here.

01 CORIOLE

One of Australia's premier cellar door experiences, Coriole Winery delivers fine food, unmatched views of the sea and vines, and some of the best examples of wine produced in the Vale. In a previous life the tiny cellar door, surrounded by a cottage garden, was an ironstone barn built in the 1860s but for the last 50 years it's been the beating heart of the vineyard. It's here that you'll be treated to samples of the wineries award-winning shiraz, grenache and chenin blanc alongside tipples of their new wave of releases such as piquepoul, fiano and negroamaro. The accompanying restaurant is one of the most awarded in the region boasting a seasonal menu of sustainably sourced produce from around the peninsula. Sit back, grab a glass of fiano and relax in the gardens while drinking in the view of the Vale's vines that appear to roll all the way down to the sea. *79 Chaffeys Road, McLaren Vale; 08-8323 8305; www.coriole.com; cellar door 10am-5pm Mon-Fri, 11am-5pm Sat & Sun; restaurant from noon daily.*

02 THE CURRANT SHED

Now this is a twist on an outdoor shed! The deceptively spacious interior of The Currant Shed is modern and sleek with simple furnishings. Each table faces directly onto views of citrus and vines that snake up a small incline to a grove of eucalypt. The best of the Fleurieu Peninsula's produce is on offer here where lunch can be a simple a la carte affair or a six-course chef selection dependent on your appetite. The summer menu bursts with character and surprises – kingfish is paired with chimichurri and sea grapes, slow cooked lamb is accompanied by rhubarb shavings, and sardines and squid make the perfect plate companions. The venue has struck up a partnership with Shottesbrooke winery and the wine list brims with regional favourites. For the beer connoisseur, local brews from Shifty Lizard and Smiling Samoyed will quench your thirst. *104 Ingoldby Road, McLaren Flat; 08-8383 0232; www.currantshed. com.au; from 11:30am Thu-Tue*

'We're pretty damn serious about making good beer and having some fun. And we are reasonably reasonable about doing it responsibly.'

Danny Strapps, Shifty Lizard

03 STAR OF GREECE

Perched atop the cliffs of Port Willunga, the Star of Greece is a South Australian institution and a must-stop on the region's culinary trail. Its focus on simple, delicious, locally sourced food has continued unabated for over 20 years and diners are treated to some of the state's best ocean views. Named after a local wreck (so, not a Greek restaurant) the Star's seasonal menu bursts with local delights, from squid sourced from the waters off Kangaroo Island and freshly caught garfish to delicious locally supplied pork and lamb – this is South Australia on a plate. With a killer wine list to boot The Star of Greece is one dining experience to savour. Oh, and they don't care if you're wearing flip-flops 'coz...it's the beach y'know'. *1 The Esplanade, Port Willunga; 08-8557 7420; www.starofgreece. com.au; lunch from noon Wed-Sun, dinner from 6pm Thu-Sat*

04 SHIFTY LIZARD TAPHOUSE

There's a lot to love about the lads that have set up Shifty. Owner-operators Danny Strapps and Lee Stone grew up in the area and had the audacity to establish one of Australia's craftiest little craft breweries in the heart of wine country. Forget the robust reds of the surrounding wineries, The Shifty Lizard Taphouse, located in the main street of handsome Willunga, is an unexpected Shangri-La for those that love the amber drop.

06 Bremerton Wines
interior

07 Bremerton Wines
exterior

08 The mighty Murray
River flows through
South Australia

Who can't resist a hearty stout named Stouty McStout Face or the citrusy styling of an IPA cheekily called Bruce Lee-zard. With both a core range and limited releases all ready for the drinking, there's plenty of reasons to come back to this brilliant brewery.
33 High Street, Willunga; 08-7079 2471; www.shiftylizard.com; noon-8pm Thu, noon-10pm Fri, 11am-10pm Sat, 11am-7pm Sun.

05 DEGROOT COFFEE

Having relocated to the beachside town of Port Elliot from suburban Adelaide over half a decade ago, DeGroot Coffee remains a low-key, hands-on, family-run affair. The family opted to establish their new roasting roots on the popular town's outskirts, escaping the craziness of the main thoroughfare. It now neighbours a jumble of eclectic businesses, including a gallery, pop-up winery and a Dutch Stroopwafel caravan. The sound of whirring coffee grinders and the aroma trail of freshly roasting coffee beans greets punters on arrival into the expansive open shed; a home where the bean is king. Offering only three single origin roasts, DeGroot's philosophy is quality over quantity and you won't leave without having downed at least two.
89 Hill St, Port Elliot; 04-0444 2722; www.degrootcoffeeco.com. au; 8am–2pm

06 BREMERTON WINES

On the edge of the Fleurieu Peninsula lies the quiet and often overlooked hamlet of Langhorne Creek. The region is thick with vines and blessed with warm summer days and cool evenings, assisted by the breeze off of nearby Lake Alexandrina, manifesting conditions that create an intensity to the wines and a treat for the drinker. Beautiful Bremerton Wines operates out of a spacious and lovingly restored 1860s stone barn off the town's main road. Commence a tasting with the crisp apple-laden Wiggy Sparkling Chardonnay or the dense CHW Sparkling Shiraz, which are produced in alternate years. With a super-dry verdelho, a cheekily named Racy Rose, and a surprising malbec all on the tasting menu, be sure to assign a designated driver. If you're a tad peckish, stay for a lunch platter or indulge in a hearty beef and red wine pie.
Strathalbyn Road, Langhorne Creek; 08-8537 3093; www. bremerton.com.au; 10am–5pm

WHERE TO STAY
OXENBERRY FARM
Located on the outskirts of the township of McLaren Vale, Oxenberry Farm dates back to the 1840s having accommodated the region's first farming settlers. The site's stunning sandstone cottages have been rejuvenated into cute self-contained B&Bs.
www.oxenberry.com

WHAT TO DO
SECOND VALLEY BEACH
One of South Australia's most Instagrammed spots, Second Valley Beach is perfect for swimming, snorkelling or jetty fishing. And, if you're lucky, you may spot a local leafy seadragon. The stunning coastline begs to be explored and the summer sunsets are next level.
www.fleurieupeninsula. com.au/second-valley

COORONG ADVENTURE CRUISE
Explore where the 'Mighty Murray River' meets the sea, discover the place that inspired

the Australian classic novel *Storm Boy* and hear the stories of local Indigenous Australians. The abundance of birdlife is best seen via the six-hour adventure cruise with a truncated 1½ hour viewing of the Murray

Mouth also available for those on tight schedules.
www.spiritofthecoorong. com.au

CELEBRATIONS
SEA & VINES
With wineries across McLaren Vale, McLaren

Flat, Yankallila and Willunga participating, this festival is a perfect celebration of the region's incredible wines paired with fresh seafood foraged from local waters.
www.seaandvines.com.au

GET THERE
Launceston airport receives
flights from across Australia;
you can rent a car here too.
But it's less than a three-hour
drive from Hobart so flying to
the state capital is an option.
For non-flyers, the Spirit of
Tasmania sails from Melbourne
to Devonport six days / week.

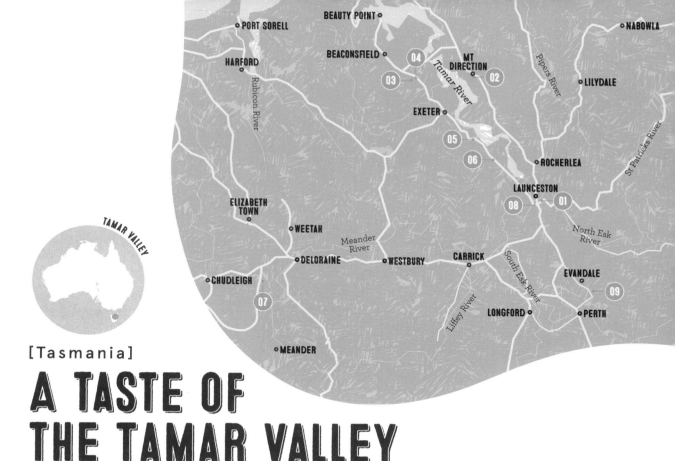

TAMAR VALLEY

[Tasmania]
A TASTE OF THE TAMAR VALLEY

Take a chilled-out road trip along the Tamar River to discover one of the world's most revered wine regions and a local food scene that focuses on high quality.

Tasmania's very first winemakers planted the island's original vineyards in the Tamar Valley, taking of advantage of the blissfully balanced Mediterranean climate of the central north of the island. It's not only grapes that thrive here – the region supplies much of Tasmania with fruit, vegetables and high-quality livestock. With such superb raw materials, local producers are able to craft excellent foods and drinks, which we explore in this trail.

Our route revolves around the Tamar River, a broad and lazy river that meanders from the regional hub of Launceston north to the sea. Over recent years Launceston (first declared a city in 1888) is in the process of catching up with Hobart as a place to enjoy great food and drinks. While it

doesn't yet have an equivalent of MONA and remains a historic country town at its heart, Launceston's restaurants, bars, cafes, markets and producers are on the way to matching the state capital. It can offer destination dining at Stillwater, one of the best farmers' markets in Australia and, of course, it is on the doorstep of one of the world's top cool-climate wine regions with pinot noir to savour. Brewers and distillers have also opened up in the Tamar.

Looping anti-clockwise around the Tamar Valley from Launceston, we'll pick our own berries, taste the most interesting of the Tamar's wines, explore some of the local producers, and drop into the best cafes and restaurants the region has to offer. With easy-going accessibility, the Tamar offers a comfortable, no-stress weekend escape.

01 HARVEST LAUNCESTON

Get a flavour of seasonal Tasmanian produce at the weekly farmers' market on Cimitiere Street, opposite Albert Hall. The line-up of stallholders varies but arrive early and start your day with coffee from Ritual, and breakfast pastries from Apiece Sourdough Bakery. Then follow your nose to discover any of the following: cherry pies, kombucha and kimchi, fresh berries, seafood, olives, nuts, ice cream, cheese, mushrooms, honey and preserves, game meat, grass-fed beef, truffles, garlic and a lot more. You can also restock your wine, beer and cider reserves. The focus is always on organic, ethical and seasonal produce and wandering the market gives an appetising introduction to what Tasmania has to offer enthusiastic eaters.
71 Cimitiere St, Launceston; 0417 352 780; www.harvestmarket.org. au; 8.30am-12.30pm Sat

02 HILLWOOD BERRIES FARMGATE

Heading up the east side of the Tamar River takes you to Hillwood Berries where owners Robin, Simon and Marcus Dornauf grow a variety of soft fruit, some of which you can pick yourself. 'Our climate is ideal for growing berries,' says Katie Mulder of Hillwood Berries. 'Not too hot, not too cold.' Being a berry farm, the picking season extends from November to May but there's also a cafe and shop selling vinegars and preserves. 'In summertime our frozen berry ice cream machine is in full swing,' says Katie.
105 Hillwood Rd; www.hillwood berries.com.au; 9-5pm daily

03 SWINGING GATE VINEYARD

Next, cross the Tamar via Batman Bridge. Swinging Gate, on top of a hill up a dirt road, is one of the most interesting and charming wineries in the region. Owner Doug Cox is known for marching to his own beat, mixing old world inspiration with new world adventure. Example: he experiments with five different types of pinot gris. The 'Skinny' stays on grape skins for eight days giving it a beautiful rose tint. Cox is inspired by Alsace-style wines, which are fruity and dry. He's most proud of

01 Stillwater restaurant near Cataract Gorge

02 Harvest farmers' market in Launceston

03 Artful dining in Stillwater's restaurant

04 Hillwood Berries Farmgate

05 Tasting platters at Loira Wines

his *pétillant-naturel*, which has no fineing, no filtering and no sulphur. And he also makes Tasmania's only frontignac-muscadet: 'Try it with scallops,' suggests Doug. The cellar door is in the old tractor shed, with some accommodation available down the hillside in a pair of geodesic domes.
103 Glendale Rd, Sidmouth; 0419 599710; www.swinginggatewines. com.au; 10am-5pm Mon-Sat, 12-5pm Sun

04 LOIRA VINES

Loira Vines, which is at the bottom of the slope below Swinging Gate, makes a good place for a pitstop thanks to the platters that owners Adrian and Mirabai Carruthers prepare for lunch guests from vegetables, meat and cheese sourced from Harvest farmers' market. 'We discovered the property on a wine-tasting tour and ended up purchasing it,' explains Adrian. Despite being the smallest vineyard with a cellar door on the island they now not only grow pinot noir, pinot gris, chardonnay and shiraz grapes but apples for their cider and hops for their beer too. They also collaborate with Doug up the hill on Swinging Gate's annual Abstract field rose blend. Loira's own pinot gris has pear to the fore, while their pinot noir goes well with duck terrine or wood-fired pizza.
3191 West Tamar Hwy, Sidmouth; 0418 477760; www.loiravines.com. au; cellar door 12-5pm daily, food 12,30-2.30pm Fri-Sun

05 TURNER STILLHOUSE

Take a break from the grape at the Turner Stillhouse in Grindelwald. Founder Justin Turner and ex-Boags brewer Brett Coulson have set up next to Tamar Ridge wines. They've fitted out a smart tasting room above the gleaming stills. You'll have to wait to try their whisky but the gin is already winning awards and fans: the Founder's Release is a contemporary style with Australian flavours of fresh lime and rose petals to the fore, while the Distiller's Release is a spicier proposition. From Friday to Sunday you can order a picnic to go from neighbouring caterers Hubert + Dan.
1a Waldhorn Drive, Grindelwald; 03 6776 1414; www.turnerstillhouse. com; 12-4pm Mon-Sat

06 VELO WINES

Rod Thorpe is a grape-growing legend in Tamar. He planted the renowned Moores Hill vineyard and now manages Velo Wines. 'I wanted to see if I could get it back to what it was when it was known as Chateau Legana,' says Rod. Using natural methods he produces shiraz, cabernet and pinot noir and the new 100% cabernet wine is a revelation. 'Over the last 20 years Tasmania has got warmer so the cabernet is getting better,' he explains. Rod started his career as a chef so he knows what pairs with his wine: duck with pinot, venison with shiraz and a rare eye fillet of beef with the cab. 'Tasmania has a very modern food scene. Its strength is a light, Mediterranean style of cooking,'.
755 West Tamar Hwy, Legana; 03 6330 1582; www.velowines.com.au; 11-4 Wed-Sat, 11-3 Sun

07 41° SOUTH

Ziggy Pyka came to Australia in 1987 and fell in love with Tasmania. So he bought some land with a river and stocked it with salmon, using the wetlands as a bio-filter to ensure there was minimal impact on the water and the environment. But Ziggy's masterstroke was hot-smoking the salmon so it could be sold in Tasmania and in Melbourne. His salmon farm lies down a tree-lined track and is worth the detour for its delicious salmon.
323 Montana Rd, Deloraine; 03 6362 4130; www.41southtasmania. com; 9am-3pm daily

08 STILLWATER RESTAURANT

Set right on the river's edge in a former mill, longstanding Stillwater restaurant occupies a special place in Tasmanian hearts for its elegant but approachable dining, which perhaps aspires to Alice Waters levels of localism. As co-owner Kim Seagram says, Stillwater serves Tasmania on a plate. It now offers seven sleek suites if you wish to stay on after dinner.
2 Bridge Rd, Launceston; 03 6331 4153; www.stillwater.com.au; 8am-2pm daily, from 5.30pm Wed-Sat

09 INGLESIDE BAKERY CAFE

Make a final stop at this outstanding bakery in a historic village close to Launceston airport. Everything is homemade so pick up some sourdough, a sandwich or slices of cake for the trip home (eating in is also an option). The cherished bakery dates from 1867 but it is not all that Evandale is famed for: the town hosts the annual Penny Farthing National Championship.
4 Russell St, Evandale; 03 6391 8682; 8am-3.30pm daily

WHERE TO STAY

PEPPERS SILO HOTEL
Times change and this nine-storey hotel on the edge of Launceston is an ingenious way of repurposing four huge grain silos overlooking the Tamar. The design is modern and spacious, with curvaceous walls adding to the effect. A great restaurant has views over the river but it's also possible to stroll into the centre in less than 30 minutes.
www.peppers.com.au

WHAT TO DO

MOUNTAIN BIKING
Adventurous types shouldn't miss the chance to drive (about two hours) to the town of Derby, which is home to world-class mountain biking trails. Bikes can be hired at Vertigo MTB, who can recommend beginner trails or more advanced routes.
www.rideblueberby. com.au

NATIONAL AUTOMOBILE MUSEUM OF TASMANIA
For those more interested in motors, this

Launceston museum has a collection of classic cars, from early British sports cars to the golden age of Aussie muscle cars.
www.namt.com.au

CELEBRATIONS

VINTAGE: TAMAR
Taking place annually over a winter weekend at the end of May,

Vintage celebrates the year's grape harvest and the great wines from previous vintages at many of the Tamar's wineries. Buses shuttle imbibers from one to the next venue, where winemakers offer classes, tours and talks.
www.vintagetamar.com.au

EVANDALE VILLAGE FAIR
Every February the Georgian town of Evandale turns over its streets to stalls, street entertainers, costumed revellers and spectators of the world's most competitive penny farthing bike race.
www.evandalevillagefair. com

GET THERE
Hourly ferries travel to
Bruny Island from Kettering,
a 30-minute drive south
of state capital Hobart,
which is the main domestic
air travel hub. A day's bike
rental on the island costs
AUD65; see https://cy-
clebrunyisland.com.au.

91

BRUNY ISLAND

[Tasmania]

A BRUNY ISLAND BUFFET

Experience Tasmania's culinary excellence in one dainty package: premium honey, cheese, wine and oysters form a delightful road trip across Bruny Island.

SNUG · DENNES POINT · Cape de la Sortie
CONINGHAM · Bull Bay
KILLORA
OYSTER COVE · · BARNES BAY · Storm Bay
ROBERTS POINT · Barnes Bay
KETTERING · Apollo Bay
05 · (North) Bruny Island
WOODBRIDGE · Great Bay
NICHOLLS RIVULET
BIRCHS BAY · 02 · 01
FLOWERPOT · D'Entrecasteaux Channel
03
MIDDLETON · Simpsons Point · Moorina Bay
Isthmus Bay · Cape Queen Elizabeth
GORDON · Simpsons Bay
VERONA SANDS · SIMPSONS BAY · Simpsons Bay
Satellite Island · ALONNAH · Tasman Sea
ADVENTURE BAY · Penguin Island
Little Taylor Bay · 04
LUNAWANNA · (South) Bruny Island
Cape Connella

To Australians, Tasmania's very name conjures up images of farmers' markets, cool-climate wines and succulent seafood. Some of the best produce is hidden away off Tassie's southeast coast, on Bruny Island.

To the island's Aboriginal people, this 362-sq-km (140 sq miles) realm of ash-white sand, eucalyptus forests and dazzling blue bays is known as Lunawunna-alonnah. While Bruny has seen successive European arrivals, with settlement gathering pace in the late 19th century, its relative remoteness has sheltered it from overdevelopment. Bruny is an island off an island state, where wildlife proliferates alongside a human population of just 600-odd souls. Echidnas are easy to spot snuffling through the bush and fur seals are a common sight, somersaulting in the frigid water. The island's a significant habitat for little penguins, swift parrots and one of the rarest birds in Australia, the forty-

spotted pardalote, while its mammalian icon is the white wallaby, found nowhere else on earth.

Against this backdrop of abundant wildlife, Bruny's produce benefits from clear waters and fertile soil. Large, meaty oysters are farmed in the D'Entrecasteaux Channel. On land, one-of-a-kind cheeses are matured, fruity chardonnays are bottled, and bees are sent out to work collecting nectar. Producers are few and standards are high, meaning a gourmet road trip of the island has an exclusive, boutique feel – if you mention the cheese place or the winery, locals will know exactly where you mean.

Day trippers inundate the island, so choosing to stay overnight offers insights into a side of Bruny that few visitors enjoy: the sight of pademelons hopping out from the bush at twilight, and the opportunity to refill your wine glass generously, knowing that there's no long drive home.

01 The causeway
between North and
South Bruny Islands

02 Fresh oysters at
Get Shucked

03 Bruny Island
lighthouse

04 Produce from the
Bruny Island Cheese
Co, and their beer

01 GET SHUCKED

The oysters farmed on Bruny Island are glistening, juicy-fat mouthfuls that slide from their pearlescent shells onto eager tongues. And they don't come fresher than at the memorably named Get Shucked, only 15 minutes' drive south of Bruny ferry terminal. *Crassostrea gigas* (aka the Pacific oyster) was introduced to Tassie in the 1940s. Ever since, these whopping bivalves have been freed from their shells, christened with a squeeze of lemon, or served Kilpatrick, with a fiery garnish of Worcestershire sauce and bacon. The pristine waters of the D'Entrecasteaux Channel are credited with nurturing the oysters – juicy, sweetish, ample in size – that are expertly shucked here. There are Tasmanian wines and beers to wash them down, and a play area to entertain kids while the grown-ups order another dozen. *Lease 204, 1735 Bruny Island Main Road, Great Bay; 0439 303 597; www.getshucked.com.au; 9.30am-4.30pm*

02 BRUNY ISLAND CHEESE COMPANY

Less than 1km (0.6 miles) south of Get Shucked is Bruny Island Cheese Company. Since 2017, all cheeses have been made from milk produced at their own organic, sustainable dairy farm. While leaning into local cheese-making styles, the specialists behind this boutique fromagerie have also drawn inspiration from far and wide across Europe. Their 'Tom' is a riff on French Alpine semi-soft cheese Tomme, while one distinctly local creation is infused with fragrant Huon pine, the '1792' cheese (named after the year the French first stepped on Tasmania). Our favourite is 'Oen', a soft cow's-milk cheese washed in pinot noir and robed in vine leaves.

No single country can lay claim to the cheese plate, but there's something truly modern Australian about a heavy wooden board laden with artisanal cheeses, cubes of quince paste and grapes. Order a selection of cheeses and pair them with beers (made behind the dairy), perhaps the raspberry stout or barley-quinoa ale, and linger a while at a table under the eucalypt trees.

'We make cheese, brew beer, bake bread, grow grass, raise cows and produce organic milk on a small island at the edge of the world. Come visit.'

Nick Haddow, Bruny Island Cheese

1807 Bruny Island Main Road, Great Bay; 03-6260 6353; www. brunyislandcheese.com.au; 9am–5pm Oct–mid-Mar, 10am-5pm mid-Mar–Sep

03 THE HONEY POT

Less than five minutes' drive south is a perfect companion to those rich, nutty cheeses: honey. 'Bruny offers a climate that is a little milder than mainland Tassie,' explains the owner and manager of The Honey Pot, Natalie Wright. 'With almost a full season of native, nectar-producing plants, the bees thrive.'

Two decades of honey production on Bruny have grown The Honey Pot into a 400-hive operation. Following the seasons, the team move the hives around

the island. Endemic Tasmanian leatherwood trees at Mount Mangana bring about a creamy, floral-scented honey, while a more aromatic golden liquor results from north Bruny's white-flowered prickly box shrubs.

'Honey produced from different areas, even from the same plant species, will always carry their own distinct flavours,' explains Natalie. 'For instance the bush honey we collect from Bruny has a strong tea tree influence, as it flowers the same time as some of the eucalyptus trees.'

Then there's manuka honey, with its renowned health-boosting properties, dense texture and rich flavour. It's more than superfood hype: each year, The Honey Pot

05 Tasting a dram at Bruny Island House of Whisky

06 Spot fur seals and other wildlife on North and Bruny Island

sends their manuka honey for laboratory tests to determine its level of MGO (methylglyoxal); that is, the antibacterial and anti-inflammatory health benefits.

'Some hospitals are using the honey on open wounds and burns, with a high success rate,' says Natalie. 'I keep a jar at home, and feed it to my children, I swear it's great for coughs and colds!'
2184 Bruny Island Main Road, Great Bay; 03-6266 0342; www. thehoney-pot.com; 10am-4pm Apr-Sep, 9am-5pm Oct-Mar

04 BRUNY ISLAND PREMIUM WINES

Twenty minutes' drive further south takes you across the Neck, the slender isthmus that separates Bruny Island into north and south, and on to the most southerly vineyard in Australia. Bruny Island

Premium Wines takes a small-batch approach: a community hand-picking effort in April, grape pressing, then at least nine months in French oak barrels before the wine is ready to be poured.

Oenophiles will find a varietal to their taste: the honeyed chardonnay with notes of fresh-baked croissants, bright and grassy sauvignon blanc, appley gewürztraminer, lightly spicy pinot noir... For something even more Tasmanian – after all, the state has been known as the Apple Isle – Bruny's only ciders are made here, too. Crisp Tasmanian Jonagold, Royal Gala and Pink Lady apples are spiked with blackberries and ginger to make lip-smacking hand-bottled thirst-quenchers. Whichever you sip, take your time at a table overlooking the vines and nibble marinated mushrooms, blackberry-cured salmon tartare, and more.

4391 Bruny Island Main Road, Lunawanna; 0409 973 033; www. brunyislandwine.com; winery 11am-4pm, restaurant lunch & dinner daily

05 BRUNY ISLAND HOUSE OF WHISKY

Now that your belly's full and your car boot is clanking with jars of honey and bottles of wine, it's time to return to the ferry. Thirty-five minutes into the northward drive, pause at Bruny Island House of Whisky to add to your stock of Bruny produce to haul home. You're only 3km (2 miles) from the ferry terminal at this point, so if you aren't driving, kill some time with a flight of whiskies by the open fire inside.
360 Lennon Road, North Bruny Island; 03-6260 6344; www. tasmanianhouseofwhisky.com.au; 9.30am-5.30pm, hrs vary seasonally

WHERE TO STAY
CLOUDY BAY CABIN
Miles of private bushland surround Cloudy Bay Cabin, a cosy, off-the-grid timber cottage just steps from a surf beach. *www.brunyisland.com. au/cloudy-bay-cabin*

43 DEGREES
Proud of its outstanding eco credentials, 43 Degrees in Adventure Bay has apartments powered by solar energy and showers that use rainwater, along with luxurious features like Balinese-inspired decor and spa baths. *www.43degrees.com.au*

WHAT TO DO
GUIDED HIKES
Hiking is an immersive way to experience this romantic, windswept island. Bruny Island Safaris offers combined bushwalking and grazing tours, complete with smoked salmon picnics at scenic overlooks and nature-spotting trails through the tangled interior. *www.brunyislandsafaris. com*

QUARANTINE STATION
Exposing a darker side of island history, this 19th-century site at Barnes Bay housed infectious people during the post-WWI global influenza pandemic. Plantlife has also been quarantined here, an early iteration of Australia's notoriously tough customs restrictions. *www.bica.org.au/bruny quarantinestation*

CELEBRATIONS
TASTE OF TASMANIA
The state's most note-worthy annual food festival is in late December and early January on the main island. The Taste of Tasmania brings Bruny's gourmet producers flocking, along with tastemakers from around the state. *www.thetasteof tasmania.com.au*

NAYRI NIARA GOOD SPIRIT FESTIVAL
On Bruny Island itself, the island's ancient cultural practices are honoured at Nayri Niara Good Spirit Festival, a coming together of artisans, musicians, dancers and foodies. Check online for this biannual festival's dates (next held in 2021). *www.nayriniaragood spirit.com*

GET THERE

There are direct flights to Launceston from Melbourne, Sydney and Brisbane. It's a 225km drive from Launceston to Stanley – break it up with a night's stop in Devonport, Penguin or Burnie.

Map labels: STANLEY 08, PORT LATTA, SMITHTON, EDITH CREEK, WYNYARD, SOMERSET, BURNIE, 07, Bass Strait, Noland Bay, Anderson Bay, BRIDPORT, GEORGE TOWN, 06, 05, 04, Tamar River, ULVERSTONE, DEVONPORT, PORT SORELL, BEACONSFIELD, SCOTTSDALE, Arthur River, CRADLE COAST, TASMANIA, 03, EXETER, SHEFFIELD, WARATAH, 02, LAUNCESTON 01, MOINA, ELIZABETH TOWN, DELORAINE, Ben Lomond National Park, CRADLE VALLEY, Lake Mackintosh

[Tasmania]

CULINARY DELIGHTS ON THE CRADLE TO COAST TRAIL

Abundantly fertile earth fuels this trip across Tasmania's northwest coast, where the only thing fresher than the air is the produce.

Drive across Tasmania's northwest coast and one of the striking features is the blood-red soil. It's this volcanic, nutrient-rich earth that gives life to much of Tasmania's fresh produce, turning this corner of the island into an epicurean delight.

The Bass Highway runs the entire length of the region, from Launceston to Smithton, and it's lined with artisan producers, while others are no more than a few kilometres off the highway. It creates an easy continuum of culinary stops as you journey towards the state's northwest tip, where the world's cleanest air – as decreed by science – blows ashore, breathing further freshness into the region's offerings.

Your guiding line along this coast can be the well-signposted Cradle to Coast Tasting Trail, which links 30 gourmet producers on the coastal plains between Bass Strait and the highlands around Tasmania's most famous peak, the bowed figure of Cradle Mountain.

Along the way are Tasmania's third- and fourth-largest cities, Devonport and Burnie. Once derided as cultural deserts, they're emerging as creative centres, with food and drink at the heart of their revivals.

Vineyards in this region tend to be dotted through the landscape rather than clustered together, and distilleries and craft brewers take advantage of the pure mountain water that pours down from the central highlands. And then, of course, there's that fertile red soil that nourishes everything. In a country more famous for bulldust and dun-brown earth, this coast and its hinterland are as plentiful as a banquet. Tasmania's reputation as arguably Australia's freshest and finest gourmet destination is founded here.

01 ASHGROVE CHEESE

The Bennett family has been farming these Elizabeth Town lands since the 1880s, and its cheeses have been one of Tasmania's farm success stories since the 1990s. Cheese wheels are stacked 15 high in the glass-fronted maturing room, and you can expect some trademark Ashgrove flavours in the cheeses on offer in the expansive tasting room (which also has an ice-cream counter) – think locally grown wasabi and native pepper berries. The provedore shelves are a what's what of Tasmanian premium products – you could just about take a gourmet tour of the state right here.
6173 Bass Hwy, Elizabeth Town; 03-6708 1012; www.ashgrovecheese. com.au; 7.30am-5.30pm

02 HOUSE OF ANVERS

Chocolate is rarely a vintage item, but House of Anvers' Fortunato No 4, created from Nacional cacao beans, which were once thought to be extinct, is claimed as the 'rarest chocolate in the world'. The exclusivity of Igor Van Gerwen's Latrobe factory ends there because it's an inviting place that's part cafe and part factory store, with a small chocolate museum attached. The chocolate production takes place inside a Californian bungalow built after WWI by Theo d'Oliveyra, who was so determined to fill it with Tasmanian blackwood features he also bought a local sawmill. Two sets of windows provide a view into the factory workings.

9025 Bass Hwy, Latrobe; 03-6426 2703; www.anvers-chocolate.com. au; 7am-5pm

03 GHOST ROCK WINES

Twice named as Tasmania's best cellar door, this isolated winery was bought by Cate and Colin Arnold in 2000, and is today in the hands of their son Justin, who has worked in the Yarra Valley, Margaret River and Napa Valley, and wife Alicia, who runs the cellar door. Ghost Rock's fine restaurant dominates the cellar door, dishing up platters with local gourmet treats such as ham and chorizo from Mt Gnomon Farm, Pyengana cheese, 41 Degrees hot smoked salmon and Rocky Gardens quince jelly. The view alone – over the vines and farmland to Bass

'We're an artisan chocolaterie that specialises in using local ingredients and very rare cacao varieties.'

Igor Van Gerwen, House of Anvers

Strait – makes it one of the state's most enticing cellar doors.
1055 Port Sorell Rd, Northdown; 03-6428 4005; www.ghostrock. com.au; 11am-5pm

04 CHARLOTTEJACK

Chef Ben Milbourne grew up in Tasmania's northwest and came to prominence on the TV reality show Masterchef. He has since produced a string of TV cooking programmes, but his latest production is this excellent restaurant named after his two children. Shared plates bring Mexican and seafood overtones to local produce, and you're pretty much in the kitchen with the chefs if you dine at the bar stools. The studio for Milbourne's production company is immediately behind the restaurant – peep through the window if filming is underway. CharlotteJack is the centrepiece of Devonport's new Providore Place, designed to become the food hub of Tasmania's northwest. The Southern Wild gin distillery and bar has set up here, while the central atrium fills with fresh produce during the Cradle Coast market each Sunday.
Providore Place, 13-17 Oldaker St, Devonport; 0436 372 287; www. charlottejack.com.au; 11.30am-3pm, 6pm-late Thu-Sun

05 TURNERS BEACH BERRY PATCH

Pick-your-own berry farms are the very symbol of a Tasmanian summer, and you barely need to

leave the Bass Hwy to find Craig and Wendy Morris' inviting seaside patch. Take a stroll among the berries to gather your own sweet feast –the beach is 400m (1300ft) away if you want a picnic on the sand – or head to the cafe, which spills outside onto picnic tables and benches. Wood-fired pizzas and berries rule the menu. Kids can climb the haystack, and summer Friday nights bring live music to the patch's outdoor stage.
4 Blackburn Dr, Turners Beach; 03-6428 3967; www.theberrypatch.com.au; 9am-5pm, to 9pm Fri

06 HELLYERS ROAD DISTILLERY

Tasmania's largest whisky distillery has curious origins, having been created by a group of local dairy farmers – thus the milk factory next door. The view over the Emu Valley from the distillery's lofty perch is lovely, but the true moment of beauty comes when you step into the rich aroma of the angels' share on the Whisky Walk distillery tour. This tour is the only way you can taste Hellyers Road's cask-strength whisky – you can even pour and wax-seal a bottle straight from the cask for yourself. Tastings include the distinctly Tasmanian flavour of the original single malt finished in a pinot noir barrel, and given the distillery's dairy origins, you might want to try the cream liqueur, blended with fresh Tasmanian cream.
153 Old Surrey Rd, Burnie; 03-6433 0439; www.hellyersroaddistillery.com.au; 10am-4.30pm

07 HURSEY SEAFOODS

Huddled at the base of the volcanic outcrop known as the Nut, Stanley is foremost a fishing town, and the Hursey family has been fishing its waters since the mid-1970s (third-generation fisherman Steve Hursey was a recent star of the screen in Foxtel's Aussie Lobster Men series). The fishing operation, which runs nine boats, is directly beneath this restaurant, meaning the crayfish, flathead and scallops have pretty much swum fresh off the boats. The downstairs takeaway counter is the perfect fish-and-chips experience. While the cavernous upstairs restaurant might seem a bit institutional, it's still serves seafood fresh from the boats.
2 Alexander Tce, Stanley; 03-6458 1103; www.hurseyseafoods.com.au; noon-2.30pm & 5.45-7.45pm, takeaway 11.30am-7.30pm

WHERE TO STAY

THE MADSEN
Along the waterfront in Penguin, this grand former bank building harbours six boutique rooms – the luxurious penthouse and beach-front spa suites are the most impressive. The lobby honesty bar stocks Hellyers Road whisky and a selection of Tasmanian wines.
www.themadsen.com

SHIP INN
Built in 1849 by the grandfather of the only prime minister from Tasmania, Joseph Lyons, this newly converted inn provides a blend of sea-side, heritage and luxury right at the foot of The Nut in Stanley. The seven suites are individually themed and styled.
www.shipinnstanley.com.au

WHAT TO DO

CRADLE MOUNTAIN
What would the Cradle Coast be without its famous namesake mountain? A 6km (3.7 mile) walking track circuits Dove Lake at its

foot, providing varying angles on the mountain, or it can be climbed in a full and challenging day of hiking. It's about an hour's drive off the Bass Hwy at Railton.

LITTLE PENGUIN OBSERVATION CENTRE
Like commuters returning home after work, little penguins shuffle ashore faithfully every night at the very edge of Burnie's city centre. The observation centre runs free interpretation tours as the penguins arrive.
www.facebook.com/BurniePenguinObservationCentre

CELEBRATIONS

TASTE THE HARVEST
A day-long Devonport celebration of Tasmanian food and drink held in and around Providore Place each March. Stalls from local eateries and wineries focus on north-west Tasmanian produce.
www.tasmania.com/events/taste-of-the-harvest

GET THERE

The Huon Valley begins just a 30-minute drive southwest of Hobart, with Huonville just shy of 40km (25 miles) away along the Huon Highway. Cygnet is another 15km (9 miles) further south.

HUON VALLEY

[Tasmania]

STAY A WHILE IN THE APPLE ISLE: HUON VALLEY

A 30-minute drive from Hobart, Tasmania's Huon Valley will quench your thirst with cider, fill you with local produce and leave you wanting more.

As the southernmost local government area in Australia, the Huon Valley might be a blip on the radar for overseas visitors, but those in the know are familiar with the scenic drive that leads to Tasmania's largest apple-growing region, which is scattered with charming heritage towns that mix old with new. Huonville is on the banks of the Huon River, surrounded by orchards and farmland; village-like Franklin attracts wooden-boat lovers at its visitor centre; artistic Cygnet is the heart of the fruit-growing region with D'Entrecasteaux Channel on one side and the Huon River on the other; Geevston is a small town near forests, rivers and Hartz Mountains National Park; and further south unspoilt Dover fishing village sits at the top of Esperance Bay.

Stumbled upon by Bruni d'Entrecasteaux in the

18th century, Cygnet was named for the swans that graced its waters – which is easier to reconcile than Eggs and Bacon Bay, a tiny suburb 17km (10.6 miles) away named after the flowers that grow along the coast (not the hangover cure you might need after the cider trail). Settlers followed in 1840, including Thomas Judd who planted the first apple orchard.

Today 80% of Tasmania's apples are grown here and the cider industry is booming. You'll also find small wineries, galleries and restaurants and cafes where cooking with local and seasonal produce isn't something that's just on trend, but a way of life. In a region lauded for its bounty and natural beauty, Cygnet makes a wonderful base. The Channel Highway cuts through the town centre, lined with quaint cafes and the region's more modern restaurants.

01 WILLIE SMITH'S APPLE SHED

Home to Willie Smith's Organic Apple Cider, this wooden shed is a triple threat with a cellar door, restaurant and museum on-site. The restaurant keeps things seasonal and local, whether its salmon fishcakes made with Huon Aquaculture salmon or a lamb shoulder to share. It's a gold coin donation to enter the museum, where a self-guided tour details the history of the Apple Isle. Charles Oates Distillery is also here, plus there's an artisan and produce market every Saturday and live music every Friday night and on the first Sunday of each month. The Apple Shed also hosts the annual Huon Valley Mid-Winter Festival.

2064 Huon Highway, Grove; 03-6266 4345; www.williesmiths.com.au; 10am-6pm Mon-Thu & Sat-Sun; to 10pm Fri

02 FAT PIG FARM

Food critic-turned-farmer, author and local television personality, Matthew Evans left his city life for Tasmania's Huon Valley, where he now runs a 28-hecatre (70-acre) family farm raising Wessex Saddleback pigs. In 2016 he opened a cookery school and farmhouse table, where Friday Feasts are hosted (sometimes on a Thursday or Saturday; AUD175 per adult). Tour the farm in between courses made with produce harvested from the garden and Matthew's own pigs, matched with local beer, wine and spirits. Booking in advance is essential. Check the website for one-off classes and events.

Glaziers Bay, Cygnet; 0432 082 631 www.fatpig.farm; from 12.30pm Friday with booking

03 GRANDVEWE CHEESES & HARTSHORN DISTILLERY

The sheep on this pristine farm graze away overlooking D'Entrecasteaux Channel and Bruny Island. From their milk, this family of farmers not only produces organic cheese, but also vodka and gin made from whey at Hartshorn Distillery. The micro distillery – the first in the world to create spirits this way – makes 80 bottles per batch and labels them by hand. Sample it at the cafe along with

'The Huon Valley is a pretty speccy part of the world, full of great produce and people wanting to share it.'

Andrew Smith, Willie Smiths's Apple Shed

local wines, or make like the sheep and graze on a build-it-yourself cheese platter, toasted sandwich or sweet treat.
59 Devlyns Rd, Birchs Bay; 03-6267 4099; www.grandvewe.com.au; 10am-5pm Mon-Thu, 9am-5pm Fri-Sun Sep-May; 10am-4pm daily Jun-Aug

04 PORT CYGNET CANNERY*

Established by a local family, Port Cygnet Cannery is a food, drink and agricultural hub that supports those who make a living from the land. Opened in late 2019, the first stage saw a restaurant, bar and beer garden powered by a wood-fired pizza oven from Naples (nicknamed Dante the Inferno) and produce from the adjoining Cannery Farm

and elsewhere in the Huon Valley. Stage two is a winery and cellar door from Sailor Seeks, which makes and sells pinot noir and chardonnay.
60 Lymington Road, Port Cygnet; 0438 663 525; www. portcygnetcannery.com; 4-10pm Fri, noon-10pm Sat, 8am-4pm Sun

05 WOODBRIDGE SMOKEHOUSE

If the Apple Isle is known for its cellar doors, Woodbridge Smokehouse could be considered an ocean door. Set on a 10-hectare (25-acre) apple orchard, the Smokehouse sells some of the best smoked ocean trout (from Macquarie Harbour on Tasmania's west coast) and Atlantic salmon (from the Huon Valley) in the world.

05 A warm welcome at Frank's Cider

06 Vegetarian dishes at Red Velvet Lounge

07 The River Derwent and the Huon Valley

Brick ovens containing three types of wood, including apple chips from the orchard, are used to smoke the fish. It's available to taste, as well as to purchase in platters best enjoyed on the picturesque deck. *59 Thomas Road, Woodbridge; 03-6267 4960; www. woodbridgesmokehouse.com. au; 10am-4pm Thu & Fri or by appointment*

06 RED VELVET LOUNGE

Located in Cygnet, this cafe-restaurant is 100% vegetarian, with plenty of vegan and gluten-free options, too. An iconic Huon Valley venue, Red Velvet Lounge closed after a devastating fire in 2014, after which the community and State Government chipped in more than AUD100,000 to help rebuild it. Now under new management, live music continues to be a drawcard – catch it on Friday nights from around 6pm. *24 Mary Street, Cygnet; 03-6295 0730; www.redvelvetlounge.com. au; 9am-4pm Sat, Sun & Wed, to 8pm Thu & Fri*

07 ILHA RESTAURANT

There's a South American influence at this casual, green-walled restaurant, opened by a former MasterChef contestant in her hometown. Like many of the restaurants here, ingredients are local and seasonal, so the menu changes regularly. That could mean wallaby tartare with beetroot, horseradish and wattleseed crackers; marinated chicken heart skewers or half spatchcock with mole and refried beans. Refer to the specials on the butcher's paper roll and ask friendly staff for their picks. *2/23 Mary Street, Cygnet; 0404 365 815; www.facebook.com/ ILHACygnet; 5-11pm Thu & Fri, 11am-11pm Sat, 11am-5pm Sun*

08 KATE HILL WINES

Just because this cellar door is small, doesn't mean it ain't mighty. Kate Hill worked in South Australia, France, California and Chile before acquiring a 100-year-old timber apple cool store in 2011, which she turned into a down-to-earth and welcoming winery and cellar door with her husband – from whom you'll receive an outpouring of knowledge when you visit. There are a number of varieties in the range, but Kate is known for her riesling. *21 Dowlings Road, Huonville; 0448 842 696; www.katehillwines.com. au; 11am-4pm Fri-Sun*

09 FRANK'S CIDER

The Clarks family was one of the first to grow apples and pears in the Huon Valley. The cafe came later in 2014. Housed in a weatherboard from the 1870s it offers rustic, local food – think nourishing soups in front of the open fire in winter, or salmon and cheese boards when it's warmer. Cider tastings are free and the mini Franklin Apple Museum is worth a look. Check the website for orchard tours, live tunes on Sunday afternoons and 'Funnies at Frank's' comedy nights. *3328 Huon Highway, Franklin; 0438 663 525; www.frankscider.com. au; 10am-5pm Sep-May, to 4pm Jun-Aug*

WHERE TO STAY
HIGHLAND GETAWAY
Two private suites on a working farm, one with a hot tub and the other with a cinema, both with king beds and valley views. Take a farm tour and feed the adorable highland cattle. *www.highlandgetaway. com.au*

CYGNET OLD BANK B&B
Set in a National Trust Victorian building from 1909, this former bank on Cygnet's main street has three airy bedrooms. Breakfast made from local produce is served in the Conservatory Cafe. *www.cygnetoldbank. com.au*

WHAT TO DO
THE FARMHOUSE KITCHEN
Southern Italian cooking classes limited to six people in a country-style kitchen. Mini classes run for a couple of hours and focus on a single dish followed by a tasting (AUD75 per person), while master-classes run from 9am to 1.30pm and are followed

by a two-hour lunch (AUD255 per person). *www.thefarmhouse kitchen-tas.com*

CELEBRATIONS
HUON VALLEY MID-WINTER FESTIVAL
Over a weekend in July, thousands gather in the middle of winter for

an old English assailing ceremony, giant bonfire and to burn a two-storey wicker man. There's also a pagan dress-up competition, storytelling, music performances, stallholders and feasts. *www.huonvalley midwinterfest.com.au*

TASTE OF THE HUON
A local celebration of food and wine bolstered by entertainment, arts and crafts. Founded in 1993, it's held at Ranelagh with more than 20,000 attendees over the two-day programme. *www.atasteofthehuon. com.au*

A.D 1823.

GET THERE
Hobart has direct flights from
most Australian mainland
capital cities, and makes the
perfect base for this trail.

The following labels appear on the map:

ROSEGARLAND · 04 · BLACK HILLS · BRIGHTON · Coal River · PLENTY · HAYES · MAGRA · BRIDGEWATER · GRANTON · River Derwent · GAGEBROOK · 05 · RICHMOND · 06 · Meehan Range · NEW NORFOLK · SORELL CREEK · CLAREMONT · OLD BEACH · MALBINA · 03 · MOLESWORTH · BERRIEDALE · 01 · OTAGO · RISDON VALE · 07 · BROOKSIDE · LACHLAN · GLENLUSK · GLENORCHY · CAMBRIDGE · GLENFERN · COLLINSVALE · NEW TOWN · LINDISFARNE · 08 · DERWENT & COAL VALLEY · 02 · Wellington Range · Organ Pipes · HOBART

[Tasmania]
TOURING THE DELICIOUS DERWENT & COAL VALLEYS

You barely need to leave Tasmania's capital city, Hobart, to get among the gourmet treats of the Derwent Valley and the parallel, wine-soaked Coal Valley.

The River Derwent is the lifeblood of southern Tasmania. The state's second-longest river, it begins flowing from Australia's deepest lake, set among World Heritage-listed mountains, and washes into the Southern Ocean through the state's capital city, Hobart. The river's upper reaches are wild and remote, but as its course flattens through New Norfolk and Hobart, it begins to assemble a gathering of gourmet experiences along its banks.

From the River Derwent's banks in Hobart, it's little more than 10km (6 miles) across the low Meehan Range to the adjoining Coal Valley and Australia's southernmost cluster of wineries. Half-a-dozen cellar doors line the Coal River's western bank between Cambridge and one of Tasmania's prettiest towns, Richmond, offering tastings of superb cool-climate wines. Complementing the vineyards are a

valley cheesemaker and a family farm that's doing all sorts of good gourmet things.

Together the twin valleys create an ideal grazing loop out from Hobart. Vineyards begin to appear even before you've found your way out of the city's northern suburbs, while the Coal Valley unspools from right beside Hobart's airport – you can pretty much step off a plane and almost directly into a cellar door.

Hobart is well established as one of Australia's most enticing cities, especially for gourmands. Once considered the poor country cousin to mainland cities, it's now renowned for the quality of its culinary offerings, utilising Tasmania's fabulously fresh produce and seafood. Great bars showcase local wines, whiskies, gins and craft beer, while Hobart is also said to boast more cafes per capita than any other Australian city, making it a fitting base from which to seek out the tastes of the Derwent and Coal Valleys.

01 The twee town of
Richmond, Tasmania

02 The Agrarian
Kitchen in action

03 The Agrarian
Kitchen

04 Moorilla, MONA's
on-site winery

01 MOORILLA

When Claudio Alcorso planted southern Tasmania's first vineyard on a small peninsula in Hobart's northern suburbs in 1958, he could not have imagined the scene six decades on. That peninsula is now home to Hobart's MONA art gallery, but atop it the vines remain, now under the ownership of gambler, self-professed maths nerd and gallery owner David Walsh. The glass-encased, 1st-floor cellar door offers tastings beneath John Olsen's painting *The Source*, which hangs on the ceiling. You can also sip your way through beers from Moorilla's brother brewery, Moo Brew, here. *MONA, 655 Main Rd, Berriedale; 03-6277 9960; www.moorilla.com. au; 9.30am-5pm Mon-Wed*

02 AGRARIAN KITCHEN COOKING SCHOOL

This offspring of the Agrarian Kitchen Cooking School opened in 2017 and within a year had been named among Australia's top 50 restaurants. The setting is incongruous – the cavernous ward of a former psychiatric hospital, complete with original pressed-tin ceiling – but the experience is par excellence. The menu is seasonal and ever-changing, but invariably highlighted by produce and meat from the Agrarian Kitchen's own farm and the community garden across the road from the restaurant. *650 Lachlan Rd, Lachlan; 03-6261 1099; www.theagrariankitchen. com; class times vary*

03 TWO METRE TALL BREWERY

Pull up at the farm bar at Ashley and Jane Huntington's 500-hectare (1235-acre) cattle property and Ashley will happily tell you that the tastes of Two Metre Tall's wild-fermented beers are 'bloody weird'. The wild fermentation produces acidic, almost white-wine-like flavours. You can sit at the outdoor bar bench and watch the hops mature, or you're welcome to set up on the lawns for a BYO barbecue or picnic – cutlery and plates are available at the bar. Brewing takes place inside an old shearing shed beside the bar. *2862 Lyell Hwy, Hayes; 0400 969 677; www.2mt.com.au; noon-4.30pm Thu-Mon*

© Courtesy of Agrarian Kitchen; Agrarian Kitchen; © Robin Barton

'Moorilla is part of MONA, but the winery came before the museum. Australia's largest private gallery is a weird but (almost) never wanky deep-dive into why humans make art.'

Danielle Gibson, Moorilla

04 POOLEY WINES

Pooley's beautiful cellar door is inside stables behind the stately, 1832-built Belmont House – the sandstone bricks for the house and stables came from the same quarry as the blocks for Australia's oldest road bridge, 1.5km (1 mile) down the road in Richmond. Anna Pooley is the family's third-generation winemaker (her grandmother Margaret was running the business well into her 90s), and her riesling is the most popular variety on a long tasting list – no sooner was the 2019 riesling in the bottle than it won gold at the Royal Melbourne Wine Show. Enjoy a wood-fired pizza behind the stables, where tables and beanbags spill out onto the lawn.

1431 Richmond Rd, Richmond; 03-6260 2895; www.pooleywines.com. au; 10am-5pm

05 WICKED CHEESE

After spending five years as production manager at the famed King Island Dairy, head cheesemaker Ashley McCoy brings impeccable credentials to Wicked's intriguing range of cheeses – the likes of whisky cheddar, Tasmanian pepperberry cheddar and chilli camembert. Alongside tastings, there's a wall of windows through which to watch production (weekdays only) and ogle the maturation room. Cheese is unsurprisingly the menu's star item at Wicked's licensed cafe, while the tasting room also functions as a

05 Some of Sullivan
Cove's prized whisky

06 Pick your own at
Coal River Farm

07 You can arrive at
MONA by water

delicatessen for local products, from Coaldale walnuts to condiments, wine and Tasmanian salt.
1238 Richmond Rd, Richmond; 03-6260 2341; www.wickedcheese. com.au; 10am–4.30pm

06 COAL RIVER FARM

Daniel and Melanie Leesong's family farm is the complete gourmet all-rounder. The tall windows of the chic cafe, which does wonderful things with the farm produce, peer over the Coal River, and in summer there's DIY pickings from the 20,000 berry bushes that stripe the slopes above the cafe. The corridor into

the cafe provides a glimpse into the farm's chocolate production, and then there are its artisan cheeses that grace the daily 'high cheese' sittings (from 2.30pm). Blankets are available if you want to bundle together a picnic feast at the top of the orchard.
634 Cambridge Rd, Cambridge; 03-6248 4960; www.coalriverfarm. com.au; 9am–5pm

07 SULLIVANS COVE DISTILLERY

The setting for this world-beating distillery could just about be any tin shed in any industrial complex, but there's magic within. Producing just

15,000 bottles a year, Sullivans Cove was awarded world's best single malt in 2014 and world's best single-cask single malt in 2018 and 2019. Stop by the shed for a tour, which takes place on a platform overlooking the lone still and includes a selection of tastings, from the wash through to the final smooth-as-velvet whisky range. You can also just visit the tasting room, which is lined with barrels, a leather chesterfield and dark blinds that block out the industrial surrounds.
1/10 Lamb Place, Cambridge; 03-6248 5399; www.sullivanscove.com; 10am–4pm

WHERE TO STAY
MONA PAVILIONS
Attached to MONA and Moorilla, these eight art- and architecture-themed chalets have wine cellars, riverside balconies and private artworks from the gallery's collection. If you stay on a Tuesday, when MONA is closed to the public, you get a private, exclusive gallery tour.
www.mona.net.au/stay/ mona-pavilions

THE WOODBRIDGE
This restored Georgian manor sits on the banks of the River Derwent in the centre of New Norfolk. It's Tasmania's only accredited five-star hotel, and has a fine private restaurant and excellent wine selection from its convict-built cellar.
www.woodbridgenn. com.au

WHAT TO DO
MONA
The art gallery that almost singlehandedly put Hobart on the world travel map is burrowed into the sandstone cliffs

of a peninsula, and features the private, eclectic collection of gambler-philanthropist owner David Walsh. Ancient antiquities mingle with contemporary artworks in a gallery that's sexy, provocative and deeply engaging. MONA also stages winter and summer festivals.
www.mona.net.au

MT FIELD
NATIONAL PARK

From New Norfolk, it's a 40km (25 mile) detour to Tasmania's oldest national park. In autumn the slopes of the Tarn Shelf glow when the native fagus – one of Australia's few native deciduous trees – turns golden. Lower down the slopes, the thick rainforest is split by the watery beauty of 45m-high (147ft-high) Russell Falls.
www.parks.tas.gov.au

CELEBRATIONS
TASTE OF TASMANIA
A week-long Hobart harbourside celebration of Tasmania's gastronomic prowess on either side of New Year's Eve that sees producers and restaurateurs dish out seafood, wines, cheese and beers. Plus there's a private New Year's Eve party.
www.thetasteof tasmania.com.au

GET THERE
It's a three-hour drive from Melbourne to Halls Gap, so aim to set off early for the 250km (155 mile) trip along the Western Hwy (M8). Once in Halls Gap, many places of interest can be covered on foot or bicycle hire. another bus on to Halls Gap.

01

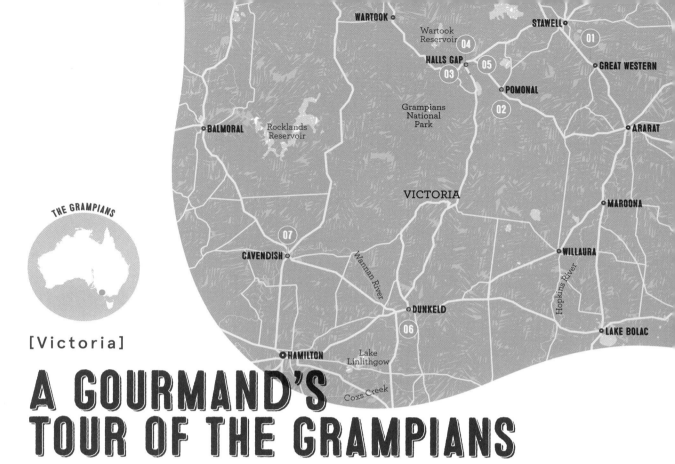

THE GRAMPIANS

[Victoria]

A GOURMAND'S TOUR OF THE GRAMPIANS

Be awed by the extraordinary vistas of the Grampians' ancient landscapes, in between stops at wineries, acclaimed restaurants, artisan food producers and breweries.

Sacred to Indigenous Australians, who've resided here for over 30,000 years, the Grampians (traditionally known as Gariwerd) is an evocative national park comprising stunning mountainous scenery set among bush. The benefits of the region's rich volcanic soils and Mediterranean-style climate have been known to farmers, winemakers and artisan producers for generations, earning its reputation as a gourmet food and drink destination.

Before you embark on any gastronomic pursuits, make sure to first strap on your boots to tackle the Grampians world-class hiking trails – ranging from a leisurely stroll to epic, week-long treks. The sense of timelessness you'll get from atop rock ledges that look out to sweeping valley views is almost transcendental. Add to this Aboriginal rock art dating back some 20,000 years, scenic waterfalls

and abundant native animals and wildflowers, and it becomes clear why the Grampians is such a special destination. Rock climbing is also a huge attraction, luring visitors from around the world to scale its peaks both here and at nearby Mt Arapiles.

Thanks to a collective of talented chefs, brewers, winemakers and cafe owners, you'll eat and drink very well out here. At the foot of the Southern Grampians, the Royal Mail Hotel in Dunkeld leads the way in the fine dining stakes, while to the northeast are vineyards dating back to the 1850s. The main tourist hub of Halls Gap has a new microbrewery, along with country pubs, and cafe-provedores specialising in quality ingredients grown on their doorstep. Furthermore, just outside of town you'll find olive groves, craft beer and cider makers, to round off a busy weekend spent visiting rustic cafes, gastropubs and boutique wineries.

01 The town of Dunkeld beneath Mt Sturgeon

02 Salmon and stout at Paper Scissors Rock

03 Cocktails at the Royal Mail Hotel

04 Wickens restaurant at the Royal Mail Hotel

05 Tasting flights and sharing platters at Pomonal Estate

① BESTS GREAT WESTERN

As soon as you step foot into this atmospheric cellar door, you get the distinct feeling that not a whole lot has changed here since they first opened their doors back in 1866. Within its historical wooden shack, built from local gum trees, you can sample its interesting range of wines, including their flagship shiraz, along with a very drinkable cab sauv, riesling and rosé, which all go beautifully with platters of cheese and locally made salamis. Leave time to take a walk through the original underground cellar featuring historical hand-dug tunnels. It's located within the Great Western winery region, a 30-minute drive east of Halls Gap.

11 Bests Rd, Great Western 03-5356 2250; www.bestswines. com; 10am-5pm Mon-Sat, 11am-4pm Sun

② POMONAL ESTATE

A rightfully popular stop for those exploring the Grampians is this newish venue that has you covered no matter what your tipple is. Part cellar door, part microbrewery and cidery, and part gastropub and cafe, it's a bit of everything rolled into one. Set on an attractive rural property, it's a short drive from Halls Gap and has a modern space to drop in for a tasting paddle of its house-brewed craft beers and ciders to go with a menu of homemade sausage rolls, lamb burgers and local produce platters. The wines are made using grapes sourced from the region and include a decent shiraz and sparkling riesling. They offer snazzy accommodation too, in well-appointed villas with an outdoor jacuzzi.

2079 Pomonal Rd, Pomonal; 0448 983 248; www.pomonalestate.com. au; 10am-5pm Wed-Sun

③ BUSHFOODS CAFÉ & RESTAURANT

The Djab Wurrung and the Jardwadjali are the traditional owners of Gariwerd, and have lived here for more than 30,000 years. In Halls Gap, the informative Brambuk Cultural Centre is a place where you can

Learn about the traditional owners of the land at the Brambuk Cultural Centre and get a taste of indigenous flavours at the bush tucker cafe.

not only learn about their culture, but also get a taste of indigenous flavours at the on-site cafe specialising in bush tucker fusion. Choose between kangaroo steak sandwiches with bush tomato chutney, emu sausages with bush herb mash, or wattleseed damper with quandong jam and cream. *277 Grampians Rd, Halls Gap; 03-5361 4057; www.brambuk.com.au/bushfoodscafe.htm; 9am-5pm*

04 PAPER SCISSORS ROCK BREW CO.

Bringing craft beer to the Grampians, this Halls Gap microbrewery only opened its doors in 2019. Their beers are big on hops for beer lovers into American-style IPAs, but the

range is rounded out with a lighter pilsner, fruity XPA and an English bitter. Grab a paddle to taste the full range, and order from the beer-friendly, seasonal menu of street food dishes. *119 Grampians Rd, Halls Gap; 03-5311 3709; www.paperscissorsrock.beer; 11am-8pm Sun-Thu, to 9pm Fri & Sat*

05 ROYAL MAIL HOTEL

Long regarded as one of regional Victoria's best restaurants, this art-deco gem is in the town of Dunkeld, right on the edge of the Southern Grampians. Hard-working chef Robin Wickens has put together imaginative menus for its two separate restaurants, but both feature

80% of produce that comes directly from its organic kitchen garden. The fine dining Wickens at Royal Mail restaurant looks out to views of Mt Sturgeon and has a cosy open-fire atmosphere. The degustation menu of modern Australian features the likes of crayfish mousse, confit ocean trout and its signature slow-cooked lamb to go with one of the best wine lists in the country. The front bistro Parker St Project has more of a pub atmosphere but without skimping on gastronomic standards. Here it's all about shared plates ranging from smaller bites of beer-pickled onions, lamb croquettes or duck-fat chips to go with larger seasonal dishes of slow-cooked brisket with bourbon glaze salsa verde, or sourdough crumpets with duck confit. *98 Parker St, Dunkeld; 03-5577 2241; www.royalmail.com.au; Wickens at Royal Mail: 6-11.45pm Wed-Sat, noon-3pm Sat; Parker St Project: 7.30am-10pm*

06 BUNYIP HOTEL

Hidden away in tiny Cavendish (population 334), the art-deco Bunyip is seemingly your classic small-town country pub (c 1840s), but with one big difference: it's being run by the former head chef of the acclaimed Movida restaurant in Sydney. Originally from the area, James Campbell has returned to his old stomping ground to put his hometown on the culinary map, creating a regularly changing menu of gourmet takes on nostalgic pub classics using fresh, local produce. Expect the likes of chips and eggs, bangers and mash with onion brandy sauce, and duck breast with housemade black pudding and tempura beetroot. It offers a cracking selection of local wines, along with a quality list of beers, and does homemade ice cream for dessert. For a full appreciation of its culinary vision, drop by on Sunday for the lunch tasting menu. *17-25 Scott St, Cavendish; 03-5574 2205; www.bunyiphotelcavendish. com; 3-10pm Wed, to 11pm Thu-Sat, noon-6pm Sun*

WHERE TO STAY

ROYAL MAIL HOTEL

It makes sense that gastronomes will want to stay on-site at the region's best restaurant. Its tastefully furnished rooms offer sweeping views of the Southern Grampians and landscaped gardens, along with offering perks that includes a luxurious pool and daily guided tour of its famed kitchen garden led by chefs.
www.royalmail.com.au

WHAT TO DO

BRAMBUK CULTURAL CENTRE

This well-curated exhibition centre offers rounded coverage on the traditional owners of the Gariwerd region and is a fantastic opportunity to engage with local Aboriginal culture. It covers pre-European history (dating some 30,000-plus years ago), along with more sobering accounts detailing British colonisation. Daily demos involve boomerang throwing, Aboriginal art classes and learning about bush tucker. It also

offers recommended guided tours of the ancient Aboriginal rock art sites that dot the region.
www.brambuk.com.au

CELEBRATIONS

GRAMPIANS GRAPE ESCAPE

Held over a weekend in May, this annual festival celebrates local food and wine. As well as getting to indulge in delicious cuisine, there are cooking demos, live music and loads of kid-centric activities.
www.grampians grapeescape.com.au

06 Wickens restaurant at the Royal Mail Hotel

07 The Brambuk Cultural Centre in Hall's Gap, Grampians National Park

GET THERE

Geelong is a 75km (46 mile) drive from Melbourne along the M1, but Torquay marks the official starting point of the Great Ocean Road (B100), 21km (13 miles) further along. The trip from Torquay to the Twelve Apostles in Port Campbell is 200km (124 miles). For the return trip, it's faster to head inland via the Princess Hwy. For public transport (www.vline.com.au), catch a train to Geelong from Melbourne, from where buses head to Apollo Bay. From here there are connections on to Port Campbell. Avalon Airport is a 25-minute drive from Geelong, with domestic flights to many cities.

Barwon River

GEELONG

OCEAN
GROVE

01

WINCHELSEA

TORQUAY

02

ANGLESEA

03

AIREYS INLET

04

LORNE

Mount Elm Creek

Lake
Corangamite

BEEAC

CAMPERDOWN

TERANG

Lake
Colac

BIRREGURRA

Barwon River

COBDEN

COLAC

DEANS MARSH

05

VICTORIA

07

Gellibrand River

FORREST

TIMBOON

GELLIBRAND

PORT
CAMPBELL

BEECH FOREST

WYE RIVER

GEELONG

Bass Strait

PRINCETOWN

LAVERS HILL

06

WONGARRA

JOHANNA

APOLLO BAY

CAPE OTWAY

[Victoria]
THE GREAT OCEAN ROAD

Get behind the wheel to embark on this iconic coastal drive that takes in natural wonders in between stops for divine food cooked up by talented local chefs.

When it comes to great road trips, they don't come more aptly named than this one. Right up there with Australia's most popular tourist destinations, the Great Ocean Road is a 189km (117 mile) coastal drive that kicks off from the surf capital of Torquay (1½ hours from Melbourne), which winds you through a series of relaxed coastal towns, forested roads and scenic detours before climaxing with the unforgettable finish as you arrive at the majestic Twelve Apostles. It's a drive defined by sweeping ocean panoramas, countless beaches, atmospheric 19th-century lighthouses and the Otway Ranges filled with koalas, platypus, wallabies and echidnas.

Along the way you'll want to take plenty of stops to admire the views, go for swims, bush walks and explore the sights, but be sure to factor in time for the region's sublime culinary offerings. Given the high

standard on offer, you'll need to be selective as you can't eat everywhere – any places you can't get to are simply reasons to return!

If you're ever wondering what constitutes Australian food, a trip down the Great Ocean Road will give you a good idea. Fish and chips, egg-and-bacon rolls, scallop pies and Otway roast lamb are merely scratching the surface until you stop by the hatted restaurants. Acclaimed chefs – enticed to the Great Ocean Road by both the fertile soils, seafood and artisan producers – draw on native coastal ingredients to whip up contemporary, innovative and divine Aussie cuisine.

Inland detours lead you into dairy country for delicious cheese and ice cream, along with chocolate, wine and whisky. Add in some ripper coastal pubs, microbreweries and gin distilleries and you're guaranteed a memorable weekend.

01 IGNI

While the main highway now bypasses Geelong, a detour to Victoria's second biggest city is highly recommended, not just for the sparkling bay views, but for one of the best restaurants in the state. Set up by local boy Aaron Turner, IGNI can put no foot wrong with this fine diner cooking up native flavours on a charcoal grill to provide a degustation menu full of surprises and original tastes, all superbly presented. The staff is exemplary and the atmosphere is distinctly relaxed minus any pretension.

Ryan Place, Geelong; 03-5222 2266; www.restaurantigni.com; 6-11pm Thu & Fri, noon-4pm & 6-11pm Sat, noon-4pm Sun

02 FISH BY MOONLITE

The opportunity to sample fish and chips cooked up by a hatted chef is one too good to pass up, and here at Fish by Moonlite they deliver with a gourmet version of every Aussie's favourite beach takeaway food. Located in the delightful coastal town of Anglesea, this boutique fish-and-chip shop cooks up the crunchiest chips and battered fish you'll ever eat. Don't miss the divine flake – freshly caught in Portland in southwest Victoria – with its juicy, snow-white flesh coated in a vodka-infused batter and fried to perfection. Enjoy it on the beach at Point Roadknight or on picnic tables by Anglesea River.

Shop 4, Anglesea; 0480 224 173; www.fishbymoonlite.com.au

03 AIREYS PUB

In the heart of the tiny, sleepy beach town of Aireys Inlet is this much-loved local pub, with a storied past that dates back to 1904. Destroyed in the 1983 Ash Wednesday fires, it was rebuilt only to go broke in 2011 before a bunch of locals chipped in to take it over and start brewing their own beer. Today they have half a dozen of its Salt Brewing Co. (www.saltbrewing.co) beers on tap, including a pale ale, blood orange IPA, golden ale and their signature Salt lager, brewed using water from the ocean. All are produced on-site and best enjoyed by the fire or out in its expansive beer garden, while tucking into their

gastropub fare. While you're in Aireys, head across the road to Great Ocean Road Gin (www. greatoceanroadgin.com.au) who make their own gin using such locally sourced ingredients as foraged kelp and honey.
45 Great Ocean Rd, Aireys Inlet; 03-5289 6804; www.aireyspub. com.au; 11.30am-11pm

04 IPSOS

The resort town of Lorne is one of the top destinations along the Great Ocean Road, featuring a beautiful beach and a thriving food and cafe scene along its main strip. One of its stars is Ipsos, a modern Greek restaurant run by the affable Dom Talimanidis, who has continued

the family legacy in Lorne by opening at the same address as the famed Kostas Taverna, formerly run by his parents. Ipsos is a very popular spot and has earned itself a chef's hat for its delectable slow-cooked lamb shoulder, fried local calamari and flavoursome dips, and a fantastic local and Greek drinks list. The family pedigree runs strong in the area, with fellow brothers running the acclaimed A La Greque (www. alagrecque.com.au) in Aireys Inlet and cafe Salonika (www.salonika. com.au) up the street from Ipsos in Lorne.
48 Mountjoy Pde, Lorne; 03-5289 1883; www.ipsosrestaurant.com. au; noon-10pm Thu-Mon

05 BRAE

Hidden away in the tiny country town of Birregurra (population 828) – a scenic 30-minute drive north of Lorne through pristine forest – Brae is not only one of Australia's gastronomic highlights, but a regular nominee in the World's Best 100 Restaurants list. Set inside a rustic-chic farmhouse overlooking acres of pastoral property, here acclaimed chef Dan Hunter sources nothing but the finest quality ingredients, usually whatever's sustainable and local, both from his bountiful organic kitchen garden or from artisan producers in the region. Drawing on what's available he designs a multi-course set menu of cutting-edge, thought-provoking, contemporary dishes

laid out before you like creations of art. Indigenous and coastal vegetables are also featured, given it a distinct local flavour. Well worth the splurge.

4285 Cape Otway Rd, Birregurra; 03-5236 2226; www. braerestaurant.com; 6.30-11.30pm Thu, noon-6pm Fri, noon-11.30pm Sat, noon-5pm Sun & Mon

06 GREAT OCEAN ROAD BREWHOUSE

With its main brewery a bit off the tourist trail – tucked away in the forests of the Otways – the team from Prickly Moses made the wise decision to bring things closer to the action with the opening of this brewhouse in Apollo Bay. One of the Great Ocean Road's most popular towns, Apollo Bay gets crammed by the busload, so its setup on the main drag within

a handsome red brick pub is the perfect spot to come by to sample their dozen or so beers. If you're here for a pub meal opt for the front bar, otherwise make your way around to its Tastes of the Region building for a selection of regional charcuterie, regional wines and craft beers. In 2020 they launched a new whisky distillery across the road, where you can also grab a woodfired pizza and locally roasted single-origin coffee.

29/35 Great Ocean Rd, Apollo Bay; 03-5237 6240; www. greatoceanroadbrewhouse.com. au; noon-late

07 12 APOSTLES GOURMET TRAIL

For most visitors, Port Campbell will mark the end of their Great Ocean Road journey. And what a finale! Here you will be treated by

a series of limestone stacks that jut out into ocean, of which the most famous is the Twelve Apostles. Once you're done sightseeing, take the road north, leading you inland to some of the region's finest artisan producers. Most notable is Timboon Railway Shed Distillery (www.timboondistillery.com.au), producer of one of Australia's finest single malt scotch whiskeys. Sample the goods at its rustic cellar door, before dining in the quality cafe specialling in local beef dishes. The trail also takes in ice cream, berry farms, fudge producers, chocolatiers and two top-notch cheesemakers, Apostle Whey (www.apostlewheycheese.com. au) and Timboon Cheesery (www. timbooncheesery.com.au).

Port Campbell/Corangamite; www.12apostlesfoodartisans. com.au

WHERE TO STAY

QDOS
Elegant ryokan-inspired (traditional Japanese accommodation) treehouses in a sublime bush setting just outside Lorne, sharing space with Qdos Art Gallery and its sculpture garden.
www.qdosarts.com

BRAE
If you're here to dine at this famed restaurant, make a night of it and stay in their boutique suites on-site, decked out with designer touches, a record player, temperature-controlled wine fridge and cocktail bar.
www.braerestaurant.
com

WHAT TO DO

AUSTRALIAN NATIONAL SURFING MUSEUM
Drop into Australia's surf capital Torquay to check out this brilliantly curated museum showcasing the history of surfing – from the countercultural heydays to current-day competitive pro circuit. From here, the world-famous surf

break at Bells Beach is a 15-minute drive away.
www.australiannational
surfingmuseum.com.au

CAPE OTWAY LIGHTSTATION
The forested leg of the Great Ocean Road leads you through a canopy of towering trees, home to many koalas, and to this beautiful 1848 historical lighthouse, the oldest on mainland Australia.
www.lightstation.com

CELEBRATIONS

APOLLO BAY SEAFOOD FESTIVAL
Getting bigger by the year is this celebration of local seafood in Apollo Bay with a weekend of food and drink featuring local artisan producers.
www.apollobayseafood
festival.com

GET THERE
The King Valley is about three hours northeast of Melbourne by car or five hours southwest of Canberra. There are good train services to nearby Wangaratta but you will then need your own transport.

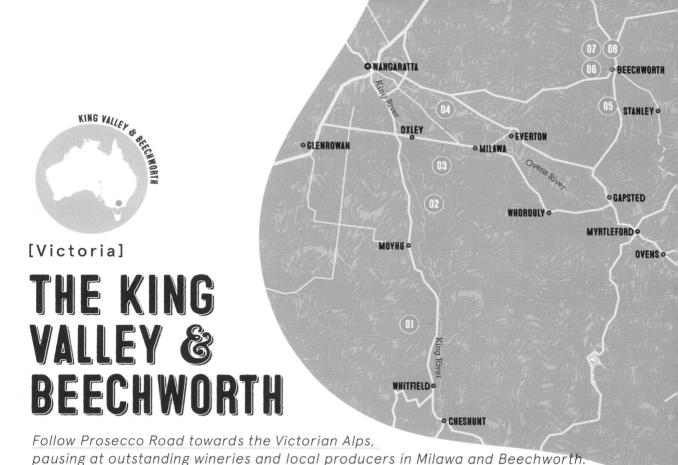

[Victoria]

THE KING VALLEY & BEECHWORTH

Follow Prosecco Road towards the Victorian Alps,
pausing at outstanding wineries and local producers in Milawa and Beechworth.

The first crops planted in the King Valley were tobacco plants. They were a good earner for the Italian families that had settled here in the 1950s until, well, you know what happened. Luckily, there was a ready-made alternative: vines. Encouraged by wine-making families such as the Brown Brothers, local families cultivated grapes and, unlike many other regions of Australia, they first tried varieties familiar from their homelands: sangiovese, nebbiolo, pinot gris and what is now known as glera, used to make prosecco. And so the roots of the King Valley's hedonistic Prosecco Road were established.

The King Valley lies along the Whitfield to Wangaratta road, three hours' drive northeast of Melbourne. The road runs alongside the fish-rich King River and on the horizon to the northeast, beyond meadows filled with grazing cattle and sheep, rise the foothills of the Victorian Alps. It's a fertile landscape that lends itself not only to grapes and grazing but also countless other crops, including nuts (which you will see advertised on the roadside), vegetables, olives and more. A new wave of producers, such as cheesemakers, distillers and brewers, has arrived and added to the appeal of the King Valley for a weekend of indulgence.

This trail begins halfway up the Prosecco Road and heads north to Milawa, at the junction of the Great Alpine Road that leads into the mountains. We've selected our favourite winery on Prosecco Road but there are plenty of others to explore the length of the King Valley so it's easy to extend a trip. We pause in Milawa a while, tasting that rare commodity in Australia, good cheese. A fine distillery in a farm shed lies down a dusty road here. Then we continue north to the regional food and wine hub of Beechworth. Spend some time in this historic town, visiting as many of the restaurants as you can manage before burning off some of the calories with a swim, hike or bike ride in the rugged landscape of this plateau.

(02)

01 RED FEET

Start the trip with a visit to one of the most fun wineries along Prosecco Road. Founded by winemaker Damien Star and managed by his sister Megan, Red Feet is one of the smallest vineyards in the King Valley but manages to cram in a lot of experiences: you can try your hand at pruning vines, crushing grapes in their hand-operated basket press or just take in the views across the valley to the Black Range mountains from the tasting room. A variety of grapes are grown: Damien started with plantings of sangiovese and the Spanish grape tempranillo – 'a bit controversial with the Italian families,' says Megan. Red Feet also offers a cool-climate shiraz. 'I want to make the best

wine that I can but I want it to be approachable,' says Damien.
49 Cemetery Lane, King Valley; 03-5729 3535; www.redfeet.com.au; 11am-6pm Fri-Sun

02 HURDLE CREEK STILL

Gin has evolved immeasurably since the days when a quarter of London homes distilled their own illicitly. At Hurdle Creek Still, gin is further refined with botanicals that reference the rural surroundings of this boutique distillery. Their Powder Monkey Navy Strength gin adds eucalyptus leaves picked from the Blaklely's red gum outside the stillhouse, plus pink peppercorns, cinnamon and aniseed myrtles. 'We usually have an idea of where we want to end up when we create a

new gin,' says owner Simon Brooke-Taylor. 'The Powder Monkey we got right first time: we wanted an old-school gin made with local botanicals and customers kept coming back for more. It's a big, punchy, juniper-forward and uniquely Australian gin'

Simon's tasting shed adds more rare delights, including a *pastis* and a cherry gin, to the local food and drink scene. 'If it can be grown, raised or harvested here, from nuts, berries, fruit, honey, to organic beef, goats or cheese, somebody will be doing it, making it or serving it their restaurant, accompanied by local wines,' he says.
216 Whorouly-Bobinawarrah Rd, Milawa; 03-5727 9106; www. hurdlecreekstill.com.au; 11am-4pm Thu, 11am-5pm Fri-Sun

01 Beer and pizza with
Ben Kraus at Bridge
Road Brewers

02 A spiritual journey
at Hurdle Creek Still

03 Delicious dairy
at Milawa Cheese
Company

04 Grape harvesting
with Damien Star at
Red Feet

03 BROWN BROTHERS

At the other end of the scale, family-owned Brown Brothers is one of Australia's biggest wine names. Beyond the polished experience of their cellar door, Brown Brothers was one of the pioneers of King Valley and there's a lot of local history to discover – their very first vines were planted in Milawa in 1885. The flagship wines are named after Patricia Brown, the family matriarch, and are released on her birthday each year. There's a truly vast number to taste (recent additions include an albariñō and an arneis from their 'kindergarten' winery) but start with a behind-the-scenes tour. *239 Milawa-Bobinawarrah Rd, Milawa; 03-5720 5547; www.brownbrothers.com.au*

04 MILAWA CHEESE COMPANY

The ideal partner to King Valley wines can be found at family-owned Milawa Cheese Company, now run by Ceridwen Brown. 'Mum and Dad set up Milawa Cheese Company after travelling through Europe and falling in love with the variety of cheeses available,' says Ceridwen. 'Coming home to cheddar and camembert in a can, they wanted to bring great local cheese to Australia.' Their first cheese was a blue cheese, now available in an aged version, both of which benefit from the quality of local milk. 'The foothills of the Victorian Alps is a beautiful place to make cheese. It's a perfect climate and the cows and goats range over lush green pastures all year. And being located in the King Valley

means we have some spectacular wines to match with our cheeses.' *17 Factory Rd, Milawa; 03-5727 3589; www.milawacheese.com.au*

05 BRIDGE ROAD BREWERS

Continue north to Beechworth and drop into Ben Kraus' brewery, which also serves some of the best pizzas in the state, such as the gorgonzola with apples from Stanley's orchards just up the road. You can see the beers being brewed before sampling them. Our picks? The Beechworth Pale Ale is a classic Aussie ale, thanks to a mix of 10 different, locally grown hops. There's always an interesting range of rarities on tap. *50 Ford St, Beechworth; 03-5728 2703; www.bridgeroadbrewers. com.au; see website for times*

05 Elizabeth and Stephen Morris at Pennyweight Wines

06 Sweet treats at Beechworth Honey

07 Lake Sambell in Beechworth

06 BEECHWORTH HONEY

At the top of Beechworth's main street, this shop is more than a place to stock up on the sweet stuff. Steven and Jodie Goldsworth bought their first bees in 1992, Jodie having grown up in the fourth-generation of a Beechworth beekeeping family. They've helped put Beechworth on the map over the last 25 years. 'I'm proud of the fact that I know my great-grandfather, who was a gold miner turned beekeeper, would be pleased to see his legacy,' says Jodie. In the Beechworth Honey shop you can taste more than 40 varieties of uniquely Australian honey, from light and fruity (such as ironbark or blue gum) to dark and bold (Northeast Victoria's red stringy bark). Honeys in the Bee Cause range are sourced from various types of location, from mountains to meadows, and 1% of the revenue to environmental causes. A small beekeeping museum at the shop explains the honey-making process. *31 Ford St, Beechworth; 03-5728 1433; www.beechworthhoney.com. au; see website for times*

07 PENNYWEIGHT WINES

Our favourite winery in Beechworth is Pennyweight for three reasons: the wine, the setting, and the hospitality from Elizabeth and Stephen Morris, from a Rutherglen winemaking family. They planted vines around this hill in 1977. 'We came here because it's cooler,' says Elizabeth. Water remains a precious resource - they don't believe in watering their vines so they cleverly planted them in arcs to save water. The Bordeaux-style cabernet blend has mouthwatering notes of dark chocolate and red fruit. But it's the fortified wines that are the souvenir-worthy surprise, especially the amazing 'Gold' white port, best served slightly chilled. *13 Pennyweight Lane, Beechworth; 03-5728 1747; www.pennyweight. com.au; 10am-5pm daily*

08 EMPIRE HOTEL

You could spend a week in Beechworth and not exhaust its excellent dining potential. There's the Press Room for tapas, the Ox and Hound Bistro and Michael Ryan's award-winning Provenance. One of best new additions is the Empire Hotel on a corner near Lake Sambell. It has been spruced up by owners Andrew Madden, Scott Daintry and Shauna Stockwell, whose cooking expertly blends classic and contemporary influences. *10 Camp St, Beechworth, 03-5728 2743; www. empirehotelbeechworth.com.au*

WHERE TO STAY

ARMOUR MOTOR INN
Beechworth makes a great base for exploring the region but lacks a lot of accommodation options. One of the best motels is this one, down by Lake Sambell. It's family-owned, clean, friendly and good value.
1 Camp St, Beechworth; 03-5728 1466; www. armourmotorinn.com.au

LANCEMORE MILAWA
Many of the wineries in the King Valley offer guest accommodation. Or you can try this large country hotel, which has spacious rooms, great views and an outdoor swimming pool.
223 Milawa-Bobinawarrah Rd, Milawa; 03-5720 5777; www.lancemore.com.au

WHAT TO DO

SWIMMING
Chill out on hot afternoons at a couple of the lakes in the area. To the south of the King Valley, Lake William Hovell has good fishing, boating and lakeside hikes. It's actually an

artificial lake where the King River has been dammed. In Beechworth, Lake Sambell is similarly human-made but no less appealing, with walking in a nature reserve and boating and fishing on the water. For a wilder watery experience, head out to Lake Kerferd near Stanley. In short, bring your swimmers.

CELEBRATIONS

LA DOLCE VITA
King Valley's annual food and wine festival is a weekend-long celebration in November of local produce along the Prosecco Road, with music, activities and tastings for the family. A shuttle bus runs between participating wineries.
www.winesofthe kingvalley.com.au

SPRING TASTING
Beechworth's vignerons show off their hard work at this annual exhibition in the town centre. Typically around 30 local producers participate and it's a great opportunity to try several wines to work out what styles you like and also talk to the winemakers.
www.beechworth vineyards.com.au

GET THERE

From Melbourne it's an hour's drive to Red Hill's wineries. The nearby beach towns of Sorrento and Portsea can be reached by train and bus from Frankston, but you'll need your own wheels for the wineries.

01

MORNINGTON PENINSULA

SAFETY BEACH

06

05

02

MERRICKS NORTH

Arthurs Seat
State Park

RED HILL

Mornington
Peninsula

03

RED HILL SOUTH

MERRICKS

04

01

MAIN RIDGE

POINT LEO

Western
Port

SHOREHAM

[Victoria]

MAKE A MEAL OF IT ON THE MORNINGTON PENINSULA

A perfect weekend escape from Melbourne, the Mornington Peninsula offers world-class wines and a bounty of local produce, hidden among beaches and bush scenery.

Kicking out from Melbourne's southeastern bayside suburbs is this boot-shaped peninsula that's long been a playground for city-dwellers seeking a seaside escape. From endless summers spent by foreshore caravan parks to weekends away in luxury holiday homes, families have been coming to the Mornington Peninsula for generations. On one side you've got a string of pretty beaches, lined with iconic bathing boxes looking out to the calm, flat waters of Port Phillip Bay, while on the other it's all the romance of a rugged coastline, with pounding waves and wild, swirling surf of the Antarctic-chilled Bass Strait.

To uncover its epicurean delights, however, you'll need to dust off the sand from your towel to head inland to the forested Red Hill area. Home to some 50-plus wineries, and accompanied by fine dining restaurants, produce farms, breweries, cider houses and distilleries, as a whole it's a region that's firmly on the map as one of Victoria's gourmet hot spots.

The drive into Mornington's wine country evokes all the senses of your quintessential Australian road trip, winding you along eucalypt-scented roads lined with gum trees and koala road signs. Known primarily for its chardonnay and pinot noir, it's been a big few years for this cool-climate wine-growing region. A lot of money has been pumped into the industry, and the bar has been risen to lofty new heights. This has resulted in a number of slick, new wineries featuring architecturally-designed cellar doors and acclaimed hatted restaurants, attracting a well-heeled clientele here for a day of indulgence.

Among it all are more rustic, family-owned vineyards keeping things real, while being equally proficient in producing a quality drop true to the region. Add in stops for craft beer, artisanal distilleries, cheese, olives and berries, and you've got yourself a weekend of culinary pleasure to look forward to.

01 PT LEO ESTATE

One of Australia's most acclaimed winery-restaurants, Pt Leo Estate has cemented the region's reputation as a top epicurean destination in Victoria. A stunning AUD50 million dollar makeover has transformed this once humble cellar door into a sleek, architectural, landscaped masterpiece, luring folk in for all of life's finer pleasures: food, wine and art, accompanied by sweeping 180-degree pastoral and coastal views.

The building's curvaceous, wave-shaped entrance – fronted by a modern sculpture showpiece and bottle tree – offers a striking first impression. Stretching across the premise are three dining options,

all under the guidance of gun chef, Phil Wood (ex Rockpool in Melbourne), including not one, but two, hatted restaurants. Fine dining Laura offers a tasteful intimate space for its set five-course menu of cutting edge, locally sourced cuisine; in contrast, the larger open-space Pt Leo Estate Restaurant does an a la carte menu featuring salivating-inducing mains such as wood-roasted snapper and slow-roasted lamb dishes. At the centre of the action is their cellar door, offering tastings of its estate-grown pinot, chardonnay and shiraz.

Even if you're not here for food, drop by for the sculpture garden. Spaced over 135 hectares (334 acres), it features 60 contemporary

works by prominent Australian and international artists.
3649 Frankston-Flinders Rd, Merricks; 03-5989 9011; www. ptleoestate.com.au; 11am-10.30pm Thu-Mon, to 5pm Tue & Wed

02 JACKALOPE

Encapsulating the new wave of boutique wineries that have swept across the Mornington Peninsula is this multifaceted venue that incorporates fine dining, luxury hotel and lulling, rolling vineyard views.

First impressions won't disappoint with a long stately driveway leading you through the estate's immaculate vines and arriving at a colossal contemporary sculpture of its

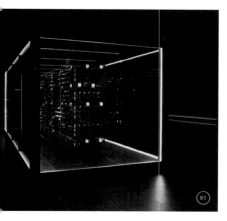

namesake creature, the Jackalope. If you're fine dining, its acclaimed restaurant Doot Doot Doot offers a more serious approach that its name may suggest. A dark-lit sumptuous affair, the five-course menu comprises highly seasonal European-inspired cuisine, but with a distinct local flavour, and paired with their estate wines. For something more casual, Rare Hare maximises views of the countryside, accompanied by a lively bistro atmosphere with roaring fire, live music and alfresco seating to enjoy the inventive menu of charcoal-roasted vegetarian, seafood and meat dishes. There is also the barrel-filled wine cellar, offering tastings of the winery's crisp whites and light reds.

166 Balnarring Rd, Merricks North 03-5931 2500; www.jackalope hotels.com; Doot Doot Doot: noon-2.30pm Sat & Sun, 6-10pm

ⓒ MAIN RIDGE ESTATE

Go back to where it all began at Main Ridge Estate, one of the region's first wineries to open up in 1975. These days it's led by hardworking winemaker James Sexton, along with his parents, who together ensure a hands-on, family-run atmosphere that you won't get at the bigger, more streamlined enterprises. Its tasteful brick cellar door offers scenic outlooks over the vines. Taste their quality range of pinot noir and chardonnay – don't miss the 2018 Half Acre pinot – while enjoying a

charcuterie board on the outdoor deck. On the way out, stop by Red Hill Cheese (www.redhillcheese. com.au), an artisan cheesemaker and cafe just across the road. *80 William Rd, Red Hill; 03-5989 2686; www.mre.com.au; noon to 5pm Fri-Sun*

ⓓ RED HILL BREWERY

Opening in 2005, Red Hill Brewery was producing non-mainstream, preservative-free ale well before it was known as 'craft' beer. Tucked away on a small bush property, this rustic brewhouse makes all its beers on-site – some using the hops you'll see growing in the front paddock – and offers tasting paddles of their IPA, pale ale, Hefeweizen, kolsch, pilsner

and a Scotch ale poured from a ye olde wooden pump. Keep an eye out for small-batch, one-off beers made using seasonal produce such as plums, truffles, honey and cherries. There's also a smoker for American-style barbecue lunches of slow-cooked brisket and pulled-pork burgers. Beer lover's bliss! *88 Shoreham Rd, Red Hill South; 03-5989 2959; www. redhillbrewery.com.au; 11am-6pm Wed-Sun*

Ø5 BASS & FLINDERS GIN DISTILLERY

One of the pioneers in kicking off Australia's artisanal gin scene, Bass & Flinders were not only the first distillery to open along the Mornington Peninsula, but one of the first to incorporate native Australian botanicals into their handcrafted gins.

Check out their 'Angry Ant' gin, made using indigenous flowers and spices, with a dash of ant pheromone to round out a truly unique concoction. Other notable releases feature regional flavours such as locally foraged kelp, Red Hill shiraz grapes and black truffles. Brandy, vodka and limoncello are other tipples they take seriously here. They also offer a distillation class 101, where you drive the flavour by choosing your own botanicals, before taking your handcrafted gin home as a keepsake! *40 Collins Rd, Dromana; 03-5989 3154; www. bassandflindersdistillery.com; 11am-5pm*

Ø6 JIMMYRUM

In this golden age of 'craft booze' where artisanal gin and whisky

makers dominate the scene, somehow rum has missed out among it all. Identifying a gap in the market, a team of rum aficionados stepped up to open JimmyRum in 2019. Set in the backstreets of Dromana's industrial complex – known locally as the Bermuda Triangle, given it's home to several breweries, a gin distillery and cider maker – here they offer tasting flights and a menu of rum cocktails to enjoy by the fire or outside on bean bags in the garden.

After a day of drinking, you may be needing a pick-me-up, in which case head across to Little Rebel (www.littlerebel.com.au) a third-wave microroaster doing the Peninsula's best coffee, brewed using single-origin beans. *6 Brasser Ave, Dromana; 03-5987 3338; www.jimmyrum.com.au; noon-6pm Tue-Sat, 10am-2pm Sun*

WHERE TO STAY
JACKALOPE

A stylish designer hotel is the one thing that's eluded the Mornington Peninsula, but the arrival of Jackalope in 2017 has righted the ship for those seeking a weekend of luxury. From the outside it could be a modern art museum – a formidable, compound-like contemporary space, sitting among vineyards, with lair-inspired suites and rooms with floor-to-ceiling windows overlooking public sculptures and an infinity pool
www.jackalopehotels. com

WHAT TO DO
PENINSULA HOT SPRINGS

A weekend down this way should be all about treating yourself, so keep the ball rolling with a visit to this day spa featuring an outdoor sanctuary of naturally heated pools sourced from the mineral waters beneath.
www.peninsula hotsprings.com

POINT NEPEAN NATIONAL PARK

At the toe of the boot-shaped peninsula is this scenic coastal park looking out to dramatic ocean vistas. Grab a bike to explore the historical Fort Nepean, a naval base where remarkably the first shot was fired not only for WWI, but also for WWII! It's also where Australia's former Prime Minister Harold Holt mysteriously disappeared back in 1967.
www.parks.vic.gov.au/ places-to-see/parks/

CELEBRATIONS
THE PENINSULA PICNIC

Showcasing the best of Mornington's wine, beer and food is this day of merriment held in March, accompanied by live bands and lawn games
www.peninsulapicnic. com.au

GET THERE

It's about half an hour's drive from Melbourne's Tullamarine Airport into the CBD by taxi or rideshare (Uber, DiDi and Ola operate in Melbourne). You can also catch the SkyBus into the centre every eight minutes from outside the terminals for AUD19.75 per adult one way, or AUD36.50 return.

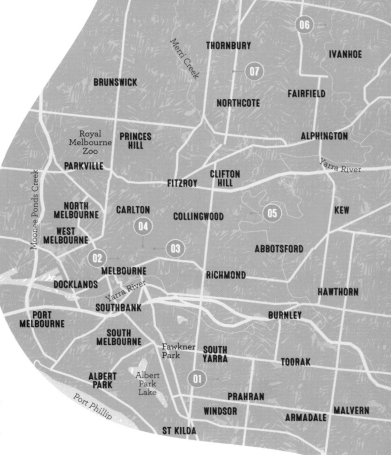

MELBOURNE

[Victoria]

MUNCHING AROUND MELBOURNE

From local legends to mesmerising markets, urban breweries and globally recognised restaurants, Melbourne's food scene is limited only by your appetite.

It would be ignorant to reference Australian food culture without first acknowledging Aboriginal and Torres Strait Islander people, who preceded Melbourne's multiculturalism by tens of thousands of years. But honing in on the last two centuries alone, waves of migrants have brought a taste of their homes to Melbourne, creating a layered dining scene backed by contemporary chefs and some of the world's best produce. It started with Chinese migration in the 1900s, which boomed with the gold rush. After WWII Italians also began to call Melbourne home, with specialist grocers opening on Lygon St and introducing the coffee capital of the world to caffeine. Simultaneously, Greek people opened fish and chip shops and milk bars in the first half of the 1900s, with the cuisine becoming popularised in the 1950s and restaurants opening about 30 years later.

The first Australian Thai restaurant opened in Melbourne in the mid 1970s, while Vietnamese refugees turned to cooking to earn an income. More recently, African communities have grown, but there's not enough space on this page to name every culture represented in Melbourne. Our melting pot of cuisines has formed a foundation that's been built upon by professional chefs, who often reference their heritage on the plate. The restaurant industry is tough here – popular strips are saturated, diners' standards are higher than ever and premium produce has a premium price tag. Still, the result is an ever-rising bar for cafes, restaurants and watering holes. Eating your way around this city should be treated as an adventure, an opportunity to enter into a meal with curiosity and leave with a piece of someone else's story. There's never been a better time to be hungry in Melbourne.

01 MAKER & MONGER

In the bustle of Prahran Market's Harvest Hall is what owner Anthony Femia dubs his 'Chapel of Cheese'. A 7m (23ft) counter proudly displays wheels of the best, while out back is a maturation room. Don't leave without eating; the seasonal grilled cheese sandwiches are the best in the country and staff take to the Wagyu brisket-filled Flamed Reuben with a blowtorch. In cooler months, Swiss raclette is scraped onto potato and shiitake mushrooms. Pull up a sought-after chair, order a Market Lane coffee to complement your brunch and soak up the marketplace atmosphere.
Stall 98, Prahran Market, 163 Commercial Rd, South Yarra; 03-9958 4830; www.makerandmonger. com.au; 7.30am-4pm Thu, Fri & Tue, to 4.30pm Sat, 9am-3pm Sun

02 MIZNON

Founded by Israeli chef Eyal Shani in Tel Aviv, you'll also find Miznon in Paris, New York, Vienna and on the cobblestones of Hardware Lane in Melbourne. What you won't find is a better pita, whether hot chickpeas and egg, lamb chops with tahini or ocean trout belly with avocado. The dinner menu has more share plates, but the signature whole roasted cauliflower is always available. The staff can come across direct, but it adds to the personality of the place, which is fresh, fun and always pumps Israeli tunes. Help yourself to the pita, tahini and pickle bar while you wait.
59 Hardware Lane, Melbourne; 03-9670 2861; www.miznonaustralia. com; noon-10pm Mon-Sat

03 SPRING STREET GROCER

Spring Street Grocer is an alimentari-style store that combines the nostalgia of the fruit and veg shop you may have visited as a kid with beautiful design. Pantry essentials and organic produce are on the fancy side, but it's a great spot to find something local with pretty packaging. On weekdays, Rolls Ready at the rear offers wholesome sandwiches, some featuring cheese from the underground cellar – descend the spiral staircase for a look; it's not to be missed. Gelateria Primavera

at the front of the shop makes the city's best gelato, while next door City Wine Shop is a wonderful spot. *157 Spring St, Melbourne; 03-9639 0335; www.springstreetgrocer. com.au; grocer 9am-9pm Mon-Sun; gelateria noon-10.30pm Sun-Thu, to 11pm Fri-Sat*

04 BAR MARGAUX

For AUD99 a feast of oysters, steak tartare, frites and champagne could be all yours with Bar Margaux's 'Beggar's Banquette'. It's available between 4pm and 6pm, and again from midnight until close at this New York–style French brasserie basement bar. Dishes such as escargot and the MGX burger – a decadent, hulking thing slathered in cheese, bacon and bone marrow –

are always on the cards. With black-and-white chequered tiles and red leather banquettes, this painfully stylish bar stays open late and is popular with the hospitality crowd. Martini, anyone?
111 Lonsdale St, Melbourne; 03-9650 0088; www.barmargaux.com. au; 4pm-3am Sun-Thu, noon-5am Fri, 4pm-5am Sat

05 FARM CAFE

Wedged between the peaceful Abbotsford Convent and Collingwood Children's Farm is this oasis of an outdoor cafe. Nowhere else in Melbourne can you enjoy eggs with goat's curd and seasonal greens or a rustic sausage roll while gazing at roaming peacocks or listening to farm animals calling

out for breakfast. Picnic baskets – complete with borrowed rugs – can be ordered online in advance. Try to time your visit with one of the farmers' markets, either on the second or fourth Saturday of the month at the farm and convent respectively. Within the Convent are also art studios, galleries and multiple cafes to explore.
Collingwood Children's Farm, 18 St Heliers St, Abbotsford; 03-9415 6581; www.farmcafe.com.au; 9am-3pm Mon-Fri, 9am-4pm Sat-Sun

06 LUNE CROISSANTERIE

Her croissants have been called the best in the world, and Kate Reid – a former Formula One aerodynamicist – is certainly consistent. The queue moves

quickly at the smaller city store on Collins St (across the road from the Grand Hyatt) but the original Fitzroy location is worth seeing for the glass cube pastry kitchen in the centre of the warehouse. The best way to skip the line and taste the creativity is by booking one of a handful of seats for the Lune Lab experience: three life-changing pastries and a hot drink for AUD65 per person. Bookings are released at the end of the month for Friday through Sunday of the following two months. Check dates online and pounce quickly.
119 Rose St, Fitzroy; 03-9077 6463; www.lunecroissanterie.com; Mon-Fri 7.30am-3pm, Sat & Sun 8am-3pm (or until sold out)

07 FREE TO FEED

For a cooking class with purpose, book in for a session with this not-for-profit social enterprise. The organisation uses food-oriented initiatives to assist refugees, new migrants and people seeking asylum to find employment and connect with the community. During a cooking experience – which could include traditional Palestinian, Sri Lankan or Syrian food – you'll not only leave with new recipes, but also a fresh perspective. There are two venues, but if you're at the Thornbury kitchen, pop across the road to Welcome to Thornbury food truck park for a drink.
763A High Street, Thornbury & 539 High Street, Northcote; 0426 252 334; www.freetofeed.org.au

08 MOON DOG WORLD

What do you call a 12,000 sq metre (130,000 sq ft) brewery that fits more than 700 people, is longer than the Melbourne Cricket Ground, has a lagoon, fountain, restaurant, playground, barrel aging room and retro arcade games hidden in shipping containers? You call it a theme park. Enter Moon Dog World. Located in the north-eastern neighbourhood of Preston, it's tricky to reach (if you're not willing to rideshare, you're going to have to bus it, then walk a kilometre), but once there Moon Dog World is heaven on earth for beer lovers. There are 72 on tap with something new subbing in almost daily. Beer nerd bar staff provide tasters and share information without making you feel like a rookie.
32 Chifley Dve, Preston; 03-9428 2307; www.moondogbrewing.com. au; 11am-10pm Mon-Wed; to 11pm Thu & Sun; to 1am, Fri & Sat

WHERE TO STAY
ZAGAME'S HOUSE
A boutique, 97-room hotel at the city end of Lygon St in Melbourne's Little Italy. All rooms have king beds, slick monochromatic palettes and were approved by a Feng Shui master. There's psychedelic artwork on the walls and room service features breakfast ramen.
www.zagameshouse. com.au

QT
Proudly reinforcing QT's brand of eccentric cool, Melbourne's edgiest hotel combines industrial design with unconventional art, an in-house restaurant, rooftop bar, cake shop and Japanese knife store for an ideal city-centre stay.
www.qthotels.com

WHAT TO DO
QUEEN VIC MARKET ULTIMATE FOODIE TOUR
To really get into the guts of Melbourne's biggest and most-loved market, opt in for a Queen Vic Market Ultimate Foodie

07

Tour (AUD69 per person). It runs for two-hours and is headed by a local guide who shines light on the market's history. You'll be treated to tastings, meet the shopkeepers and leave with a shopping bag and AUD5 voucher. Aside from the tours, Vic Market also holds weekly night markets during the summer months. And it's brilliant to browse

at any time of day. As closing time approaches, traders will be offering discounts, if you can think of anything to do with a whole tray of mangos. See the website for opening hours.
www.qvm.com.au/tours

CELEBRATIONS
MELBOURNE FOOD AND WINE FESTIVAL
Held in March over 10

days, this food festival brings the biggest and brightest local and international culinary names together for a program of 140-plus one-off events, ranging from free talks and long lunches to mini festivals and impressive collaboration dinners.
www.melbournefood andwine.com.au

FINE ART GALLERY

BALLARAT
FINE
G

SHOP Art Gallery
of Ballarat

GET THERE
Ballarat is a 1½-hour drive from
Melbourne along the M8. From
here it's a further hour to Castlemaine. Beyond Castlemaine,
it's a further 30 minutes to
Bendigo, from where it's under
a two-hour drive back to Melbourne via Kyneton. The region
is well connected by regular
trains (www.vline.com.au).

01

THE GOLDFIELDS

NEWBRIDGE · · BENDIGO · 04
LOCKWOOD · 05
DUNOLLY · · RAVENSWOOD ·
MALDON · · HARCOURT ·
MARYBOROUGH · 07 · CASTLEMAINE ·
NEWSTEAD · 06
TALBOT · MALMSBURY ·
CAMPBELLTOWN · KYNETON · 08
VICTORIA
LEXTON · CLUNES · TYLDEN ·
DAYLESFORD · WOODEND ·
WAUBRA · SMEATON · TRENTHAM ·
LEARMONTH · CRESWICK · BLACKWOOD · GISBORNE ·
Lake Burrumbeet 02
00 · BALLARAT · GORDON · BALLAN ·
03 BACCHUS MARSH

Bet Creek
Loddon River
Campaspe River
Loddon River

[Victoria]

STRIKE GOURMET GOLD ON THE GOLDFIELDS

Immerse yourself among the grandeur of yesteryear in gold-rush-era towns, now reinventing themselves with lures of fine dining, breweries, distilleries and wine bars.

An hour or so drive west from Melbourne leads you into a corridor of the state's most attractive countryside, zipping you through bucolic farmland and bush landscapes in between a sequence of charming gold-rush-era towns filled with history. Like many parts of regional Victoria, it's undergoing an epicurean renaissance, coming-of-age as a food destination as talented producers and chefs put the region on the map for foodies.

The likes of Ballarat, Bendigo, Castlemaine and Maryborough are all grand affairs founded from the spoils of the 1850s gold rush, a moment in time that elevated them as being among the richest towns on Earth. The magnificence is still on show, particularly in the larger cities of Ballarat and Bendigo with their grandiose streetscapes that look straight out of a movie set. The region's resplendent 19th-century architecture comprises heritage hotels,

banks, theatres and art galleries. And recognising the potential of such palatial buildings, in recent times savvy proprietors and chefs have moved in to convert many into refined restaurants, cafes and pubs, breathing new life into these historic towns.

Attracted by the fresh air and country charm, many 'treechangers' have made the move to the Goldfields in recent years, and with this influx, Melburnians have brought with them urban tastes, which has helped to shape the food-and-drink scene. Where before your choice was deciding between Chinese or takeaway pizza, now it's all degustation menus, gastropubs, wine bars and provedores that focus exclusively on local produce and regional wines. And it's not just the 'blow in' cityslickers adding to the scene either – a lot of talented local chefs who grew up here are being lured back to their hometowns, well aware of the bounty of fresh quality produce to draw upon.

01 RED DUCK BREWERY & KILDERKIN DISTILLERY

When it comes to producing inventive, chemical-free beers and interesting gins, the team at Red Duck was well ahead of the game – they've been brewing in their Ballarat tin shed since 2005. At the no-frills cellar door you can make your way through its sought-after collection, including core and seasonal releases big on hoppy, fruity flavours, made with anything from blood orange and sparkling wine to raspberry hibiscus and coconut blossom. The attached Kilderkin distillery produces its Larrikin gin range, infused with interesting botanicals and very well received. Sample it with a tasting flight or rosemary-spiked G&T. Meanwhile, they have a single-malt scotch ageing in the barrels to be released in 2021. Informal tours can be arranged for those interested in the production process. *11A Michaels Dr, Ballarat; 03-5332 0723; www.kilderkindistillery. com.au; www.redduckbeer.com. au; noon-5pm*

02 UNDERBAR

Representative of Ballarat's rise as a culinary destination is this intimate, 16-seat fine diner set up by chef Derek Boath. He boasts a C.V that includes a stint at the Michelin three-star restaurant Per Se in New York. It's one for those seeking the full gastronomic experience, with a degustation menu featuring innovative modern Australian dishes, executed with flair and focused around locally sourced, seasonal ingredients. *3 Doveton St North, Ballarat; www.underbar.com.au; 7-11pm Fri & Sat*

03 MITCHELL HARRIS

Despite an abundance of wineries with cellar doors found across the fertile volcanic soils, somehow the Victorian Pyrenees wine-growing region has managed to fly under the mainstream radar. In-the-know oenophiles are the exception, and are well aware of the quality coming out of the area, and this includes the folk from Mitchell Harris, a well-respected local winemaker

'Mitchell Harris is a collaboration between two families. It started with purchasing a parcel of pinot noir and chardonnay fruit and the idea of making a flagship sparkling wine created by John Harris, our winemaker.'

Alicia Mitchell, Mitchell Harris

who've set up one of the best wine bars you'll find in regional Victoria. Here they showcase the best wines from both the immediate area and across Victoria. It's set in Ballarat's city centre, where they've done a great job of converting a former mechanics shop into am attractive red-brick space where you can enjoy a glass or a bottle, accompanied by a menu of fantastic food produced by talented, local purveyors.
38 Doveton St North, Ballarat; 03-5331 8931; www. mitchellharris.com.au; 11am-8pm Wed-Sun

04 THE DISPENSARY

Melbourne isn't the only city to be blessed with cool laneway bars, with this intimate Bendigo gem being of the same ilk. And what it lacks in size, this tiny bar makes up for with a big drinks list featuring some of the finest booze selections you'll find anywhere. Its fridge is crammed with hard-to-find craft beers from across Australia, NZ and beyond, including a few rippers from Bendigo. If you're not a beer drinker they'll mix you up a stiff drink from the excellent cocktail menu, many featuring local gins, vermouth and Australian craft spirits. Drinks are accompanied by a fine array of food options, from smaller bites such as confit

05 Stroll up to
Shedshaker in
Castlemaine

06 Beer tasting at
Shedshaker

07 Go back in time at
Sovereign Hil

duck leg bao, to something more substantial such as a Black Angus eye fillet flavoured with a shiraz-and-tarragon butter.
9 Chancery Lane, Bendigo; 03-5444 5885; www. dispensarybendigo.com; noon-11pm Tue-Sat, to 4pm Sun

05 SHEDSHAKER

Opening in 2016, within a historic red-brick mill, Shedshaker's taphouse is a top spot for flavoursome, well-made beers ranging from its Frailty Pale Ale and Celtic Red to Knucklehead Rye IPA and Hempathy hemp ale. The Holy Grail Cloudy Ale, meanwhile, was named in reference to one of the owners being a member of Aussie band Hunters & Collectors. It's part of the Mill Complex (www. millcastlemaine.com.au), sharing space with an artisanal ice-cream maker, vintage stores, coffeehouse, bakery and a microwinery, a modest 20-minute (but uphill) walk from the centre of Castlemaine; visit the Botanical Gardens across the road.
9 Walker St, Castlemaine; 0487 860 060; www. shedshakerbrewing.com; 2-8pm Tue & Wed, to 10pm Thu, to 11pm Fri, noon-11pm Sat, 2-9pm Sun

06 SOURCE DINING

Kyneton's Piper St has undergone a culinary boom that's transformed this once sleepy country town into a foodie hotspot. Among the strip of fine dining, authentic multicultural cuisine, alluring cafes, cool bars and a gin distillery, the hatted Source Dining ranks among the best. Named in reference to its approach of sourcing its products and ingredients locally and seasonally, owner-chef Tim Foster does a stellar job in putting together a menu that takes in anything from slow-roasted pork belly, Asian influences in the handmade dumplings and Lombok chicken curry, to modern European such as wild hare ragu, all accompanied by fresh produce from its kitchen garden. They've also taken over Goldmines Hotel (www.goldmineshotel.com) in Bendigo, an historical pub with a similar philosophy and menu, but with a main point of difference being the bistro component, where you can tuck into pimped-up pub classics such as burgers stacked with double grass-fed beef patties and a side of duck-fat potatoes.
72 Piper St, Kyneton; 03-5422 2039; www.sourcedining.com.au; noon-11pm Thu-Sat, to 3pm Sun

WHERE TO STAY

CRAIG'S ROYAL HOTEL

If you're wanting to experience gold-rush-era opulence, there's no better place than this imposing, grand Victorian-style hotel that's a fixture along Ballarat's main strip. Dating to 1862, it's a place steeped in history, hosting luminary guests from prime ministers and members of the royal family to literary figures such as Mark Twain. The boutique rooms have period features, balanced with modern comforts, while diners are spoilt for choice with the multiple eating options ranging from a formal restaurant and a character-filled front bar to the house cafe and provedore.
www.craigsroyal.com.au

WHAT TO DO

HEATHCOTE WINERIES

The Goldfields is blessed with wineries spread across the district, many with cellar doors to enjoy tastings. The Heathcote region, a short drive east of Bendigo is known for its warm-climate red soil, which produces the state's best full-bodied shiraz. Home to some 40 wineries, a typical day here involves a blissful programme of wine tasting, visiting breweries, gastropubs and gourmet provedores.
*www.heathcote
winegrowers.com.au*

SOVEREIGN HILL

A Ballarat institution, and one of Victoria's most famous tourist attractions, Sovereign Hill is a reconstruction of a gold-rush-era settlement. Here you can take a step back in time while ambling down its historical streetscape lined with ye olde shoppes and folk dressed in period costume. Try your fortune panning for gold, among many family-friendly activities.
www.sovereignhill.com.au

CELEBRATIONS

PLATE UP BALLARAT

A month-long festival of culinary events in May showcasing local producers, regional wines and craft beer.
*www.plateupballarat.
com.au*

GET THERE
The Bellarine Peninsula is just under a 1½-hour drive from Melbourne via Geelong along the M1. Frequent trains (www.vline.com.au) depart from Melbourne's Southern Cross to Geelong station from where connecting buses await to reach the towns along the Bellarine. Otherwise take a ferry (www.searoad.com.au) from Queenscliff to get to Sorrento across the bay on the Mornington Peninsula. Avalon Airport is a 25-minute drive from Geelong, which offers domestic flights to many cities.

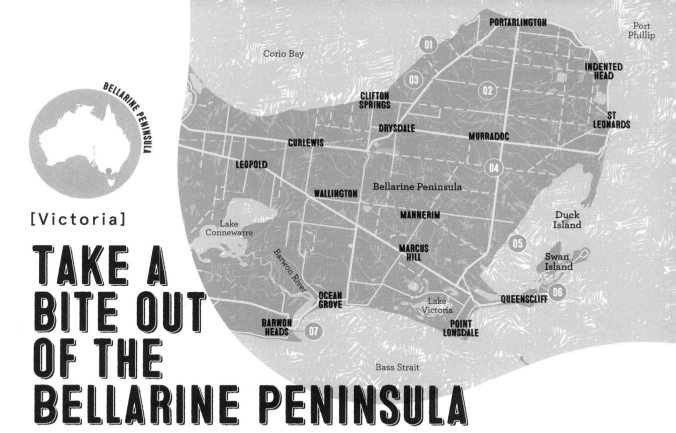

PORTARLINGTON

Port
Phillip

Corio Bay

01

INDENTED
HEAD

03

CLIFTON
SPRINGS

02

DRYSDALE

ST
LEONARDS

MURRADOC

CURLEWIS

LEOPOLD

04

Bellarine Peninsula

WALLINGTON

Duck
Island

MANNERIM

Lake
Connewarre

05

Swan
Island

MARCUS
HILL

Barwon River

QUEENSCLIFF

06

OCEAN
GROVE

Lake
Victoria

BARWON
HEADS

07

POINT
LONSDALE

Bass Strait

BELLARINE PENINSULA

[Victoria]

TAKE A BITE OUT OF THE BELLARINE PENINSULA

A treasured beach destination for Melburnians for generations, the Bellarine Peninsula has established itself as a wine-growing region and offers other epicurean delights.

The Bellarine Peninsula has been attracting tourists ever since the 19th century, when well-heeled Melburnians would arrive on luxury paddle steamers to take their annual holidays. It's a tad easier to get here these days (though much less glamorous), and remains a sought-out beach destination where people come to spend days lazing on the sand in between swims, long walks, exploring rock pools and scoffing fish and chips.

But well before you could order minimum chips (at least 20,000 years, to be precise) the indigenous Wathaurong people roamed these coastal plains, hunting and cooking charcoal meats, fish, oysters and foraged vegetables. And today it remains a fertile ground for food and drink, with a heap of delicious local produce to be enjoyed along the Bellarine Taste Trail (www.thebellarinetastetrail.com.au). The route leads you away from the beach to explore the region's inland treasures of wineries, gin producers, breweries, restaurants and rustic cafes, along with stops for cheese, olives and smoked fish.

While wine is still a relatively new industry, with vineyards only planted in the latter half of last century, the cool-climate 'maritime' wines – namely pinot noir and chardonnay – have fast gained a reputation as being quality drops. There are some 15 cellar doors here to visit and taste local wines that span the full spectrum from sparkling to shiraz. Most wineries have on-site restaurants or cafes offering lovely views and platters of Bellarine produce to enjoy with a glass of vino or two.

The Bellarine's small coastal towns also have their charms, offering a relaxed seafaring atmosphere to enjoy fresh local food to a backdrop of heritage architecture, lighthouses and tales of shipwrecks.

01 Point Lonsdale
lighthouse

02 Fresh cuisine at
Jack Rabbit

03 Fresh air and sea
views at Jack Rabbit

04 Destination dining
at Merne at Lighthouse

01 JACK RABBIT

If you're looking to pair a glass of wine with a fine view, Jack Rabbit is up there with the Bellarine's best. This highly rated winery-restaurant looks out to the translucent waters of Port Phillip Bay, framed by mountain views of the You Yangs and the distant skyline of Melbourne. When the weather's nice the outdoor patio is the place to be for a glass of chardonnay or pinot noir, accompanied by cheese platters, bowls of Portarlington mussels and locally caught, cider-battered gummy shark. There is also a fine dining restaurant doing a menu of creative cuisine. Cider lovers will want to sample their Flying Brick range, produced at the slick cider house, a 15-minute drive away.

85 McAdams Lane, Bellarine; 03-5251 2223; www.jackrabbit vineyard.com.au; 10am-5pm

02 SCOTCHMANS HILL

Leave the beach behind to head inland and visit the Bellarine's oldest winery where you trade coastal views for pastoral outlooks. Its cellar door restaurant is within an atmospheric converted barn and offers tastings of their well-regarded cool-climate shiraz (a rarity out this way) to go with its signature estate-grown pinots and chardonnay. Grab a table outdoors to graze on produce platters or mains such as smoked fish and bowls of soup.

190 Scotchmans Rd, Drysdale; 03-5251 4431; www.scotchmans.com. au; 11am-5pm

03 THE WHISKERY

At a place called The Whiskery, who would've thought gin would be the star of the show?! But as their single malt sits maturing in the barrels (with 2021 the estimated release date), the Teddy & the Fox gin has stolen the limelight, winning all kinds of awards since its launch in 2018. The Whiskery is set on a rural property inside a stylish, rustic tin shed fitted with couches, a fireplace and a bar opening out to a deck, where you can stop in for a tasting flight of gins or a G&T – pair it with a woodfired pizza for lunch. Their full range of bottled gins is for purchase, too.

1 Scotchmans Rd, Drysdale; 0468 926 282; www.bellarinedistillery. com.au; 11am-5pm Thu-Sun

'The Whiskery is located in the heart of the northern Bellarine Peninsula and is a beautiful, rustic environment in which to enjoy our new whisky.'

Russ Watson, The Whiskery

04 MERNE AT LIGHTHOUSE

While many of the wineries in this region have their own restaurants, Merne is one of the few Bellarine standalone gastronomic dining options to focus squarely on produce sourced from the area. It offers casual fine dining in a relaxed setting overlooking olive groves and is all about set menus designed to share, with an option of two- or four-course dishes, showcasing seasonal, creative, contemporary modern Australian cuisine. Expect the likes of slow-cooked kangaroo tail, sea vegetables and local snapper, along with its estate-grown olives. Settle in for a long lunch and treat yourself with the paired Bellarine wine option.
650 Andersons Rd, Drysdale; 03-5251 5541; www.merne.com. au; noon-2pm Thu-Mon, 6-8pm Fri & Sat

05 BASILS FARM

A winning combination of fruit and flower gardens, coastal views, quality wines and food, Basils draws in regulars and tourists for brekkie, brunch and bottles of bubbles. As well as its shiraz, pinot and chardonnay, Basil's point of difference is its sparkling wine, enjoyed on the lawn or cottage with a cafe menu showcasing local produce. Resident llamas and farm animals keep the kids entertained.
43-53 Nye Rd, Swan Bay; 03-5258 4280; www.basilsfarm.com.au; 10am-4pm Mon, Thu & Fri, 10am-5pm Sat & Sun

05 Barwon Heads town and beach

06 Steamy scenes on the Bellarine Railway

06 QUEENSCLIFF BREWHOUSE

After a day of wine tasting, a crisp cold ale may be in order to cleanse the palate. In which case drop into the historical town of Queenscliff to check out this microbrewery set in a double-storey terrace hotel (c 1850s), where the team from the Prickly Moses brewery have moved in to open a brewhouse showcasing its Otways beers, along with locally brewed ales. There are a dozen or so beers on tap, and recently they have fired up a distillery in the basement to launch a small batch gin, along with an eagerly anticipated single malt. Food's also a feature, with a menu of gourmet pub classics and platters of local produce. Dig in outdoors in the beer garden or indoors by the fire. The upstairs whisky bar with terrace balcony is also a good place to relax with a stiff drink. *2 Gellibrand St, Queenscliff; 03-5258 1717; www.queenscliff-brewhouse.com.au; 11am-11pm Sun-Thu, to midnight Fri & Sat*

07 AT THE HEADS

Where the river meets the sea you'll find the laidback coastal hamlet of Barwon Heads, a Bellarine treasure and home to one of the region's most scenic restaurants. Built onto the edge of the pier overlooking the water and the town's iconic bridge, At the Heads' glassed-in space and outdoor deck is just the place to enjoy a sunset cocktail, local wine or craft beer, along with delicious burgers and seafood mains. It's also a popular brekky and brunch spot with well-made coffees, breakfast bowls and hearty cookups. *1A Ewing Blyth Drive, Barwon Heads; 03-5254 1277; www.attheheads.com.au; 9am-10pm Tue-Sun, to 4pm Mon*

WHERE TO STAY

LON

A game changer for the region is this luxurious getaway in Point Lonsdale that recently underwent a dramatic conversion from family farm to boutique spa resort. In the family for seven generations, here they've capitalised on the natural geothermal waters deep beneath the ground to develop a boutique day spa, and tastefully furnished rooms done out in its casual brand of high luxury. *www.lonretreat.com.au*

WHAT TO DO

QUEENSCLIFF FORT

One of the best places to soak up the town's rich heritage is Queenscliff's historical fort (constructed in 1860). Guided tours take you through the fort's fascinating history, built by the military initially to protect from a feared Russian invasion in the 19th century before serving an important role in the ensuing two world wars. *www.fortqueenscliff.com.au*

BELLARINE RAILWAY

Riding the rails in Queenscliff isn't just for train buffs – trips offer scenic stream train rides and dining on the Q Train (www.theqtrain.com.au) and live music on the Blues Train (www.thebluestrain.com.au). *www.bellarinerailway.com.au*

CELEBRATIONS

QUEENSCLIFF MUSIC FESTIVAL

Held in November, this is one of the most anticipated weekends of the year and features a stellar line-up of acclaimed singer-songwriters from Australia and across the globe. *www.qmf.net.au*

GET THERE

If you're coming from Melbourne's city centre, count on an hour's drive to the wineries via the M3 and Maroondah Hwy; the journey is much shorter if you're based in the suburbs. Healesville can be reached by a train-bus combo, disembarking at Lilydale train station from where you take bus 685 or 965. If you don't have a car (or a designated driver), consider one of the winery tours such as Yarra Valley Winery Tours (www. yarravalleywinerytours.com.au).

[Victoria]

VINO AND VIEWS IN THE YARRA VALLEY

This short trip from Melbourne will lead you a world away, among pastoral surrounds and rolling vineyards, home to some of the country's finest cool-climate wines.

For oenophiles and gourmands seeking to be charmed by bucolic outlooks and a temperate year-round climate, yet without the long car journeys, then the Yarra Valley is your place. All it takes is a 10-minute drive from Melbourne's outer suburbs to find yourself among rolling farmland scenery and vines reminiscent of northern Italy, but mixed in with kangaroos and an unmistakable Aussie bush landscape.

Dating back to the 1830s, the Yarra Valley is one of Australia's oldest wine-growing regions. Over the journey it has evolved into an unstoppable epicurean force, producing not only some of the country's finest cool-climate wines, but sublime cellar-door restaurants that capitalise on the region's fresh bounty of produce.

The region is best known for its buttery chardonnays and fragrant pinot noir, but talented winemakers are also getting fantastic results in producing traditional sparkling whites, along with cabernet sauvignon, pinot gris and some interesting varietals. Most wineries have scenic cellar doors that are open throughout the week for tastings; either free, or a $5 charge, which is redeemable against any bottle purchases. Visit wineyarravalley.com.au for the full list of 80 or so wineries in the region.

From fine dining to gastropubs and award-winning cheese from rustic farm doors, the Yarra Valley is also famed as a culinary destination. Its fertile soils yield quality seasonal produce, used by talented locavore chefs to create gastronomic dishes featured on degustation menus for foodies looking to splurge. Even at your everyday country pubs and cafes you'll be treated to gourmet local fare, from succulent steaks to authentic woodfired pizzas, along with Yarra Valley wines, artisanal gins, craft beers and ciders.

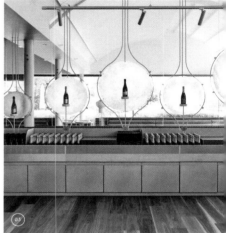

01 Take a balloon ride over the Yarra Valley

02 The homestead at Domaine Chandon, built in 1880

03 Yering Station tasting room

04 Learning about wine at Yering Station

05 Delightful dishes at Yering Station

① COOMBE

A must not only for those into their pinot noir and chardonnays, but also for culture vultures with an interest in history, this garden estate was the former home of Dame Nellie Melba (1871–1931), Australia's famed opera singer. Here you can settle in for a glass of wine to enjoy with a cheeseboard and game of croquet on the lawn, or come by for its popular Devonshire tea served inside the elegant house. There's also a restaurant dishing up a menu of modern Australian meets British-inspired cuisine with an assortment of roast meats and veggies picked from its kitchen garden. Leave time to tour the pristine gardens, dating back to 1909 and designed by William Guilfoyle who also created

Melbourne's Botanical Gardens. *673 Maroondah Hwy, Coldstream; 03-9739 0173; www. coombeyarravalley.com.au; 9.30am-5pm Tue-Thu & Sun, to 3pm Fri & Sat*

② YERING STATION

Established way back in 1838, Yering Station is Victoria's first winery and one of the earliest in Australia. Drop by its historic cellar door – which also houses a contemporary art gallery – for tastings of its estate-grown wines and those sourced from across the Yarra Valley. Make a reservation for lunch at its fine-dining restaurant, within a stunning contemporary glassed-in space overlooking vineyards, for a tasting menu of gastronomic

modern Australian using ingredients sourced from local growers. Within the adjoining 1854 Chateau Yering mansion, Eleanore's Restaurant (www.chateauyering.com.au/dining/eleonores) is another upmarket option with which to treat yourself. *38 Melba Hwy, Yarra Glen; 03-9730 0100; www.yering.com; 10am-5pm Mon-Fri, to 6pm Sat & Sun*

③ NAPOLEONE BREWERY & CIDERHOUSE

Offering an alternative to the saccharine 'cider' you mostly find on the Australian market, this boutique third-generation family-owned cidermaker has been producing apple and pear varietals since the 1940s. All its fruit is estate grown and its top quality

'The Cider House sits in our orchard and serves up a selection of our New World ciders, aperitifs and cocktails.'

Annie Field, Napoleone

has won various awards, particularly for its sparkling pear *méthode traditionnelle*. They do a decent beer too, including a great pale ale, paired beautifully with woodfired pizzas and their Punt Road wines to indulge in at the contemporary restaurant with glass-atrium design. *10 St Huberts Rd, Coldstream; 03-9739 0666; www.napoleone.com. au; 11am-5pm Mon-Fri, from 10am Sat & Sun*

04 DOMAINE CHANDON

One of the big players in the Yarra Valley is this subsidiary of French champagne maker Moët, who for over 30 years have been producing its quality sparkling whites. Its slick, multifaceted complex comprises cellar door, restaurant and a terrace

looking out to magnificent vineyard vistas. Take a self-guided tour to get the low down on its *méthode traditionnelle* production process, before doing a tasting, and then moving on to the contemporary French cuisine restaurant. If you're around on a Sunday, enquire about their winemaking classes, too. *727 Maroondah Hwy, Coldstream 03-9738 9200; www.chandon.com. au; 10.30am-4.30pm*

05 OAKRIDGE WINES

Another of the Yarra Valley's finest, Oakridge's cellar door dazzles with its panaromic vineyard views – exactly what you'd hope for when tasting some of the region's best chardonnay and pinot noirs. Its restaurant is also highly regarded,

with chefs Matt Stone and Jo Barrett nailing a truly modern Australian menu featuring the likes of crocodile, kangaroo, desert lime, kelp, macadamia and saltbush. Or just drop by for cheese and charcuterie plates with a glass of wine. *864 Maroondah Hwy, Coldstream; 03-9738 9900; www.oakridgewines.com.au; 10am-5pm*

06 LEVANTINE HILL ESTATE

Bringing his high-end urban dining concept to the country, here top chef Teage Ezard has teamed up with Levantine Hill to design a menu sourced from seasonal, local produce to create one of the Yarra Valley's best restaurants. The setting is stunning – floor-to-ceiling windows offering sublime vineyard views combined with industrial chic decor, including wine-barrel inspired booth seating to sink into and gorge on the cutting edge seven-course degustation chef's menu.

Otherwise, opt for the more relaxed bistro offering an a la carte menu. If you're not here for food, it's still worth visiting for wine tastings accompanied by those views. *882 Maroondah Hwy, Coldstream; 03-5962 1333; www.levantinehill.com.au; 10am-6pm Wed-Mon*

07 FOUR PILLARS GIN

One of the leaders in Australia's craft gin scene, this international award-winning distiller brings in visitors by the busloads. Set in the town of Healesville, a short drive north of the Yarra Valley wineries, Four Pillars boasts an impressive space combining bar and cellar door, alongside the production area that you can peek in at through the giant portholes. Tastings of gin flights are led by knowledgeable staff, and can be backed up with ordering a G&T. Nab a keepsake for back home with a range featuring the likes of Spiced Negroni, Bloody Shiraz, Chardonnay

Barrel gin and Navy Strength, along with interesting seasonal releases. *2A Lilydale Rd, Healesville; 03-5962 2791; www.fourpillarsgin.com.au; 10.30am-5.30pm Sun-Wed, to 5pm Thu, to 9pm Fri & Sat*

08 HEALESVILLE HOTEL

No self-respecting foodie visits the Yarra Valley without popping in for a meal at the historic Healesville Hotel. Choose between a formal dining room of polished dark woods, or the cosy front bar with fireplace, to order the likes of wood-fired grilled chicken cooked on red gum, or house cheeseburger and sirloin steaks made using local ingredients. A quality drinks list tempts with the region's finest. The weekend garden wood-fire barbecue lunch, featuring American style slow-cooked meats. *256 Maroondah Hwy, Healesville; 03-5962 4002; www.yarravalleyharvest.com.au; noon-late Wed-Sun*

WHERE TO STAY
HEALESVILLE HOTEL
In keeping with its refined restaurant ambience, here at Healesville Hotel they offer a boutique version of your average upstairs pub rooms, spruced up with luxurious king-sized beds, crisp linen and designer touches. If you're seeking something more self-contained, they have the attached Furmstone House for added space and privacy. *www.yarravalleyharvest. com.au*

WHAT TO DO
TARRAWARRA MUSEUM OF ART
One of Victoria's best galleries for modern art is this privately owned museum that shares space with the upmarket TarraWarra winery and restaurant. Exhibitions feature big name Australian and international artists from the mid-20th century to current day. *www.twma.com.au*

HEALESVILLE SANCTUARY
Featuring many of

Australia's native wildlife under the one roof, animal lovers won't want to miss this well-regarded zoo. Its enclosures are home to wombats, koalas, kangaroos, wallabies and dingoes, along with endangered species such as platypus, Tasmanian devils and the orange-bellied parrot. Check the website for the daily schedule of informative demonstrations that are led by the park keepers. *www.zoo.org.au/ healesville*

CELEBRATIONS
SHEDFEST WINE FESTIVAL
In a scene dominated by the larger, multimillion dollar wineries, this is a weekend every October that is all about the small guys – namely family-run wineries without cellar doors that open to the public once a year. *www.yarravalley smallerwineries.com.au*

GET THERE
Margaret River is a three-hour drive southwest of Perth, best tackled by rental car. Jetstar flies direct from Melbourne to Busselton in the Margaret River region, which is a four-hour journey.

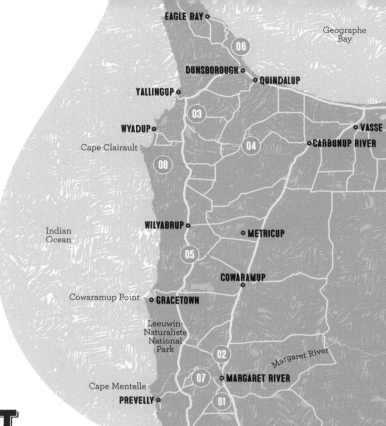

EAGLE BAY
Geographe Bay
06
DUNSBOROUGH
QUINDALUP
YALLINGUP
03
WYADUP
VASSE
Cape Clairault
04
CARBUNUP RIVER
08
Indian Ocean
WILYABRUP
METRICUP
05
COWARAMUP
Cowaramup Point
GRACETOWN
Leeuwin-Naturaliste National Park
02
Margaret River
Cape Mentelle
07
MARGARET RIVER
PREVELLY
01

MARGARET RIVER

[Margaret River]

THE BEST OF THE WEST

In just 50 years Margaret River has become synonymous with first-class wine the world over, but the region is also Western Australia's culinary capital.

Margaret River produces more than a quarter of Australia's premium wine across some 200-plus vineyards. A three-hour drive southwest of Perth, the region produced its first vintages in the early 1970s but has already become an international heavyweight. Affectionately known as 'Margs', it's recognised for cabernet sauvignon, chardonnay, semillion and sauvignon blanc. Wineries such as Vasse Felix, Moss Wood Wines, Cullen Wines, Cape Mentelle and Leeuwin Estate are legendary locals with cellar doors. Many established wineries also have fine-dining restaurants on-site, complete with postcard-perfect views of vineyards and manicured gardens. With fertile soils girt by sea, Margaret River is a food-lovers' paradise, too.

The restaurants, cafes and produce stores are run by smiling folk who are always happy to chat and offer insight into the region they adore. Although there's a town called Margaret River, driving from the top of the region to the bottom takes 1½ hours across six main towns: Margaret River, Busselton, Dunsborough, Yallingup, Cowaramup and Augusta. There are plenty of opportunities to try native Australian ingredients whether you're shopping for produce or eating out, while the entire region swells with passionate foodies when Gourmet Escape food festival comes around in November. Supplement all of that with a craft beer trail, distilleries, some of the country's most stunning beaches, native forests, hikes and indigenous Aboriginal culture and there's no denying that Margaret River is a unique Australian destination. You can research your favourite cellar doors easily online (there are around 95 of them), but this gourmet trail will provide some tips on what to eat and sip.

① MIKI'S OPEN KITCHEN

Book a couple of weeks in advance to dine at Miki's, an unexpected restaurant from Japanese-born Mikihito Nagai. He's known for tempura (it could be mango, a nori roll, chicken hearts or something else entirely) and the best seats are at the bar by the open kitchen. Here, Mikihito uses ingredients direct from farmers to create his refined, local version of Japanese cuisine. Choose from three tasting menus (there's a fourth for mini gourmands) and, if inclined, add sake or wine pairings, or BYO wine for AUD10 corkage per bottle.
Shop 2, 131 Bussell Highway, Margaret River; 08-9758 7673; www.mikisopenkitchen.com.au; 6pm or 8pm sittings Tue-Sat

② CHOW'S TABLE

Located at House of Cards winery and right next to Gabrielle Chocolate (don't leave without one of their cookies), Chow's Table surprisingly serves contemporary Chinese and Malay cuisine. Although eating dishes such as book tripe in chilli oil and black vinegar, mapo egg tofu with minced pork and Hainan-style chicken might not be what you expected in Margaret River, this is some of the best Asian food in the state – and it goes down a treat with the house chardonnay
12/5 Quininup Road, Yallingup; 08-9755 2681; www.chowstable.com.au; noon-3pm & 6-10pm Fri & Sat, noon-3pm Wed, Thu & Sun

③ MARGARET RIVER FARMERS' MARKET

This community farmers' market is a hot spot for those eager to see, shop and taste the best produce in the region, all in one locale. You won't find kitschy crafts here – this market is strictly about edible goodies, with every seller growing and handling their own products. Join the queue at Combi Coffee van and juice bar, or skip breakfast and order poffertjes (mini Dutch pancakes), dumplings from Má Là Dumpling truck or Jindong Free Range Pork's locally famous banh mi and loaded fries.
Margaret River Education Campus, Lot 272 Bussell Highway, Margaret River; 0438 905 985; www.margaretriverfarmersmarket.com.

'We follow the seasons, not in a 'dance to the sound of the moonlight' kind of way but by remaining true to the milk throughout its shifts during the year.'

Alana Langworthy, Yallingup Cheese

au; 8am-noon Sat Apr-Oct; 7.30-11.30am Sat Nov-Mar

04 SETTLER'S TAVERN

'The Tav' seems like an average Aussie pub, but discount it and you'll miss one of Australia's best and most affordable wine lists. Boasting more than 600 bottles, it's little wonder this is where winemakers drink when they knock off. There are also 16 beers on tap and another 60 in bottles, along with a menu of sustainable Western Australian seafood, free-range meats, eggs and local produce. The American Yoda smoker is responsible for the Texas-style beef brisket, but don't fill up before getting your groove on – there are live tunes on Friday and Saturday nights and every other Sunday afternoon. Gigs are usually free. *14 Bussell Highway, Margaret River; 08-9757 2398; www.settlerstavern. com; 11am-midnight Sun-Thu, 10am-1am Fri & Sat*

05 WILDWOOD VALLEY COOKING SCHOOL

What do you get when you cross a woman who's cooked at famed Australian restaurants such as Longrain and Rockpool with a man who's passionate about his Tuscan roots? A cooking class like no other. Join Siobhan and Carlo Baldini in one of three kinds of 10-person classes from December through March: Tuscan, Thai or wood-fired food. Each is hands-on and runs for a day, culminating in a five-course

feast with take-home recipes. Better yet, the lack of liquor license means it's BYO.
1481 Wildwood Road, Yallingup; 08-9755 2120; www.wildwoodvalley.com.au/cooking-classes; class times vary

06 YALLINGUP CHEESE COMPANY

For the best cheese in the region, try the small-batch, organic cow's and goat's milk varieties from Yallingup Cheese Company – all made with local milk, of course. The fresh curd is edible euphoria and you can try the range before you buy. Pick up supplies for a picnic or borrow a rug from the shop and have one on the spot overlooking a serene lake. There are local wines to wash it all down and cheese-making workshops for those eager to learn the ins and outs (check online for dates).
1071 Wildwood Road, Yallingup; 08-9755 2121; www.yallingupcheese.com.au; 10am-5pm Wed-Sun

07 BETTENAY'S MARGARET RIVER

This family-owned and operated property started as a vineyard in 1989 and has received more than 40 Australian wine medals in the last decade. Although wine is plentiful in Margaret River, its other specialty, nougat, is not. In 2012 the nougat kitchen, tasting area and shop were added. A couple of nougat varieties are put out each day to taste, but we recommend indulging in a whole bar by the lake.
248 Tom Cullity Drive, Cowaramup 08-9755 5539; www.bettenays margaretriver.com.au; 9.30am-5pm

08 YARRI RESTAURANT & BAR

Since opening in 2018, Yarri has quickly become one of Margaret River's go-to restaurants for a unique experience that speaks to the region's native ingredients and forward-thinking dining attitudes. A collaboration between chef Aaron Carr, who previously worked at famed winery Vasse Felix, and Snake + Herring Wines, the menu uses indigenous products and celebrates local produce. It's strictly seasonal but might include dishes such as emu with native pepper and quandong or wood-roasted lamb rump with harissa.
6/16 Cyrillean Way, Dunsborough; 08-9786 5030; www.yarri.com.au; 4pm-late Mon-Wed, noon-late Thu-Sun (dinner from 5.30pm)

WHERE TO STAY

EMPIRE SPA RETREAT

With hot tubs in most rooms and a sauna and day spa on-site, Empire Spa Retreat is very couple friendly. The stone and timber farmhouse is set among vineyards and native gardens with a view of the lake from the glass atrium-style dining room.
www.empireretreat.com

CAVES HOUSE HOTEL & APARTMENTS

Heritage-listed Caves House is parked on 14 hectares (35 acres) of gardens just a five-minute walk from Yallingup Beach. There are eight room types, from self-contained apartments to luxe spa suites, plus a decent restaurant with live music, and breakfast is included.
www.caveshousehotel yallingup.com.au

WHAT TO DO

KOOMAL DREAMING

Josh Whiteland (Koomal is his traditional Wadandi name), hosts a three-hour Aboriginal Food Cave and Didge Tour

that includes foraging for native bush foods and medicines, a visit to Ngilgi Cave where the acoustics are just right for didgeridoo playing, and more, finishing with a traditional barbecue lunch around the campfire (AUD155 per adult).
www.koomaldreaming. com.au

CELEBRATIONS

GOURMET ESCAPE

Held in Perth, Swan Valley and Margaret River over 10 days, the events at this highly-regarded food festival vary from

beach barbecues to forest feasts to international collaborations at stalwart wineries. Past international chefs have included Nigella Lawson, Marco Pierre White and David Chang.
www.gourmetescape. com.au

GET THERE

The Swan Valley is around 23km (14.3 miles) northeast of Perth. The area is spread out and best explored with your own transport. Another option is to catch a train on the Midland line from Perth to Guildford and join a tour or arrange to pick up an e-bike. See www.swanvalley.com.au.

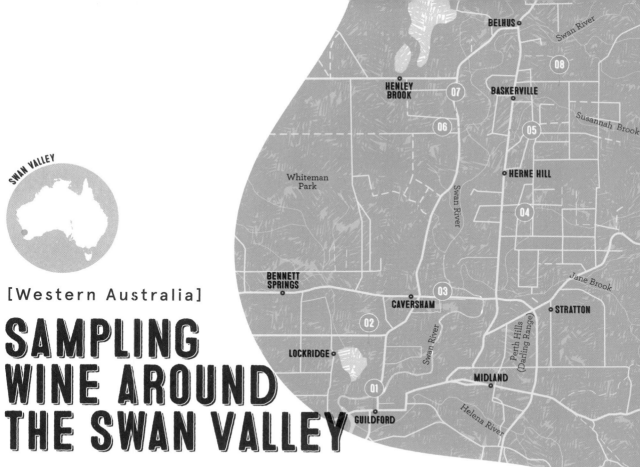

SWAN VALLEY

BELHUS
Swan River
08
HENLEY BROOK
07
BASKERVILLE
Susannah Brook
06
05
Whiteman Park
HERNE HILL
Swan River
04
Jane Brook
BENNETT SPRINGS
03
CAVERSHAM
STRATTON
02
Swan River
Perth Hills (Darling Range)
LOCKRIDGE
MIDLAND
01
Helena River
GUILDFORD

[Western Australia]

SAMPLING WINE AROUND THE SWAN VALLEY

A relaxed companion to the dynamic eating and drinking scene of nearby Perth, the Swan Valley combines vineyard dining, craft beer and artisan produce.

Closer to Singapore and Bali than the big cities of Australia's eastern seaboard – and now linked by direct 17-hour flights to London – the Western Australian capital of Perth is one of the country's most dynamic cities.

Complementing Perth's restaurants, craft distilleries and recently opened eating and drinking precincts, the nearby Swan Valley is a laid-back gourmet hub that's hugely popular with locals on weekends. Bordered by the forested escarpment of the Perth Hills, the rural area is flat and relatively spread out, making it a good place to ride an e-bike around its array of vineyard cellar doors, breweries and other artisan producers.

Compared to other stellar Western Australian winemaking areas such as Margaret River and the Great Southern region, Swan Valley wines are solid without being truly spectacular, but the area proudly

compensates with other excellent opportunities for eating and drinking. Now spread across all of Australia, the country's craft beer scene actually kicked off in the mid-1980s in the port town of Fremantle to the south, and Swan Valley brewers have been at the vanguard of the scene since 2002. From humble beginnings, Feral Brewing Company is now one of Australia's favourite breweries, but their Swan Valley taproom is still firmly focused on creating bold and interesting brews. Recent additions to the Swan's beer heritage is a craft distillery and a cider-house.

Visiting the Swan Valley also provides an opportunity to learn about the culture and culinary history of the region's original inhabitants, the indigenous Noongar people. Factor in vineyard restaurants, gourmet producers and interesting art galleries, and it's an essential escape from the urban bright lights of Perth.

01 ALFRED'S KITCHEN

When Perth locals are happy to drive around 30 minutes just for a burger, you know they're onto something special. Established in 1946 in the heritage town of Guildford, Alfred's was launched just after WWII by Englishman Alfred Cook. Now his humble caravan has expanded to include a dining area located in a 1906 train carriage, and it's a longstanding Swan Valley icon. We're big fans of the 'Hawaiian Special' crammed with an egg and a grilled pineapple ring, but the stonking steak burger with egg, cheese and bacon is a late night classic. In cooler weather, sitting outside around Alfred's toasty outdoor fire is the place to be. *cnr Meadow & James Sts,*

Guildford; 08-9377 1378; www. alfredskitchen.com.au; 5pm-midnight Mon-Fri, noon-midnight Sat-Sun

02 FUNK CIDER

Complementing the wine and craft beer produced in the Swan Valley, Funk Cider's modern takes on the refreshing tipple are both preservative-free and unpasteurised. Forget the sweet, mass-market ciders you may have tried before, and adjourn to Funk's rustic cider-house for flavoursome pints infused with funky wild yeasts or subtly aged in American or French oak barrels. Beyond a focus on apples, other ingredients including passionfruit, mango, lime and pineapple are all harnessed for

Funk's decidedly different drinks list. Interesting beers and cold-pressed juices are also served to partner pizza, platters and gourmet burgers. *55 Benara Rd, Caversham; 08-9377 4884; www.funkcider.com. au; 11am-5.30pm Mon-Fri, 10am-6.30pm Sat, 10am-5.30pm Sun*

03 MANDOON ESTATE

One of the most versatile of the wineries dotted around the Swan Valley, Mandoon Estate's manicured lawns include fine dining at Wild Swan restaurant and interesting craft beers at the sleek Homestead Brewery. Award-winning wines include shiraz crafted from 70-year-old Western Australian vines, and brews such as the Thunderbird American Pale Ale partner well

with seared squid or a Middle Eastern—inspired lamb and eggplant pizza. To learn about the food and culture of the area's indigenous Noongar people, book a bush tucker talk and tasting session with a Noongar elder. There's also modern accommodation available onsite at The Colony.
10 Harris Rd, Caversham; 08-6279 0500; www.mandoonestate. com.au; 10am-8.30pm Mon-Fri, 7.30am-8.30pm Sat-Sun

04 MORISH NUTS

Started out of a suburban Perth home back in 1988, Morish Nuts is a bona fide Western Australia success story. More than three decades on, the Morish Nuts mini-empire has now expanded to three outlets, but the Swan Valley factory store is the best place to try spicy wasabi-laced macadamia nuts or caramel-coated cashews. Beyond the big flavours that team well with bold Western Australian craft beers, there's a wide range of sweeter offerings including nougat and praline. An almost bewildering array of gift packs and hampers make this a great place to pick up something for friends and family back home.
640 Great Northern Hwy, Herne Hill; 08-9221 0214; www.morish. com.au; 9.30am-5pm

05 THE CHEESE BARREL*

Associated with the adjacent Olive Farm Wines, The Cheese Barrel offers a huge selection of both international and Australian cheeses. Indecisive travellers may find it challenging choosing, but The Cheese Barrel's friendly team steers visitors through a tasty maze including brie and blue and chèvre and cheddar. Compile your own tasting plate or select one of the day's special platters for two to four people including lavash flatbreads, crunchy baguettes and local fruit pastes. Wine flights are also available. Stock up on both cheese and wine for on-the-road picnics. Western Australian cheeses to look for include organic camembert from Margaret River and Nullaki raclette from the Dellendale Creamery in WA's Great Southern Region.
920 Great Northern Hwy, Millendon; 08-9296 4539; www. thecheesebarrel.com.au

Ø5 Welcome to Old
Young's tasting room

Ø6 Looking out over
the Swan River

06 MAALINUP ABORIGINAL GALLERY

Aboriginal art and culture combine here with walking tours and garden visits explaining the traditional bush tucker ingredients of the region's indigenous Noongar people, and there's also a shop selling food products made from local fruits and herbs such as lemon myrtle, bush tomato, quondong, wattleseed and mountain pepperberries. Check the website for in-depth cultural experiences including a three-course bush tucker dinner.
10070 West Swan Rd, Henley Brook; 08-9296 0711; www.maalinup.com. au; 10am-5pm

07 OLD YOUNG'S DISTILLERY

One of Australia's newer distilleries is also one of its most-awarded, and since their 2016 launch Old Young's have secured a stellar reputation both in Australia and internationally for their gins and other distilled spirits. Juniper from the Italian region of Tuscany underpins the distillery's gin range, but Western Australian citrus fruits and lemon myrtle herbs are also used for a local provenance. Other innovative spirits include a vodka made with local sugar cane and Swan Valley grapes, and a fruity spirit infused with passionfruit, strawberries and kiwi fruit reflecting the flavours of pavlova, a meringue-based dessert popular in both Australia and New Zealand.
10581C West Swan Rd, Henley Brook; 08-9296 6656; www. oldyoungs.com.au; 11am-5pm

08 FERAL BREWING COMPANY

One of Western Australia's pioneering craft breweries, Feral's rustic, rural tasting room is a popular weekend destination for Perth locals. The bold Hop Hog Pale Ale is now available across the country, but of more interest to travelling beer fans are seasonal and one-off brews best enjoyed locally. Perfect for a Swan Valley summer, Feral's Watermelon Warhead is a refreshing German-style wheat beer enlivened with local watermelons, while barrel-aged surprises include Barrique O'Karma, an oaked India Black Ale. Partner a tasting rack of different beers with shared plates including mushroom terrine and chargrilled octopus.
152 Haddrill Rd, Baskerville; 08-9296 4657; www.feralbrewing.com. au; 11am-5pm Sun-Thu, 11am-late Fri-Sat

WHERE TO STAY
KELLER'S B&B
A relaxing stay in the ensuite rooms of this limestone farmhouse includes saying g'day to the cows, pigs and sheep all living the good life on the adjacent working farm. Excellent breakfasts often include eggs and dairy products from the sustainability focused spread, and freshly baked Swiss-style bread and delicious housemade muesli. *www.kellersbed andbreakfast.com.au*

WHAT TO DO
WHITEMAN PARK
Arrayed over 26 sq km (10 sq miles), Whiteman Park is a versatile destination on the Swan Valley's western edge. With more than 30km (18.6 miles) of walking trails and bike paths, it's a good spot for scenic gentle exercise, and family-friendly attractions include the Caversham Wildlife Park and the Revolutions Transport Museum. *www.whitemanpark. com.au*

GOMBOC GALLERY SCULPTURE PARK
Leafy surroundings combine with an ever-evolving outdoor gallery of contemporary sculpture at this thought-provoking alternative to Swan Valley's gourmet attractions. There's also an interesting indoor gallery with painting, sculpture and mixed media works from both established and emerging artists. *www.gomboc-gallery. com.au*

CELEBRATIONS
GOURMET FEAST IN THE VALLEY
Aligned with November's hugely popular Gourmet Escape held annually in Margaret River, this two-day weekend celebration at the Sandalford Estate winery includes artisan producers, local wine and beer, and entertainment on the main stage from top Australian bands and musicians. *www.gourmetescape. com.au*

NEW ZEALAND

GET THERE
Wellington has direct international flights from Singapore, Fiji and the east coast of Australia, and is linked by frequent domestic flights to Auckland and Christchurch.

KELBURN

06 Civic Square

Chaffers Marina

Lambton Harbour

01

05

Waitangi Park

03 02

TE ARO

ARO VALLEY

07

MOUNT VICTORIA

04

Central Park

MT COOK

Basin Reserve

Charles Plimmer Park

08

WELLINGTON

[Wellington]

EAT WELL IN WELLINGTON

Coffee, craft beer and a diverse dining scene combine amid the easily walkable laneways and waterfront location of New Zealand's arty and cosmopolitan capital.

Nowhere in New Zealand packs as many essential eating and drinking experiences into such a compact area as the nation's harbourfront capital. Cool cafes dispense coffee made from locally roasted sustainable and fair trade beans, while the country's best craft beer scene is easily explored on a DIY walking tour bar hopping between laneway taprooms. NZ's diverse population is reflected in food trucks and weekly night markets, while flavours and ingredients inspired by the country's indigenous Māori people are harnessed to stunning effect in one of NZ's most innovative and interesting restaurants.

It wasn't always this way. The capital's old reputation as a grey government town was only shaken up in the 1990s by a few pioneering chefs and brewers, and then enhanced by the arrival of startup business culture and the gaming and film industries early in the 21st century.

Movie-making and web design apparently demand damn fine coffee and decent post-work libations, and the city's coffee and craft beer scenes grew along with excellent cafes, bistros and restaurants. Factor in a growing awareness of local and sustainable ingredients, and it's now reckoned Wellington has more cafes and restaurants per capita than New York City. Pretty good for a city of about 200,000 at the bottom of the world.

Wellington's small size encourages local businesses to collaborate. Craft brewers might experiment with a stout made with cacao beans from artisan chocolate makers, while the same two companies could commission local artists to create packaging for their products. Visit in August for the city's two most important eating and drinking festivals, and there's the opportunity to combine specially brewed beers with limited edition burgers at venues around town.

(02)

01 THE HANGAR

Wellingtonians take their coffee seriously and Flight Coffee's inner city base is one the best places to find out what the java-fuelled fuss is all about. Ethically traded beans are sourced from Flight's fair trade farmers in Colombia, Rwanda and Myanmar, roasted in Wellington, and then served as single origin filter and espresso coffee at The Hangar here and around NZ and Australia. There's a strong local focus with the food menu, too. The kumara (sweet potato) pancake with coconut yoghurt, seasonal fruit and toasted walnuts is a great way to start the day.
119 Dixon St, Te Aro; 027 535 0084; www.hangarcafe.co.nz; 7am-4pm Mon-Fri, 8am-5pm Sat-Sun

02 WELLINGTON CHOCOLATE FACTORY

Who doesn't like a chocolate factory, especially when there's a focus on using organic and fair trade cocoa beans sourced from around the world? Proud to be NZ's first craft bean-to-bar factory when they launched in 2013, WCF is still the only company making organic-certified chocolate in the country. Learn about the process on a tour – book ahead for most Saturdays at 11am – and sample bars blending milk chocolate with star anise or dark chocolate with salted caramel. Many of the ingredients come from NZ's South Pacific backyard, and the brand's colourful packaging showcases the work of NZ artists.
5 Eva St, Te Aro; 04-385 7555; www.wcf.co.nz; 11am-5pm Mon-Fri, 10am-4pm Sat, noon-4pm Sun

03 WELLINGTON NIGHT MARKET

As the nation's capital, Wellington is one of the country's most cosmopolitan cities. Experience this cultural diversity at the weekly Wellington Night Market on Friday and Saturday nights. Buskers and street performers are regular attendees, working hard to entertain locals feasting on flavours from around the world. Standout stalls infused with the aromas of South America, Asia and the Indian subcontinent include empanadas from Ar-Chi, mie goreng noodles from Garuda Truck, and Indian and

The Garage Project are regular collaborators with some of the planet's most interesting breweries and their Wild Workshop project is dedicated to crafting bold beers by harnessing wild yeasts.

Sri Lankan treats from Roti Bay. *116 Cuba St; 021 0281 8785; www. wellingtonnightmarket.co.nz; 5-10pm Fri-Sat*

04 MOORE WILSON'S

Established in 1918, Moore Wilson's is the city's pre-eminent provedore and grocery and a big supporter of independently produced and gourmet artisanal produce. Here's where to come to discover new trends in the local food industry and to also pick up a few edible souvenirs for the team back home. Only-available-in-Wellington treats include sweet and salty peanut brittle from Miramar bakers Piece of Cake, and tomato chilli jam from local caterers, Ruth Pretty. Check the

Moore Wilson's website under 'What's On' for their regular Pop Up Food Pods featuring a variety of local food trucks. *cnr Tory & College Sts; 04-384 9906; www.moorewilsons.co.nz; 7.30am-7pm Mon-Fri, 7.30am-6pm Sat, 8.30am-6pm Sun*

05 HASHIGO ZAKE

Founded in 2009 when NZ's craft beer scene was in its hop-fuelled infancy, Hashigo Zake has been a key driver in making Wellington one of the planet's best cities for craft beer. Now tart sour beers or barrel-aged surprises are available at bars and brewpubs around town, but the subterranean bar named after the Japanese phrase for 'bar hopping' is still an essential

Visit their Aro Valley taproom for 18 taps of GP deliciousness and plenty more canned and bottled surprises. A good place to start is Hapi Daze – Hāpi is the Māori word for hops – a Pacific ale crammed with zesty NZ hops
91 Aro St, Aro Valley; 04-802 5324 www.garageproject.co.nz; noon-7pm Sun-Mon, noon-8.30am Tue-Thu, 10am-9.30pm Fri-Sat

08 HIAKAI

After a stellar career in New York, Wellington chef Monique Fiso returned home to open Hiakai in 2019. With just 30 seats and a focus on harnessing indigenous NZ forest herbs such as kakakawa and horopito, the restaurant's ethos of 'inspired by the land, sea, and people of Aotearoa' is a unique reflection of NZ cuisine. Fiso's family background is Māori-Samoan, and her six-, eight- and 10-course degustation menus showcase Māori and Polynesian ingredients in modern and innovative dishes. Proteins could include kina (sea urchin) or titi (muttonbird), and optional beverage menus are equally surprising. Booking well ahead is essential for a restaurant that travellers to NZ should not miss.
40 Wallace St, Mt Cook; 04-938 7360; www.hiakai.co.nz; 5.30pm-late Wed-Sat

Wellington destination for travelling beer fans. Beers and ciders from around NZ are served from ten rotating taps, and superior bar snacks include world-famous-in-Wellington savoury pies. Try the chorizo, onion and porter one.
25 Taranaki St, Te Aro; 04-390 7300; www.hashigozake.co.nz; noon-9.30pm Sun-Mon, to 11pm Tue-Thu, to 1am Fri-Sat

06 DENIZEN URBAN DISTILLERY

Located in one of Wellington's repurposed laneways, Denizen Urban Distillery opened in 2018 to complete the inner city's artisan trifecta of craft beer, coffee and spirits. Rainwater and native NZ botanicals are used in the distillation process, and Denizen's flagship gin brand Te Aro Dry is also stocked at the best of the

city's restaurants, brewpubs and cocktail bars. Drop by the distillery for craft cocktails on Friday nights from 4pm to 8pm.
10 Lombard St, Te Aro; 0210 464 764; www.facebook.com/pg/denzienurbandistillery; noon-6pm Wed & Thu, to 8pm Fri, to 4pm Sat & Sun

07 GARAGE PROJECT TAPROOM

Founded in a disused automotive garage in a heritage Wellington suburb in 2011, Garage Project have grown to become one of NZ's most innovative craft breweries. They're regular collaborators with some of the planet's most interesting breweries and their Wild Workshop project is dedicated to crafting bold beers by harnessing wild yeasts occurring naturally in the local environment.

WHERE TO STAY
QT WELLINGTON
The capital city's most idiosyncratic and arty place to stay is also overlaid with a subtle layer of luxury. Black lifts and darkened corridors serve to accentuate the colourful and flamboyant rooms, while quirky decor includes shimmering Italian motorbikes and a bronze hippo on the exterior. Hippopotamus is also the name of the QT's excellent French-inspired bistro.
www.qthotels.com

WHAT TO DO
ZEALANDIA
Hidden in verdant hills just 4km (2.5 miles) from central Wellington, the vision for this groundbreaking 225-hectare (556-acre) eco-sanctuary is to return the area's forests and freshwater ecosystems to as closely as possible as their pre-human state. Over 20 different species have been reintroduced, some that have been absent on mainland NZ for over a

century. Guided tours are the best way to explore this resurgent valley.
www.visitzealandia.com

WETA CAVE
Cinema buffs should make the journey 8km (5 miles) east from central Wellington to learn about the Academy Award– winning special effects magic created by local company Weta

Workshop in films such as *The Hobbit*, *King Kong* and *Thor: Ragnarok*.
www.wetanz.com

CELEBRATIONS
BEERVANA
Held in August, this wintertime celebration of craft beer is packed with seasonal, one-off NZ brews and also regularly attracts breweries from craft brewing hotspots

such as the Pacific Northwest in the US.
www.beervana.co.nz

WELLINGTON ON A PLATE
Also held every August, this food festival features special menus and events for 17 days in restaurants, cafes and bars around the city.
www.wellingtononaplate. com

GET THERE
Hawke's Bay is roughly a five-hour drive from either Auckland or Wellington; daily one-hour flights with Air New Zealand connect both cities to Napier.

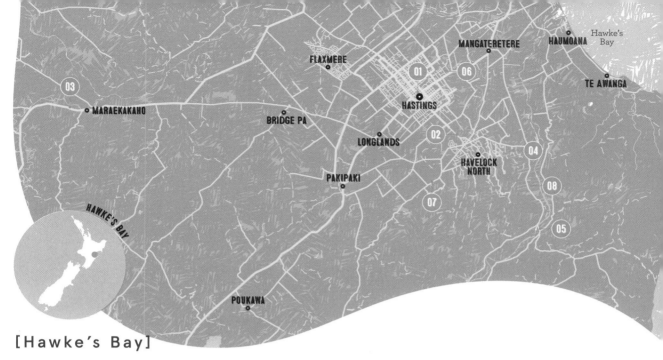

[Hawke's Bay]

FINDING THE FAT OF THE LAND IN HAWKE'S BAY

Farm to table is a way of life in NZ's rural Hawke's Bay, where vineyards, orchards, olive groves and artisan producers inspire an exciting community of local chefs.

The land has always been pivotal to the people of Hawke's Bay. Centuries ago, it was fought over by Māori tribes who lived in *pa* (fortified villages) on the Heretaunga Plains and in coastal Waimarama. Legend has it that Te Mata Peak, caught between the two, is the prostrate body of Waimarama's tribal leader, a giant called Te Mata who was choked by the earth while trying to chomp his way through the cliffs in an act of devotion for his lover Hinerakau. It takes little imagination to see his bite mark in The Gap, or Pari Karangaranga, along the clifftops.

It is striking geological features like this – crumpled cliffs shooting out of flat valleys – that have given Hawke's Bay the sheltered plains and microclimates needed to thrive in agriculture and winemaking. Today this area is one of New Zealand's largest fruit bowls, an organic-food champion and the country's oldest wine region, with more than 200 vineyards. Fruit farms and olive groves feed into a thriving network of farmers' markets, artisan food producers have taken root in the region's small towns, and fine-dining restaurants are amassing awards among the vines.

The landscapes of Hawke's Bay also make it a joy to tour. Rows of pancake-flat vines can quickly morph into gently rolling green hobbit hills. Forty-metre-high redwoods decorate the foot of Te Mata Peak and over the cliffs there's a scattering of golden beaches.

The gateway town to Hawke's Bay is art deco Napier, but the region's farm-to-table scene is strongest around the southerly inland vineyard areas of Hastings and Havelock North. These towns are not on the tourist circuit, which is arguably why Hawke's Bay's honest-to-goodness culinary prowess remains largely off the beaten track for all but in-the-know Kiwis.

01 OM GOODNESS

When everyone else in Hastings is sleeping, the bakers of OM Goodness are firing up their ovens to make speciality breads. Nutrition is at the heart of the bakery's recipes, which are refined-sugar free, gluten free, organic and mostly vegan. The basic mix is buckwheat, chia and linseed, with a sprinkling of mineral-rich kelp powder. Drop by for a manuka honey and walnut loaf, to buy a pre-mix to make at home, or for healthy sweet treats.

OM Goodness sells its goods at weekend farmers' markets. During the week it doubles as a lunch hangout with kombucha on tap. *106 Queen St East, Hastings; 027 342 0013; www.omgoodness.co.nz; 9am-2pm Mon-Fri*

02 STRAWBERRY PATCH

Fruit farms like Strawberry Patch have helped cultivate Hawke's Bay's reputation as New Zealand's fruit bowl. This one grows three varieties of strawberries and offers pick-your-own during the summer season, from October to May. There's also a farm shop on-site, but the main reason why it's always busy is the fresh-fruit ice-cream and smoothie counter. The waffle cones topped with a bee-hive whip of creamy, bright-purple berry ice cream are pretty as a picture, best enjoyed at a picnic table under the leafy roadside canopy. *96 Havelock Rd, Havelock North; 06-877 1350; www.strawberry patch.co.nz; 8.30am-5.30pm, shorter weekend hrs in winter*

03 GODSOWN BREWERY

Rachel and Godfrey's beer appreciation journey started in England, travelled via Nigeria and Perth, and ended here in Rachel's home country. The pair live on-site with their kids, and what they have built since 2010 is a delight – a rural beer garden with a safari tent for wood-fired pizzas, outdoor seating areas and a relaxed, family-friendly vibe where drinkers can get ad hoc tours of the brewing facility.

The brewery doesn't use fining agents or filtering, resulting in flavoursome, vegan-friendly beers. Its range is seasonal and dabbles with local ingredients. In winter you'll find heavier styles such as the Silent Night Espresso Stout made with Bay Espresso coffee; summer

'Our unfiltered,
vegan-friendly beers
are perfect with
brew-grain crackers
and wood-fired pizza
in the hop garden.'

*Rachel & Godfrey Downes, Godsown
Brewery*

brings Garden of Eden Farmhouse Ale, which uses local oranges. *3672 State Highway 50; 027 931 1042; www.godsownbrewery.co.nz; 3-10pm Fri, from noon Sat, noon-8pm Sun*

④ BLACK BARN

Backed by the Te Mata Hills, Black Barn is the type of winery where you could settle in for the day and night. An annual highlight is the winery's outdoor cinema in December/January, with food trucks in Black Barn's own natural amphitheatre. And every summer Saturday there's a grower's market. Despite what's going on around the periphery, it's a small, intimate operation. Black Barn's wines are estate grown and many are only available at the cellar door. Combine a wine tasting with dinner at the award-winning Black Barn Bistro overlooking the vines. Its unpretentious, modern interior and seasonal menu championing local farmers and artisans epitomises everything that's great about the Hawke's Bay food scene. *Black Barn Rd, Havelock North; 06-877 7985; www.blackbarn. com; 10am-5pm Sun-Wed, to 9pm Thu-Sat mid-Oct-Easter, closed Mon-Tue Easter-mid-Oct.*

⑤ RED BRIDGE COFFEE

Red Bridge Coffee serves some of the best coffee in Hawke's Bay from a paddock beside an intersection in the Tuki Tuki Valley. Ideally placed to catch passing traffic, business owner Melissa Campbell decided all

she needed was a modified shipping container and a coffee machine to create a rural meeting place. She serves local Hawthorne coffee alongside sticky doughnuts, flaky croissants and toasted sandwiches. Grabbed your morning flat white and take it to the grassy knoll in the hope of meeting Mollie the coffee dog. *Cnr Tuki Tuki & Waimarama Rds, Havelock North; 027 521 8214; www. redbridgecoffee.co.nz; 7am-3pm Mon-Fri, from 8am Sat & Sun*

06 HAWKE'S BAY FARMERS' MARKET

Set up by local producers in 2000, the Hawke's Bay Farmers' Market is the heart of the food community. It is one of New Zealand's oldest and the loveliest place in the bay to spend a Sunday morning. During the warmer months stallholders settle into shady spots in Waikoko Gardens. The community descends in droves, not just for the weekly shop, but also to listen to live music, munch on sausage sandwiches and slurp berry smoothies. Look out for

products featuring New Zealand's feijoa – an aromatic lime-green, egg-shaped fruit that tastes like the lovechild of a guava and pineapple. *Hawke's Bay Showgrounds, Kenilworth Rd, Hastings; www. hawkesbayfarmersmarket.co.nz; 8.30am-12.30pm Sun*

07 BIRDWOODS GALLERY

If Birdwoods looks like a country church, that's because it started life as one in 1894 in nearby Waipawa. Transplanted to just outside Havelock North, the wooden church hall has been converted into a cafe-cum-concept store with a sculpture garden. Inside a colonial cottage find an ice-cream parlour and sweet shop. In summer, the cafe spills onto the back lawn like a tea party. Come for lemonade scones in the afternoon, or feijoa juice and hash browns made with kumara (New Zealand sweet potato) at lunch. *298 Middle Road, Havelock North; 06-877 1395; www.birdwoods.co.nz; 10am-5pm mid-Dec-March, to 4pm Apr–mid-Dec*

08 CRAGGY RANGE

The drive to the door of Craggy Range winery creates quite the impression, passing a large lake with a pair of lounging bronze bulls at the foot of Te Mata Peak. The winery itself is architecturally bold, but it features in this trail because of its two-hatted restaurant run by Casey McDonald, one of Hawke's Bay's most coveted chefs. Casey worked at Michelin-starred restaurants in London and San Francisco, and then under Andrew McConnell in Melbourne (for the famed Cumulus, Cutler & Co, etc), before returning home to New Zealand in 2017. Hawke's Bay produce is front and centre on his menu, and much of the fruit, vegetables and herbs you'll find on the plate come from the kitchen gardens. These gardens are also used for seated wine tastings with dramatic Te Mata views. *253 Waimarama Road, Havelock North; 06-873 7126; www. craggyrange.com; 10am-6pm summer, 11am-5pm winter*

WHERE TO STAY

BLACK BARN LUXURY RETREATS

There are 16 different lodge options around Black Barn, including heritage properties, open-plan modern units with pools, and a beach house. Some are close enough to stumble between the cellar door and bed. A great option for groups.
www.blackbarn.com/retreats

CRAGGY RANGE COTTAGES

The Te Mata Hills look close enough to reach out and grab at Craggy Range, and the vineyard's cottages have big windows to show off their natural environment. Stays come with private cellar tours and gourmet breakfasts.
www.craggyrange.com

WHAT TO DO

WAIMARAMA MAORI TOURS

The Māori guardians at Waimarama live according to the principles of kaitiakitanga – a traditional way of managing the environment that they share with visitors through low-impact eco-tours of their conservation reserve in Hawke's Bay.
www.waimaramamaori.co.nz

MTG HAWKE'S BAY MUSEUM

Rebuilt after a 7.8 magnitude earthquake in 1931, Napier is New Zealand's art-deco pin-up. The town's flagship museum makes a good starting point for explorations, with displays on local Māori culture and Napier's social history.
www.mtghawkesbay.com

CELEBRATIONS

NAPIER ART DECO FESTIVAL

Hawke's Bay's biggest celebration is this annual heritage knees-up in February. Grab your flapper costume and follow the jazz music to find tea parties, open houses and architecture tours.
www.artdeconapier.com

BRIDGE PA WINE FESTIVAL

Seven wineries in the Bridge Pa Triangle Wine District pull together for one day each January to create the ultimate no-driving vineyard crawl. Hop-on, hop-off buses whisk drinkers between venues, and each one has a different food, wine and music offering.
www.bridgepatriangle.nz

07

GET THERE

Auckland's international airport is the largest in the country and the domestic airport is located a 10-minute walk from the terminal. Car rental companies operate out of the International Terminal and it's advisable to rent a car to get around. Parking can be tricky in the CBD so ensure your accommodation provides off-street parking.

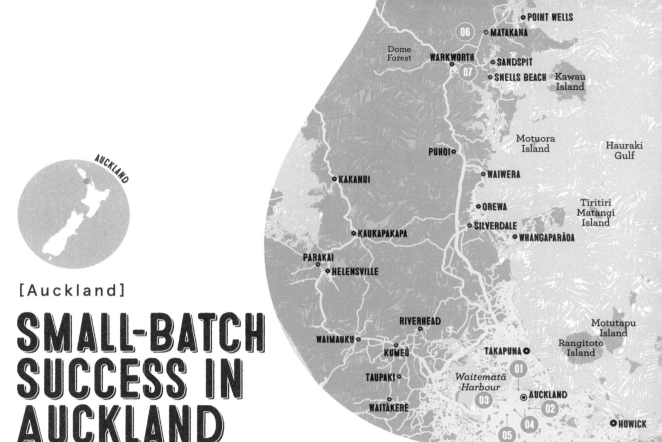

Map labels:
POINT WELLS
06 · MATAKANA
Dome Forest
WARKWORTH
07
SANDSPIT
SNELLS BEACH
Kawau Island
PUHOI
Motuora Island
Hauraki Gulf
KAKANUI
WAIWERA
OREWA
Tiritiri Matangi Island
SILVERDALE
KAUKAPAKAPA
WHANGAPARĀOA
PARAKAI
HELENSVILLE
RIVERHEAD
Motutapu Island
WAIMAUKU
Rangitoto Island
KUMEÛ
TAKAPUNA
01
Waitematā Harbour
TAUPAKI
03
AUCKLAND
02
WAITĀKERE
HOWICK
05
04

AUCKLAND

[Auckland]

SMALL-BATCH SUCCESS IN AUCKLAND

A thriving cafe culture awaits in New Zealand's largest city where local produce, old-school techniques and new flavour combinations will entice and excite.

New Zealand's largest city is dramatically positioned on a narrow isthmus and bordered by oceans to the east and west. Consistently rated as one of the world's most liveable cities, Auckland hums with a plethora of small, inventive producers. For its size, the diversity, quality and volume of ventures located within the compact surrounds is, frankly, mindboggling. Surrounded by fertile land, passion pulses through the veins of local proprietors determined to showcase New Zealand produce on a global scale.

With the ocean lapping at the city's edge, Auckland's waterfront is home to three distinct precincts, North Wharf, the Viaduct and Britomart, all offering various culinary delights. From the bustling no-fuss hubbub of the food vendors at the Auckland Fish Market hawking local oysters from the Hauraki Gulf to the convivial stylings of the slick bars and restaurants that line the Viaduct, there's a venture here for every taste persuasion. Things are not limited to the city centre alone, with dining strips in super-suave Ponsonby drawing crowds year-round determine to eat, drink and play. Further afield wineries are sprinkled around the north and south where vineyards, laden with rich fruit, wind down emerald green slopes to the sea.

From boutique, small-batch coffee roasters to plant-based cafes and brilliant bakers who made baking cool way before reality TV cottoned on, Aucklanders don't appear to follow trends, they set them. From this broad range of businesses there's a treat for every palate, informed by indigenous, Pacific and Asian influences. Yet, despite being cutting edge, Auckland's culinary scene has not lost the laidback Kiwi style that visitors adore.

01 The Hauraki Gulf and Auckland

02 The courtyard of Auckland Fish Market

03 Billypot at Auckland Fish Market

04 Seek out sculpture by Ray Haydon at Brick Bay Wines

05 Perfect pick-me-up at Ozone Coffee Roasters

01 AUCKLAND FISH MARKET AND SEAFOOD SCHOOL

Established in 1904 the recently refurbished Auckland Fish Market is an easy stroll from the city centre. The airy waterfront setting is crammed with vendors, food stalls and a full service pub at the rear. With a 'eat at the source, learn at the source' philosophy, food stalls offer sea urchin, freshly shucked oysters, fish tacos and, to keep the kids amused, popcorn prawns. The seafood school's cooking classes, located on-site, are a celebration of local produce where themed courses include The Ultimate Surf 'n' Turf Combo. Bookings are essential as space is limited.
22-32 Jellicoe St; 0493 791 497; www.afm.co.nz; 7am-9pm

02 LITTLE & FRIDAY

New Zealand baking is next level. Boutique operator Little & Friday were pioneers of the baking renaissance way before any pie-making reality shows had hit our screens. Starting out from humble beginnings operating out of a small vacant butchers shop in the suburbs, this humble venture is the jewel in New Zealand's baking crown. With multiple locations across Auckland, the thriving empire's philosophy of making everything from scratch and providing the punter with the provenance of ingredients was somewhat ahead of its time. A trip to Little & Friday is not complete without chomping down on their best known baked treat – the doughnut. These huge balls of brioche dough are filled with various filling combinations, such as raspberry and cream or banana and caramel.
11 McColl St, Newmarket; 0495 248 742; www.littleandfriday.com; 7am-3:30pm Mon-Fri, 8am-4pm Sat & Sun

03 OZONE COFFEE ROASTERS

If your blood type is coffee then this is your tribe. When New Zealand's largest provincial coffee roaster, Ozone, needed to set up supply out of Auckland they happened upon a large airy space a short detour out of Auckland's downtown. If you like your coffee tasting notes sprinkled with flavour descriptors such as

'Auckland Fish Market remains the beating heart of New Zealand seafood. The only way to eat fresher fish, is to be another fish!'

Anna Burson, Auckland Fish Market

butterscotch, plum and cherry then you may need to set aside a full morning to indulge. The batch filter changes daily and there's cold brew on tap – perfect for the summer months. Ozone's philosophy of creating a 'collision of coffee, food and company' has successfully manifested in this chic space.

1/18 Westmoreland St West, Grey Lynn; 0493 608 125; www. ozonecoffee.co.nz; 7am-3pm Mon-Fri, 8am-3pm Sat-Sun. Check website for seasonal hours

04 BLUEBELLS CAKERY

You had me at 'raspberry lemonade cupcake'. Bluebells Cakery is an Auckland phenomenon having burst onto the New Zealand baking scene in 2011. It's now a cupcake empire with cafes in multiple Auckland locations, a rocking baking school and a bestselling sweet treat cookbook.

Cupcake and cake decorating classes are on offer at Bluebells Academy where kids and adults alike can dress their cupcakes like unicorns or fiesta llama's. Bluebells cafes are brimmed with baked goodies with savoury scones, huge cream-filled eclairs and multi-coloured macarons all fighting for you sugar-kick attention. Polite warning, you may need to schedule in a jog post-visit.

361 New North Rd, Kingsland; 0493 773 429; www.bluebellscakery. com; 7am-4pm Mon-Fri, 8am-4pm Sat, 8:30am-3:30pm Sun

05 MORNINGCIDER

The crew behind Morningcider are
so community focused that they
have donated over 100 apple trees
to residents around Auckland's only
cider bar. Promising to harvest all
unwanted fruit from these trees,
their ambition is to create a truly
local cider. The bar, tucked away
behind plant-based cafe Kind,
offers a cider flight or tasting
board, which is the most fun way
to experience the vast variety
of blends on offer. With brews
including pineapple-jalapeño, feijoa
and pomegranate your taste buds
are in for a wild ride. For those
less enthusiastic about cider, the
bar offers apple wine and for the
more experimental there's the bar's
spin on a Negroni, the aptly named
Cideroni – a combination of iced
cider and sweet vermouth – and a
refreshing cider moijto.

*16 McDonald St, Sandringham;
0427 360 6780; www.morningcider.
co; 5pm-late Tue-Thu, noon-late
Fri-Sun*

06 MATAKANA VILLAGE'S MARKET

For those Saturday morning feels
head out to Matakana Village's
famous farmers' market. A short
40-minute drive north of Auckland
city centre this thriving market,
perched on the picturesque
Matakana River, has a focus on
fresh, sustainably sourced or grown
local goods and is a zero-waste
venture. It's standing room only
at stalls such as Matakana Coffee
Roaster, Puhoi Cheeses and Orata
Oysters. With samplings of feijoa
wine, manuka honey, local seaweed
and indigenous New Zealand herbs
all available, you'll want to make sure
you arrive early. The boisterous

atmosphere, variety of produce on
offer and welcoming stall operators
make this truly authentic farmers'
market a must-visit.
*2 Matakana Valley Rd, Matakana;
www.matakanavillage.co.nz/
market; 8am-1pm Sat*

07 BRICK BAY WINES & SCULPTURE TRAIL

Set against emerald hills that
slope down to the ocean there's
something a bit special about Brick
Bay Wines, home to a fabulous
sculpture trail. Lined with dense
tree ferns, the large open-air
exhibition showcases over 60 works
from both established and emerging
Kiwi artists. Frank Lloyd Wright
would approve of the winery's
restaurant, The Glass House,
cantilevered over a shimmering lake.

Focusing on the midday meal
the restaurant's seasonal menu
highlights items sourced from
their own gardens and nearby
providers. Beetroot-cured salmon
accompanied by kumara crisps is
perfectly paired with a lively pinot
gris. Succulent lamb cutlets, from
animals raised at Brick Bay's farm,
team effortlessly with the winery's
Martello Rock with its hints of
cherry and cacao. Bookings for the
restaurant are essential and allow for
a long, long lunch.
*17 Arabella Lane, Snells Beach,
Warkworth; 09-425 4690; www.
brickbay.co.nz; 10am-5pm*

WHERE TO STAY
SO AUCKLAND
In recent years, the city has been a bit scant on high-end accommodation but new kid on the block So Auckland has claimed a plethora of regional boutique hotel awards. Featuring harbour views, a five-star restaurant, spacious rooftop bar and quirky avant-garde design throughout, this is a little bit of luxury worth splurging on.
www.so-auckland.com

WHAT TO DO
AUCKLAND ART GALLERY TOI O TAMAKI
Centrally located and home to New Zealand's largest collection of historic and contemporary art, the diversity of pieces on display at the Auckland Art Gallery create a stunning visual history of the land of the long white cloud.
www.aucklandartgallery.com

TIRITIRI MATANGI ISLAND DAY TRIP
Auckland is bordered by ocean and it would be criminal not to spend at least a day on the water while you're visiting. A day trip to the stunning open sanctuary of Tiritiri Matangi – visitor numbers are limited – is a perfect alternative to the crowds that flock to the wineries on Waiheke Island. Opt for guided walks or simply laze on sheltered sandy beaches.
www.tiritirimatangi.org.nz

07

GET THERE
Bay of Islands is a 3½-hour drive from Auckland. To reach Russell take the Fullers car ferry which runs every 10 minutes from Opua between 6am and 9pm. Alternatively, Air New Zealand flies from Auckland to Bay of Islands (Kerikeri) Airport.

01

[Northland]

BOUNTY FROM THE SUN AND OCEAN IN THE BAY OF ISLANDS

The Bay of Islands is blessed with lush weather for fishing, harvesting, and creating delicious dishes – with matching beverages – best enjoyed outdoors, year-round.

Called 'the Winterless North', the Bay of Islands region is a favourite New Zealand summer-time destination, with its sparkling azure waters scattered with 150 lush green islands. Most of the action is out on the water, whether you're yachting, fishing, kayaking, paddle boarding, diving or cruising in the company of whales and dolphins.

Back on land, with its subtropical environment and fertile soils, the Bay of Islands is home to dozens of artisan producers, a handful of standout wineries, and a host of excellent restaurants bringing it all together and serving punters with genuine Kiwi hospitality.

This is also one of New Zealand's most historically significant regions. The site of NZ's first permanent British settlement is at Russell; it is ground zero for European colonisation in this country. From the outset the British struggled with farming the land in New

Zealand. Some only survived with the assistance of the Māori people, who grew imported crops for the early settlers, particularly potatoes – exchanging these for European items they considered more valuable, including weapons. If you strike up a friendship with any local in this bicultural region today, you're more likely to be offered some freshly caught fish in exchange for some conversation and a shared meal.

Looking after the land is key to the region's Māori people: *kaitiakitanga* (guardianship) can be observed here in the sustainable production practices, and the ubiquitous commitment to cutting unnecessary waste – particularly plastic. Even buying a simple take-away fish and chips at the beach, if you haven't brought your own receptacles (locals do!) expect cardboard boxes and wooden spoons, and no litter. Bring your own re-usable coffee cups and cutlery if you can.

01 AKE AKE

Kerikeri is the agricultural heartland of the region surrounded by orchards of peaches, avocados and kiwi fruit, as well as an abundance of small vineyards. The farmland setting is perfectly complemented by traditional New Zealand country fare at this upmarket restaurant. We're talking slow-cooked lamb shanks, wild game pie, confit duck and steak. After you've overindulged on a three-course Sunday roast, the only thing to do is work off some of those hearty calories on the 1km (0.6 mile) self-guided trail through the vineyards before hitting the cellar door. *165 Waimate North Rd, Kerikeri; 09-407 8230; www. akeakevineyard.co.nz; 11.45am–2pm & 5.45–8pm Mon-Sat, lunch only Sun, tastings 10am-4.30pm*

02 PLOUGH & FEATHER

Famed for its agriculture, Kerikeri also plays a significant part in the North Island story with its well-preserved historic sites, particularly Kerikeri Mission Station and Kororipo Pā. Next door, also located on Kerikeri Basin, is the popular Plough & Feather, occupying an old homestead with sweeping views from the verandah tables. The location is everything. Mains here run the gamut of bistro favourites like burgers, steak and fish of the day; plus there's a good selection of vegan options. There's also an excellent range of NZ craft beers. *215 Kerikeri Rd, Kerikeri; 09-407 8479; www.ploughandfeather. co.nz; 9am-10pm summer*

03 OLD PACKHOUSE MARKET

What looks like any old fruit-packing shed on the outskirts of town, turns into a heaving farmers' market every Saturday morning with local producers, winemakers and farmers selling direct to the public. Follow the hand-written chalkboards to try local wines, craft beer, baked goodies and delicious gourmet street food. Check online for regular themed night markets on a Thursday, too. *505 Kerikeri Rd, Kerikeri; 09-401 9588; www.facebook.com/ theoldpackhousemarket; 8am-1.30pm Sat*

01 Some of the 144 islands in the beautiful Bay of Islands

02 The view from Charlotte's Kitchen

03 Dessert at Sage @ Paroa Bay

04 The Gables restaurant in Russell

Russell, once a one-horse town filled with pirates, prostitutes and outlaws, is now a genteel village of historic streetscapes.

04 MAKANA CONFECTIONS

At this chocolate shop and cafe, opposite the Old Packhouse Market, you can watch the artisans at work through the factory window as they pop out another batch of colourful confections. After taste-testing these melt-in-your-mouth chocolates, with unusual flavours and ingredients, it won't matter that being preservative-free they don't last longer than a week – you will have gobbled them up well before then.
504 Kerikeri Rd, Kerikei; 09-407 6800; www.makana.co.nz; 9am-5.30pm

05 CHARLOTTE'S KITCHEN

Leaving Kerikeri behind, head to Paihia for all the peak water-based tourism experiences in the Bay of Islands, and you'll be spoiled for dining out experiences from around the globe. Charlotte's Kitchen – named after an escaped Australian convict who was NZ's first white female settler – is a vibey restaurant and bar that occupies a cheeky perch on the main pier. While tucking into the Asian-influenced dishes such as steamed pork buns and Vietnamese rolls (not to mention the freshly shucked oysters) you'll hear the wash from ferries under your feet as they moor up and deliver day trippers back to the mainland.
Paihia Wharf, 69 Marsden Rd, Paihia; 09-402 8296; www. charlotteskitchen.co.nz; 11.30am-10pm Mon-Fri, to 11pm Sat & Sun

06 THE GABLES

The next stop is across the bay at
Russell. Once a one-horse town filled
with pirates, prostitutes and outlaws,
it's now a genteel village of historic
streetscapes. The Gables occupies
an 1847 building (formerly a brothel)
on the waterfront – built using
whale vertebrae for foundations.
Today it serves exceptionally good
Kiwi classics (mainly lamb, beef, and
seafood) with an excellent wine list
and local cheeses. Book a table by
the windows for maritime views,
especially if dining when the sun is
going down.
*19 The Strand, Russell; 09-403
7670; www.thegablesrestaurant.
co.nz; noon-3pm & 5.30-10pm
Wed-Mon*

07 DUKE OF MARLBOROUGH HOTEL

A popular, historic hotel and
restaurant, the best reason for
stopping here on your gourmet
tour, is to watch the water activity
while tasting your way through the
NZ craft beer selections on the
sunny deck. Try hyper-local brews
such as Kainui Pilsner, a Kerikeri
thirst quencher, big on hops, oozing
citrus; or the Phat House Pale Ale
from Waipapa, with a rich and
complex toffee malt finish. In winter
you can take it inside and cosy up in
a chesterfield by a roaring fire.
*35 The Strand, Russell; 09-
403 7829; www.theduke.co.nz;
11.30am-9pm*

08 SAGE @ PAROA BAY

It's a 15-minute drive along winding
roads into the hinterland behind
Russell to Paroa Bay, but the views
alone – over the turquoise waters
of the Bay of Islands away from
the hubbub of Paihia and Russell
– make the extra effort worth
it. Once you arrive at this winery
restaurant, overlooking manicured
lawns and rolling green farmland,
and drink in the briny sea air gusting
up the hillside, you'll know what
we mean. The limited mains menu
has a seafood focus, with quality
ingredients and punchy flavours:
a side salad comes with dukkah,
pickled vegetables and balsamic
beetroot, for example. But we'd
recommend the dramatic cheese
and charcuterie tasting board, and
an afternoon grazing while sampling
the Paroa Bay wines. If you can't
organise a designated driver, book
a night at the villa accommodation
on-site, which comes with private
beach access and an infinity pool.
*31 Otamarua Rd, Paroa Bay; 09-
403 8270; www.thelindisgroup.
com/paroabaywinerysage; noon-
5pm Wed & Thu, to 8pm Fri-Sun*

WHERE TO STAY
ARCADIA LODGE
A characterful 1890 hillside house kitted out with interesting antiques. Meals are complemented by spectacular views over sailboats bobbing on the water from the deck. Grab a bottle of local wine from the honesty bar, and find a quiet spot in the garden.
www.arcadialodge.co.nz

MOON GATE VILLA
Modern accommodation set amid tropical foliage and a water feature, with a huge spa bath in the larger suite. There is also a compact self-contained cottage in the gardens, and a solar-powered swimming pool.
www.moongatevilla.com

WHAT TO DO
DISCOVER THE BAY CRUISE
Take a four-hour Discover the Bay cruise to the jaw-dropping Hole in the Rock; or alight at Urupukapuka Island for nature walks and sheltered beach swimming.
www.exploregroup.co.nz

KERIKERI MISSION STATION
Two of the nation's most significant buildings nestle on the banks of Kerikeri Basin: the Stone Store (NZ's oldest stone building) and Kemp House a pretty wooden Georgian-style house and NZ's oldest (built in 1822). Around the inlet, Kororipo Pā is the site of Hongi Hika's *pā* (fortress) and village.
www.historic.org.nz

CELEBRATIONS
WAITANGI DAY
Ceremonial events are held at the Waitangi Treaty Grounds to mark Waitangi Day on February 6th. Expect a naval salute and an annual outing for the huge Māori *waka taua* (war canoe) Ngātokimatawhaorua followed by food, music and cultural performances.
www.waitangi.org.nz/ whats-on/waitangi-day

GET THERE

The Wairarapa is best explored with your own wheels...and getting here is half the fun! The drive up over the Remutaka Range from Wellington is jaw-droppingly beautiful. Alternatively, regular Metlink (www.metlink. org.nz) commuter trains run to Masterton from Wellington via Carterton. Metlink buses join the dots to Greytown and Martinborough (your best bets for accommodation).

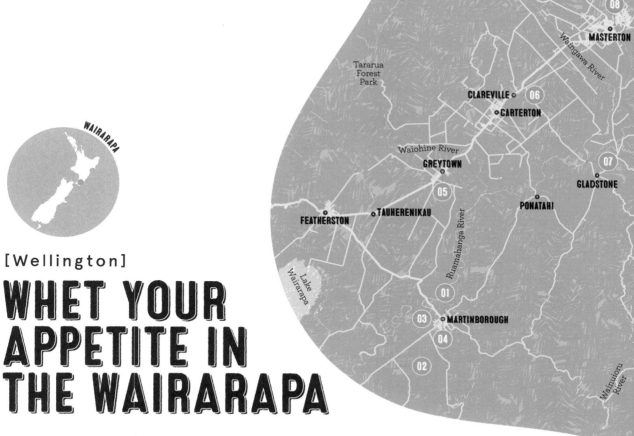

Tararua
Forest
Park

Wangawa River

08
MASTERTON

CLAREVILLE ○ 06
○ CARTERTON

Waiohine River

GREYTOWN
○

07
○
GLADSTONE

05

PONATAHI
○

○ TAUHERENIKAU
FEATHERSTON

Ruamahanga River

Lake
Wairarapa

01

03 ○ MARTINBOROUGH

04

02

Wainuioru River

[Wellington]

WHET YOUR APPETITE IN THE WAIRARAPA

*Over the hills and (not so) far away from Wellington, New Zealand's lush Wairarapa
wine region bottles-up perfect pinot noir, with foodie culture to match.*

The Wairarapa is the sprawling tract of land northeast of Wellington on New Zealand's North Island, just a one-hour drive over the craggy, mist-shrouded Remutaka Range. The unhurried lifestyle here is a real gear-shift down from Wellington's urban buzz – but it's the local vineyards and attendant foodie haunts that have turned the region into Wellington's favourite naughty-weekender.

Photogenic Martinborough is the hub of the action. Laid out in the shape of a Union Jack around a leafy square, the town is laced with gorgeous heritage architecture and surrounded by a patchwork of pastures and pinstripe grapevines. It's possible to walk between the big-ticket wineries here, but the classic Martinborough sight is of pelotons of cheery cyclists becoming increasingly wobbly as their wine-tasting afternoon progresses. Nearby Greytown and Clareville

offer some excellent cafes and bakeries, while the wineries around Gladstone and Masterton are also on the up (...and don't miss the Gladstone Inn!).

Interestingly, the Wairarapa wine industry was nearly crushed in infancy. The first vines were planted here in 1883, but in 1908 the prohibition movement put a cap on that corker of an idea. It wasn't until the late 1970s that winemaking took off again. A few commercial vineyards soon sprang up, the number since ballooning to around 30 across the region. Pinot noir is the Wairarapa's raison d'être, but sauvignon blanc also does well here, as do aromatics and syrah.

The Wairarapa's well-oiled cellar doors swing open for tastings. Most wineries charge a tasting fee (usually waived if you buy a bottle), although some will let you taste for free. Some have a cafe or restaurant; others will rustle up a picnic platter to enjoy outside.

01 Wine-tasting by
bicycle in the Wairarapa

02 In the saddle at the
Gladstone Inn

03 Reasons to stop at
Clareville Bakery

① MARTINBOROUGH VINEYARD

Kick off your Wairarapa foodie
tour in Martinborough, with a
visit to the first vineyard to plant
pinot noir here – an event that
transpired way back in 1980. The
founders conducted a detailed
survey across NZ to determine
the best place to grow pinot
noir vines, seeking to match the
climate of Burgundy in France,
the home of perfect pinot –
warm days, cool nights, low
rainfall and free-draining soils.
The Wairarapa wine industry was
born, and Martinborough Vineyard
is now a local legend with a
sterling international reputation.
The cellar door is on-site at Te
Kairanga vineyard.

*Te Kairanga Cellar Door, 89
Martins Rd, Martinborough; 06-
306 9122; www.martinborough-
vineyard.co.nz; 11am-4pm*

② CONEY WINES

Sure, Martinborough does a fine line
in stylish, upmarket cellar doors,
but there's also room here for a
little quirkiness and offbeat humour.
Welcome to Coney Wines! Fingers
crossed that your tasting host will
be the inimitable Tim Coney (older
brother of NZ cricketing legend
Jeremy) – an affable character
who makes a mighty shiraz and may
randomly burst into song. It's also
home to the excellent Trio Cafe;
bookings recommended.

*A107 Dry River Rd, Martinborough;
06-306 8345; www.coneywines.
co.nz; 11am-4pm Fri-Sun Dec-Mar,
Sat & Sun only Oct, Nov & Apr-Jul*

③ MESITA WINE BAR

Hankering for another vino and the
last cellar door has closed for the
evening? Make a beeline for Mesita,
a tiny side-street wine bar in
central Martinborough (follow the
vintage rock from the main street).
Inside are excellent wines – mostly
locals with some far-flung stars
– plus craft beers, killer cocktails
and Mexican-inspired nibbles.
Four-pinot tasting flights are a
good way to sample the vineyards
that got away.

*14c Ohio St, Martinborough; 06-
306 8475; www.mesita.net; 4pm-
late Mon, Thu & Fri, from 2pm Sat
& Sun*

'Our guiding principle – small is beautiful – turns out to be a metaphor for hard labour, but what else are ex-city dwellers good for?'

Tim Coney, Coney Wines

04 MARTINBOROUGH BREWERY

It's hard to go anywhere in NZ these days and not find a craft brewery bubbling away in the corner. Martinborough is no exception – and if you're more into pilsner than pinot, this little side-street brewer is the place for you. Actually, the vibe here is more complimentary than contra when it comes to Martinborough's wineries: the beer here is awesome (try the Black Nectar oatmeal stout), but no one is under any illusions as to why the Wairarapa is on the foodie tourism map! Sip a tasting paddle or a pint on the sunny terrace out the front. Tours by arrangement.

10 Ohio St, Martinborough; 06-306 6249; www.martinboroughbeer. com; 2-7pm Mon & Tue, 11am-8pm Thu-Sun

05 FOOD FOREST ORGANICS

In recent years this picturesque slice of New Zealand's rural heartland has gained an unlikely Hollywood connection, with blockbuster movie directors Sir Peter Jackson and James Cameron both putting down Wairarapa roots. The ecofriendly sentiments in Cameron's Avatar series aren't an aberration: Cameron is a committed vegan, and this health-food store in photogenic Greytown, 18km (11 miles) north of Martinborough, features organic products from the Cameron Family Farms (www.cameronfamilyfarms.

04 Castlepoint lighthouse in the Wairarapa is New Zealand's tallest

05 The historic frontage of Martinborough Hotel

nz): fresh Wairarapa produce, nuts, honey, candles, moisturisers... Call in for a not-chicken pie, a salad bowl or some borscht for lunch. There's also apartment accommodation upstairs if you feel like a snooze.
101 Main St, Greytown; 06-304 9790; www.foodforestorganics. co.nz; 9.30am-4.30pm Wed-Sun

06 CLAREVILLE BAKERY

On the highway just north of Carterton, around 8km (5 miles) north of Greytown, this outstanding little bakery-cafe is a Wairarapa institution, famous for sourdough bread, lamb-cutlet pies, steak sandwiches and lavash-style crackers. If you're looking to shake off the remnants of yesterday's cellar-door pursuits, look no further. There's also garden seating, a kids' play zone, regular live music and an ocean-sized car park (a huge car park

being the primary indicator of a bad pub or a good cafe). Shovel into some Basque eggs and tune-in to the local conversation: fields, vines, fields with vines in them...
3340 SH2, Clareville; 06-379 5333; www.theclarevillebakery.co.nz; 7.30am-4pm Mon-Sat

07 GLADSTONE INN

Gladstone, 15km (9 miles) east of Clareville, is less a town, more a state of mind. There's actually very little here except a handful of vineyards, some sheep-filled paddocks, a few fences and this classic old timber pub – actually a replacement for the original 1871 boozer, which burned down in 1934. These days it's a haven for thirsty locals, back-road bikers, Sunday drivers and lazy afternoon sippers, who hog the tables in the glorious garden bar by the river. Plenty of crafty beer on tap, plus bodacious steaks and pizzas. A

Wairarapa foodie classic.
571 Gladstone Rd, Gladstone; 06-372 7866; www.gladstoneinn.co.nz; 11am-late Tue-Sun

08 WAIRARAPA FARMERS' MARKET

Drive 16km (10 miles) north of Gladstone and wind up your foodie tour in Masterton, the Wairarapa's biggest town and service hub. It's a far cry from Martinborough's gourmet offerings – Masterton is more business than boutique – but there's a great little cinema here (www.thescreeningroom.co.nz) plus the region's best farmers' market. Near the Waipoua River, this effervescent mart fills the trestle tables to overflowing every Saturday morning, rain or shine. Bring your hunger, and an appreciation for buskers of varying repute.
4 Queen St, Masterton; 06-377 1107; www.waifarmersmarket.org. nz; 9am-1pm Sat

WHERE TO STAY
MARTINBOROUGH HOTEL
After a hard day's wine tasting, work your way into a quiet beer at this handsome 1882 pub – Martinborough's pride and joy. A handful of plush suites await upstairs. *www.martinboroughhotel.co.nz*

CLAREMONT
A classy accommodation enclave 15 minutes' walk from downtown Martinborough, the Claremont has self-contained units, mod studios and sparkling two-bedroom apartments. Bike hire, too (handy). *www.theclaremont.co.nz*

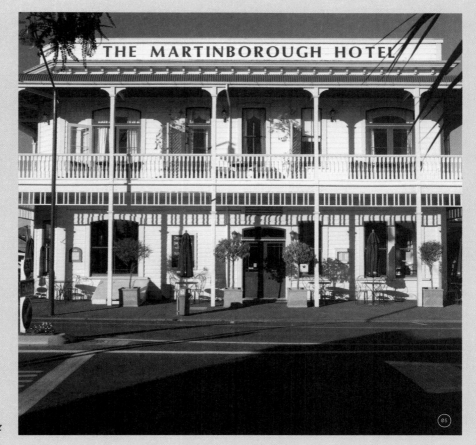

WHAT TO DO
MARTINBOROUGH WINE WALKS
Martinborough's compact wine zone can be explored on foot... and you won't need to nominate some poor sucker to drive! Walking tours visit three or four cellar doors and include tastings and lunch (with wine).

www.martinborough winewalks.com

CAPE PALLISER LIGHTHOUSE
Burn some calories on the 250-step climb to the base of this candy-striped lighthouse (1897) on the Wairarapa's southern fringe. Fab views! *www.wairarapanz.com/cape-palliser*

CELEBRATIONS
WAIRARAPA WINES HARVEST FESTIVAL
Celebrates the start of the harvest (mid-March) with an extravaganza of wine, food and family fun. It's held on a remote riverbank 10 minutes from Carterton; shuttles depart from major Wairarapa towns.

www.wairarapaharvest festival.co.nz

TOAST MARTINBOROUGH
A hugely popular wine, food and music event held on the third Sunday in November; book accommodation a long way in advance *www.toastmartin borough.co.nz*

GET THERE
Passenger ferries with Fullers (www.
fullers.co.nz) run from the Ferry
Building in Auckland. Cars and e-bikes
can be rented on the island. Sealink
(www.sealink.co.nz) run vehicular
ferries from Half Moon Bay in east
Auckland and from Wynyard Wharf.

The map shows Waiheke Island with the following labels:

Hooks Bay, Cactus Bay, Onetangi Bay, ONEROA, BLACKPOOL, PALM BEACH, SURFDALE, Huruhi Bay, OSTEND, ONETANGI, OMIHA, Rocky Bay, Waiheke Island, Pakatoa Island, Hauraki Gulf, Rotoroa Island, COWES, Waiheke Channel, Awaawaroa Bay, Te Matuku Bay (McLeods Bay), ORAPIU, Tamaki Strait

Map markers: 01, 02, 06, 07, 04, 03, 05, 08

WAIHEKE ISLAND

[Auckland]

WINING & DINING ON WAIHEKE ISLAND

A favourite retreat for Aucklanders, Waiheke's menu of eating, drinking and activities plays out amid an island landscape of sandy beaches and expansive harbour views.

Less than 45 minutes from downtown Auckland by ferry and enhanced by a dry microclimate, Waiheke has transitioned from a raffish, bohemian escape into one of New Zealand's most interesting food and wine destinations.

Winemaking began on the island in the late 1970s with an emphasis on Bordeaux-style red wines. In recent decades a wide range of other varietals have been planted, and Waiheke's talented winemakers have also coaxed award-winning chardonnay, syrah and sauvignon blanc wines from the island's versatile terroir. Rustic vineyard sheds and barns have been replaced by architecturally spectacular cellar doors and restaurants where sophisticated menus showcasing local produce and island seafood combine with views of the Hauraki Gulf and Auckland's skyline.

Inspired by the winemaking industry's trailblazing spirit, Waiheke's eating and drinking scene has also expanded to include locally roasted coffee, innovative craft beers, and the perfect holiday treat of gourmet ice cream. Visit mid-week outside of the Christmas—New Year period, and the island's beaches are quiet. Explore Waiheke with a car and even more spectacular beaches such as Man O'War Bay can be discovered.

Reflecting the island's Mediterranean-style climate, there's a touch of Southern Europe meets the South Pacific in Waiheke's restaurant scene, but relaxed Kiwi hospitality and a focus on local ingredients means they remain a fully NZ experience. Entrepreneurial arrivals from other countries helm food trucks offering global eats from wood-fired pizza to Sri Lankan curries, while Waiheke's combination of island scenery and opportunities for active adventure bookends leisurely hours enjoying the island's gourmet attractions.

01 ISLAND GELATO COMPANY

Opened by a finalist in Masterchef New Zealand, Island Gelato's frozen summertime sensations are dispatched from a repurposed shipping container at the southern end of Oneroa village. Flavour combinations are both bold and interesting, often harnessing seasonal ingredients, and always incorporating global influences. Check out the 'Flavour Archive' on the website for past combinations such as Blueberry and Sake, Chocolate Truffle Black Forest, and Thai Basil and Mandarin. Good coffee and bagels from well-known NZ chef Al Brown are also served, and there's another Island Gelato branch in Auckland's downtown Ferry Terminal if you need a fix before or after the short journey to the island.

124 Ocean View Road, Oneroa; 021 536 860; www.islandgelato.co.nz; 7.30am-5pm Mon-Fri, 7.30am-8pm Fri Sun

02 DRAGONFIRED

One of Waiheke's prettiest and most compact beaches is also a top spot for an al fresco snack. Wood-fired excellence including pizza, calzones and pocket breads crammed with ingredients are all served from Dragonfired's humble oceanside location. The owners are originally from Argentina, but there's a world of flavours including feta cheese, Mexican beef and Greek lamb. Pick up a NZ craft beer or local bottle of wine from the Waiheke Wine Centre in nearby Oneroa, and ease into the island twilight. Just don't feed the seagulls OK?

Little Oneroa Beach; 021 922 289; www.dragonfired.co.nz; 10am-8pm daily Nov-Mar, 11am-7pm Fri-Sun Apr-Oct

03 TE MATUKU BAY OYSTERS

The sheltered bays and cooler Southern Hemisphere waters surrounding Waiheke are ideal for aquaculture, and oysters from the unpolluted Te Matuku Marine Reserve on the island's southeast coast are some of NZ's best. They're served at vineyard restaurants around the island, but the best place to try them is at Te Matuku's seafood

01 Oneroa beach in Waiheke's northwest

02 The must-visit Island Gelato Company

03 Dreamy icecream

04 Island Coffee exterior

05 Baked delights from Island Coffee

delicatessen. Order up a dozen freshly shucked oysters and enjoy them straight from the shell with a splash of lemon juice or a dash of Tabasco sauce. Other fresh seafood including plump green-lipped mussels are also available, and during cooler months there's a steady stream of locals lunching on warming soups and chowder. *13 Belgium St, Ostend; 09-372 8600; www.tematukuoysters.co.nz; 9am-5pm Mon-Sat*

04 ISLAND COFFEE

The best coffee on the island is locally roasted in this humble setup tucked away in Ostend's compact scattering of shops. You'll probably smell if before you see it, so push the door open and

team a creamy NZ-style flat white with excellent homestyle baking including still-warm cinnamon brioches. There's also a turntable with lots of vinyl records to play, and in the back of the cafe the coffee roasting magic takes place. Island Coffee is very popular with locals and can get crowded, so maybe order coffee to go and make the short 5km (3 mile) drive to Onetangi Beach. *21B Belgium St, Ostend; 09-372 9988; www.islandcoffeenz.com; 8.30am-12.30pm Tue-Sat*

05 TANTALUS ESTATE

Crowning a hilltop like a historic European homestead, Tantalus is a thoroughly modern place offering some of the island's best wines and fine dining. Book ahead for lunch in the airy dining room and combine dishes such as NZ lamb rump with sweet potato, miso and fermented chilli and stellar wines including the Voillé Reserve Syrah. Underneath the restaurant, craft beers from the Alibi Brewing Company are served in a brick-lined taproom. Standout brews include the spicy Rya IPA, and there are always interesting seasonal beers to try. *72 Onetangi Rd, Onetangi; 09-372 2625; www.tantalus.co.nz; 11am-4pm*

06 Waterfront vines at Man O' War winery

07 Villa with a view at Man O' War winery

08 Discover Waiheke's many beaches over a long weekend

06 CASITA MIRO

Enlivened by sea breezes and framed by vineyards and olive groves, there's definitely a hint of the Mediterranean at Casita Miro's hilltop location, and the restaurant's food and decor both conspire to maintain the illusion. A wrought-iron and glass pavilion combines with a mosaic garden with echoes of Barcelona's Park Güell, while the menu presents Spanish flavours including tapas and larger raciones shared plates. Much of the menu uses ingredients from local and sustainability focused producers, and the wine list features exemplary vintages from Casita Miro's own syrah, malbec and cabernet franc grapes.

72 Onetangi Rd, Onetangi; 09-372 7854; www.casitamiro.co.nz; 11.30am-4pm Sun-Thu, to 8pm Fri-Sat

07 THREE SEVEN TWO

Named after the first three letters of Waiheke Island phone numbers, Three Seven Two's spacious waterfront location showcases seasonal bistro menus with many local ingredients. The flavours of Southeast Asia, the Middle East and Mediterranean Europe often star, and there's a very good selection of local Waiheke wines and beers. Head out to the shaded rear courtyard for the most relaxed ambience. On cooler nights outside of summer, there's a lovely outdoor fire to cosy up next to.

21 The Strand, Onetangi Beach; 09-372 8846; www.threeseventwo. co.nz; noon-late

08 MAN O' WAR

Tucked away on the island's more isolated east coast, it's a mini-mission to get to Man O' War Bay, but definitely worth the effort. Either negotiate a winding unsealed road with brilliant hilltop views of the Coromandel Peninsula or secure a short flight with Auckland Sea Planes from downtown Auckland. Visitors are rewarded with the vineyard's beachfront location and tastings including the much-lauded Valhalla chardonnay. Man O' War's island vineyard holdings comprise just 60 hectares (148 acres), but their diverse production also includes superb Bordeaux-style blends. Charcuterie and cheese platters and good pizzas are ideal for a leisurely lunch.

725 Man O' War Bay Rd; 09-372 9678; www.manowar.co.nz; 11am-4pm Mon-Fri, 11am-6pm Sat-Sun

WHERE TO STAY

CABLE BAY VIEWS

These three modern self-contained studio apartments have harbour views and are handily close to a couple more of Waiheke's excellent vineyard restaurants. The property is also conveniently close to the passenger ferry wharf at Matiatia and the island's main settlement of Oneroa. For families and groups, the larger Cable Bay Lodge and Cable Bay House are recommended.
www.cablebayviews.co.nz

WHAT TO DO

ECOZIP ADVENTURES

With vineyard, native bush and ocean views, EcoZip's three separate 200m (656ft) zip lines make for an exciting ride, and there's a gentle 1.5km (0.9 mile) walk back up through the bush after the thrills. Costs include transfers from Matiatia Wharf or Oneroa if you don't have your own transport. Book ahead online.
www.ecozipadventures. co.nz

POTIKI ADVENTURES

These guided tours explore Waiheke Island from a Māori cultural perspective, including beaches, a bush walk, a vineyard visit and demonstrations of traditional musical instruments and weaving.
www.potikiadventures. co.nz

CELEBRATIONS

SCULPTURE ON THE GULF

Usually held in March every odd-numbered year – although the 2020 event was delayed to 2021 – this 2.5km (1.6 mile) clifftop walk negotiates an outdoor gallery of interesting and innovative sculptures.

Check the website for details of special shuttle buses providing access to the beginning of the walk. There's also a dedicated festival information centre adjacent to the passenger ferry terminal at Matiatia.
www.sotg.nz

GET THERE
Cromwell is less than an hour's drive from Queenstown, and is also well served by bus. If you don't want to drive, there are plenty of guided tours available to take you through the wine region – inquire at the local i-SITEs, or check www.centralotagonz. com/activities-tours/wine-tours. transport.

01

Map labels:
- Lake Dunstan
- Dunstan Range
- LOWBURN
- 06
- CROMWELL
- Kawarau Gorge
- 04
- 05
- 01
- 02
- 03
- BANNOCKBURN
- Carrick Range
- Clyde Dam
- OMAKAU
- CHATTO CREEK
- CLYDE
- 07
- CENTRAL OTAGO
- Fraser Dam
- 08
- ALEXANDRA
- Butchers Dam

[Otago]

SENSATIONAL CENTRAL OTAGO

World-famous pinot noir awaits you in Central Otago – presented with a truly Kiwi combo of professional pride and down-to-earth charm.

Central Otago's early boom was financed with gold. Many of the elegant pubs, stores and public buildings date from the Otago Gold Rush of the 1860s. A century later, the region struck gold for the second time when winemakers discovered it was the perfect match for the notoriously fickle pinot noir grape.

The world's southernmost wine region is surrounded by snow-capped peaks, which not only make it highly picturesque, they also create New Zealand's only true continental climate zone. Lying in the rain shadow of the mountains, this is the driest region in the country, with high daily and seasonal temperature variations. The soil, too, is famously varied, with anything from schist to lime, clay, gravel and sand found naturally here. And when the gold diggers arrived they turned everything upside down, with water races built and

tailings piled in new places. As in California, this turned out to be a bonanza for viticulture.

Around 75% of Central Otago's vines are pinot noir – when you're onto a good thing, why mess with it? There's also some riesling, pinot gris, sauvignon blanc and chardonnay. With more than 60 wineries in the area (even Australian actor Sam Neill has bought in near Alexandra at Two Paddocks) it's wise to pick up the Central Otago Wine Map, available at local i-SITEs.

The region's other famous attraction is the wonderfully naff (and somehow a little bit rude) collection of giant fruit that graces the highway at Cromwell. It celebrates the area's status as the Fruit Bowl of the South. In summer, local orchards overflow with cherries, apricots, peaches, nectarines and plums. If you're visiting at this time, you'd do well to wrap your lips around some – fresh off the tree.

01 MT DIFFICULTY

Why not start with the poster child of the Central Otago Wine Region – Mt Difficulty has made a name for itself by offering both premium single-vineyard pinot noirs, known for complex and subtle layering, as well as the more accessibly priced 'Roaring Meg' range. You can taste them at its cellar door and modern restaurant enjoying spectacular views over the Cromwell Basin. The winery dates to the early 1990s, when five growers collaborated to produce wine from the promising but unproven Central Otago region. Head winemaker Matt Dicey joined the winery in 1998, the same year it produced its first vintage.

Purchased by California wine baron Bill Foley in 2019, there's set to be expansion of the tasting room and restaurant in the years to come, as well as a strong push of the brand in the US market. Book ahead for lunch.
73 Felton Rd, Bannockburn; 03-445 3445; www.mtdifficulty. nz; tastings 10.30am-4.30pm, restaurant noon-4pm

02 CARRICK WINES

Certified-organic Carrick has achieved acclaim for producing rich, toasty chardonnays and citrusy rieslings, alongside the pinot noir that made this region famous. Carrick's stylish restaurant (book in advance), opens out onto a terrace and lush lawns, while inside there's a roaring winter fire. The top picks on the seasonal menu, which features house-grown and organic vegetables, are the excellent share platters; they overflow with local produce and are the perfect complement to the wine range.
247 Cairnmuir Rd, Bannockburn; 03-445 3480; www.carrick.co.nz; tastings 10am-5pm, restaurant 11am-4pm

03 CHEEKI CHERRIES

Come Christmas time, the cherry trees around Cromwell are sagging with the glorious weight of the fruit clustered on their branches. Local growers set up roadside fruit stalls and put out PYO ('pick your own') signs. What better way to spend an

01 Lake Dunstan and
the town of Cromwell

02 Heavenly wines
come from these vines
at Mt Difficulty

03 Chef Gwen's apple
pie at Carrick Wines

04 Pick up a bottle of
Mt Difficulty wine

05 Organically
cultivated contours at
Carrick Wines

afternoon than wandering about in the dappled shade of a cherry orchard, gathering big juicy fruits right off the tree?
247 Ripponvale Rd, Cromwell; 021-808 747; www.cheekicherries. co.nz; mid-Dec–Feb

04 CROMWELL FARMERS' MARKET

Cromwell's famous produce is best sampled on Sunday (rain or shine!) at this fantastic farmers' market held in the warmer months. Just-picked veg, homemade chutney, smoked salmon, goats cheese, artisanal breads – can you feel a picnic coming on? What makes this market special is the strong sense of community, with local buskers strumming tunes and little kids

selling treats at their own stalls.

Plus, the market is held in the unique Cromwell Heritage Precinct, created after the Clyde Dam flooded Cromwell's historic town centre in 1992, inundating 280 homes, six farms and 17 orchards. Many historic buildings were disassembled before the flooding and have since been rebuilt in this pedestrianised precinct beside Lake Dunstan. Some of these, including a stable, blacksmith shop and newspaper press, have been set up as period museum pieces; others house cheerful cafes and creative galleries.
Melmore Tce, Cromwell; 027-496 0375; www. cromwellheritageprecinct.co.nz; 9am–1pm Sunday Oct–Apr

05 CLOUDY BAY

Opened in 2018, this beautiful outpost of one of New Zealand's biggest names in Marlborough wine sits right on the edge of Lake Dunstan, and its tasting room enjoys mesmerising views through massive floor-to-ceiling windows. Cloudy Bay's Te Wahi pinot noir in particular has drawn praise for its lush and brooding flavours. Stop in for lunch, or take a 75-minute tour to learn about the local terroir and winemaking techniques.
45 Northburn Station Rd, Cromwell; 03-777 6059; www. cloudybay.co.nz; 10am–5pm daily Dec-Apr, 10am–4pm Tue-Sat May-Nov

'Overlooking the Bannockburn inlet, we're an idyllic setting for lunch and wine tastings.'

Rosie Menzies, Carrick Wines

06 OLIVERS

Atmospherically housed in an 1860's general store made of local schist stone, this bar, cafe-deli and bistro is a local institution, and a fabulous place for a big chatty lunch. The menu relies heavily on local produce with dishes such as braised hare leg and apricot-frangipani pie, and the atmosphere is friendly and convivial. Find a seat either in the fire-warmed dining room or out under the sun umbrellas in the garden. There's also a craft brewery on-site. Be sure to book ahead.
34 Sunderland St, Clyde; 03-449 2805; www.oliverscentralotago. co.nz; restaurant noon-2pm & 6-8pm, bar noon-late, shorter hrs Jun-Aug

07 COURTHOUSE CAFE

Housed in the heritage-listed Alexandra Courthouse (1878), this cafe is a beloved local gathering spot, and an award-wining dining destination. It took out the 'Best Main Meal' award in the 2019 Eat Taste Central awards, for 'Panning the Nevis Valley' ($24), a medley of succulent beef, mixed mushrooms, poached egg yolk and scattered flowers, which pays homage to the gold rush history of the region. This is also a charming coffee-and-cake stop with outdoor tables and an interior decorated with bountiful botanical displays.
8 Centennial Ave, Alexandra; 03-448 7818; www. thecourthousecafealex.yolasite. com; 6.15am-4pm Mon-Fri, 9am-4pm Sat

WHERE TO STAY
OLIVERS
Step into the gold rush glory days at this 1860s merchant's house and stone stables. Luxurious rooms are decked out with old maps, heritage furniture and claw-foot baths, and most open onto a secluded garden courtyard. It's behind the eponymous restaurant.
www.oliverscentral otago.co.nz

DUNSTAN HOUSE
This restored late-Victorian balconied inn has cosy lounge areas, a magnificent kauri wood staircase and stylish rooms decorated with William Morris wallpaper.
www.dunstanhouse. co.nz

WHAT TO DO
OTAGO CENTRAL RAIL TRAIL
This year-round, mainly gravel cycling trail follows an old train line, disassembled in the 1990s, for 150km (93 miles) between Clyde and Dunedin. Culverts, beautiful old rail bridges, viaducts, dramatic rock cuttings

and spooky tunnels remove most of the ups and downs, making this a very accessible trail popular with families, older folks and weekend cyclists.
www.otagocentralrail trail.co.nz

THE ALEXANDRA–CLYDE 150TH ANNIVERSARY WALK
This 12.8km (7.9 mile) trail follows the river and provides welcome shady respite in the hot dry region.

CELEBRATIONS
CROMWELL WINE & FOOD FESTIVAL
Held in early January in the Cromwell Heritage Precinct, this is a great festival for enjoying local wines, gourmet bites and live music.
www.cromwellheritage precinct.co.nz

CENTRAL OTAGO PINOT CELEBRATION
Later in January the area shows off its pinots at this exclusive festival –

book in advance.
www.pinotcelebration. co.nz

CLYDE WINE & FOOD FESTIVAL
This Easter festival showcases the region's produce and brings folks from across the island.
www.promotedunstan. org.nz

GET THERE
Christchurch has direct
international flights linking the city
to Singapore, China, Dubai, Los
Angeles and Australia, and frequent
domestic services to/from
Auckland and Wellington.

Pegasus
Bay

07

05 **02** **01**

04 ○ CHRISTCHURCH ○ SUMNER

03

HALSWELL

Port Hills

GOVERNORS ○ LYTTELTON
BAY
Lyttelton Harbour

06

○ DIAMOND HARBOUR

ALLANDALE ○

○ TAITAPU ○ TEDDINGTON ○ PORT LEVY

○ GREENPARK ○ LITTLE AKALOA

○ PIGEON BAY

○ OKAINS BAY

○ MOTUKARARA

Lake Ellesmere
(Te Waihora) HILTOP DUVAUCHELLE

LITTLE BARRYS BAY ○ ○ ROBINSONS BAY LE BONS BAY
RIVER
○ KAITUNA FRENCH FARM ○ Akaroa ○ TAKAMATUA
Harbour
Kaituna
Lagoon Lake
Forsyth ○ AKAROA

Kaitorete Spit WAINUI ○ **08**

○ BIRDLINGS FLAT ○ ONUKU

South
Pacific
Ocean

South
Pacific
Ocean

[Canterbury]

A TASTE OF CHRISTCHURCH & THE BANKS PENINSULA

A dynamic dining scene and local markets selling the best of the region combine amid the exciting urban renewal of New Zealand's second-biggest city.

Following a city-changing earthquake in 2011, the biggest urban centre on the South Island has been transformed into one of the country's most dynamic and interesting destinations. Complementing Christchurch's post-earthquake re-emergence anchored in bold, modern architecture and the edgy creativity of street art, there's also been a renaissance of the city's eating and drinking scenes.

Local entrepreneurs have developed unique locations showcasing the cosmopolitan diversity of the city, often repurposing existing buildings to re-energise city fringe neighbourhoods, and the iconic frontage of the city's leisurely Avon River is once more a focus for cafes, restaurants and bars. Farmers' markets and an exciting new riverside development are important social hubs for the city's resilient locals, with stallholders from around the region selling gourmet produce from the greater Canterbury region.

As the country's second largest city, Christchurch's restaurant scene is also a major drawcard for some of NZ's best chefs, and they're contributing to the redevelopment of the city. Local, sustainable, and often organic ingredients are harnessed for menus in cosmopolitan bistros or for innovative shared plates subtly evoking the country's heritage and food culture. More recent arrivals to the city from around the world are providing a taste of their own culinary story, reinforcing Christchurch's increasing cultural diversity.

A short drive from the city, Christchurch's leafy Hagley Park, cycle-friendly terrain and well-planned avenues give way to the spectacular and more rugged landscapes of the Port Hills and Banks Peninsula. Walking trails and oceangoing activities abound, and gourmet experiences include sampling award-winning chocolate and excellent cooking classes with a backdrop of the region's French colonial history.

01 LITTLE HIGH EATERY

One of the first new hospitality projects to rise during the city's post-earthquake renewal, Little High Eatery is a versatile and energetic spot for street food flavours from around the world. Eight different gourmet businesses offer everything from gourmet burgers at Bacon Bros to chargrilled Venezuelan-style barbecue at El Fogón. Handmade Taiwanese dumplings feature at Eightgrains, while Noodlemonk combines Thai flavours with local craft beers. Sit outside in the beer garden and also explore the growing range of other new cafes, bars and restaurants in close proximity. It's also a good spot for the morning's first coffee or the last cocktail of the night.

255 St Asaph St, Christchurch; 021-0208 4444; www.littlehigh. co.nz; 8am-10pm Sun, 7am-10pm Mon-Thu, 8am-1pm Sat

02 EARL

The flavours of the Mediterranean blend on the menu of this relaxed bistro. Lunch options include matching slow-cooked lamb and smoked yoghurt with a salade Niçoise, or shared plates of taleggio cheese croquettes and Italian-style meatballs. At night the menu broadens to feature housemade pasta and bistro classics like market fish with a puttanesca sauce inspired by the eclectic cuisine of Naples. There's an Italian provenance to the cocktails too, including drinks specials during daily aperitivo sessions from 3pm to 5pm. Look forward to a focus on local wine, with a different NZ vineyard being showcased most weeks. Secure a spot in one of the booths for easygoing good times.

128 Lichfield St, Christchurch; 03-365 1147; www.earl.co.nz; noon-late Tue-Sat

03 RIVERSIDE MARKET

Opened in late 2019, Christchurch's new Riverside Market is an essential destination to understand the city's increasingly diverse and multicultural makeup, and the multi-level building has also helped to re-energise the central city's riverfront. Fresh produce stalls sell local and seasonal ingredients

© Courtesy of The Akaroa Cooking School; Inati; Riverside Market

'Riverside Market brings the very best produce from the foodie region of Canterbury into the heart of Christchurch.'

Mike Fisher, Riverside Market

from around Canterbury, while the city's best food trucks have relocated inside to offer flavours including Greek souvlaki, Argentinean barbecue and grilled chicken. A craft beer filling station, good coffee and a rooftop bar with excellent views are other drawcards. Nearby, the bars and restaurants of the revitalised Oxford Terrace precinct are a good option for end of day drinks and dinner.
96 Oxford Tce, Christchurch; 022 367 1242; www.riverside.nz; 9am-6pm Mon-Wed, 9am-9pm Thu-Sat, 10am-4pm Sun

04 INATI

Playful and innovative reinterpretations of NZ ingredients and food memories feature at the stylish Inati restaurant. Sit at the elegantly curved bar and experience leisurely four- to eight-course tasting menus of shared plates divided into 'Earth, Land and Sea'. Inati's signature dish of Bouef-nuts features delicately braised beef in a surprising doughnut blending sweet and savoury flavours, while smoked mutton tartare and milk, cornflakes and popcorn sugar are both whimsical culinary reinventions. One of the city's best wine lists is equally grounded in NZ, with many excellent varietals from around Canterbury and the South Island.
48 Hereford St, Christchurch; 03-390 1580; www.inati.nz; noon-2pm & 5-11pm Tue-Fri, 5.30-11pm Sat

05 Craft beers at the Laboratory in Lincoln

07 The Chalice sculpture in Cathedral Square

06 Chefs at work at Earl

05 CHRISTCHURCH FARMERS' MARKET

Held amid the riverside surroundings of Riccarton House, one of the country's first farmers' markets is still one of NZ's best. During warmer months gourmet ice cream from Utopia Ice cools down loyal locals, while winter favourites include ramen noodle soups from Cluck Cluck Slurp. Live music – usually with a blues or Americana vibe – is a regular Saturday morning attraction, and there's a huge range of artisan gourmet produce on offer from the Canterbury region. Here's where to come if you're looking for edible gifts and souvenirs to take home.
Riccarton House, 16 Kahu Rd, Riccarton; www.christchurch farmersmarket.co.nz 03-348 6190; 9am-1pm Sat

06 THE LABORATORY

Definitely worth the journey 23km (14 miles) southwest of central Christchurch, The Laboratory combines some of the city's most interesting craft beers with excellent wood-fired pizza. The charmingly eclectic structure was constructed from building materials rescued and reused from around the city following the 2011 earthquake, and plenty of repurposed furniture creates a cosy heritage vibe. The Laboratory's versions of popular beer styles including IPA, pilsner and stout are all well-crafted, but it's also worth trying their eclectic range of seasonal brews including the Red Flanders sour ale aged in French oak. Order a tasting tray of seven beers for the full Laboratory experience.
17 West Belt, Lincoln; 03-325 3006; www.thelaboratory.co.nz; 11am-10pm Tue-Fri, to 11pm Sat-Sun

07 SHE CHOCOLATERIE

After 15 years in Governors Bay, sitting pretty above Lyttelton Harbour, this much-loved chocolaterie has moved to the Riverside Market in central Christchurch. The views may not be as dreamy, but the bean-to-bar offerings certainly are. Perennial winners in the NZ Chocolate Awards, She's buzzing, busy cafe is the perfect spot to try handcrafted cacao-infused goodness or their signature chocolate hot drinks – sample the Salted Caramel or Mayan Chilli Spice ones.
84 Cashel St, Christchurch; 022 590 3350; www.sheuniverse.com; 10.30am-4pm

08 THE AKAROA COOKING SCHOOL

Around 90km (56 miles) southeast of central Christchurch, the Banks Peninsula harbourside town of Akaroa was the country's first French settlement, and a focus on good eating and drinking lingers. Cookery classes include flavours inspired by the owners' travels in Italy, France, Spain and Thailand, and seasonal options incorporating local produce across autumn and spring are popular. Classes are held in a heritage building right on Akaroa's spectacular waterfront.
81 Beach Rd, Akaroa; 021 166 3737; www.akaroacooking.co.nz

WHERE TO STAY

ECO VILLA

In a quiet residential neighbourhood just a short stroll from central Christchurch, this classy renovated two-storey wooden villa has eight individually decorated rooms. Throughout the building there's a focus on sustainable, ecofriendly design features, and excellent shared spaces include a lounge and a sunny garden packed full of fragrant herbs. Organic and locally sourced breakfasts are served. www.ecovilla.co.nz

WHAT TO DO

WATCH THIS SPACE

Following the devastating earthquake that damaged the city in 2011, the urban renewal of Christchurch now includes many fine examples of street art. There are interesting works all around the inner city, but the High St precinct is especially worth a stroll. See the website for a map showing street art locations or join a guided tour of the city's street art scene. www.watchthisspace. org.nz

PUNTING ON THE AVON

For a relaxing glimpse into Christchurch's British heritage, sit back and enjoy a peaceful time being punted on the Avon River by a local decked out in Edwardian attire. You can also rent a canoe, kayak or rowing boat at the nearby 1882-vintage Antigua Boat Sheds and negotiate your own leisurely route on the slow-moving river flowing through the city.. www. christchurchattractions. nz/avon-river-punting

CELEBRATIONS

BREAD & CIRCUS

Also known as the World Buskers Festival, talent from around NZ and the world entertains locals and visitors across several weeks. Check the website for who's on, and don't forget to throw money in the hat. www.breadandcircus. co.nz

GET THERE
Air New Zealand has direct flights
linking Blenheim to Wellington and
Auckland. If you're exploring NZ by
car, Blenheim is 30km (18.6 miles)
south of the inter-island ferry
terminal in the South Island town
of Picton.

[Marlborough]
GOURMET-BLESSED BLENHEIM & MARLBOROUGH

Best explored by bicycle, the heartland of New Zealand's most famous wine is also a focus for fine dining, farmers markets and craft beer.

Synonymous with New Zealand's most familiar wine style – zingy and vibrant Marlborough sauvignon blanc – the region around the South Island agricultural town of Blenheim is also a fine destination for gourmet travellers and craft beer fans. Warm days and cool nights combine with balmy spring and summer conditions to provide the ideal growing environment for Marlborough's cool climate wines, and the region's benign terrain of vineyard plains framed by the Wither Hills is easily explored on two wheels. The mild climate also supports other local produce, best sampled at one of NZ's top farmers' markets.

Marlborough wine may now be famous but in global terms its acclaim is still relatively recent and the area's first commercial sauvignon blanc vineyards were only planted in 1974. The easy-drinking but elegant wine style is still hugely popular, but other award-winning wines crafted from riesling, pinot noir and pinot gris grapes continue to enhance the area's already stellar reputation. Some of the country's most spectacular cellar doors also feature restaurants, and drifting between tasting rooms and dining amidst the wines is a quintessential NZ experience.

The Marlborough region is also one of NZ's best places for a picnic. Pick up artisanal produce and delicious homestyle baking at provedores around this compact area and combine with a local wine or craft beer. Walking or mountain biking amid the views and well-marked trails of the Wither Hills Farm Park balances out Marlborough's more indulgent pleasures.

01 THE VINES VILLAGE*

This multi-business complex around 15km (9.3 miles) west of Blenheim has plenty to offer the gourmet traveller. Sample craft beer at the Golden Mile Brewing Taproom, gin and artisan bitters at Elemental Distillers, and Appleby Farms gourmet ice cream at the Deli. Plenty of other made-in-Marlborough artisanal products are also available at the Deli including local olive oil, cheese and charcuterie. Pick up a bottle of wine from the adjacent Whitehaven Cellar Door. There's also bicycle rental available and Bike Hire Marlborough can advise on recommended routes touring the region's flat vineyard country. *193 Rapaura Rd, Rapaura; 03-572 7170; www.thevinesvillage.co.nz; 8.30am-5.30pm Nov-Apr, 9am-4pm May-Oct*

02 ARBOUR

A perennial inclusion in Cuisine magazine's list of NZ's top restaurants makes Arbour one of the nation's most consistent dining experiences. Surrounded by vineyards in the heart of Renwick wine country, Arbour's multi-course tasting menus showcase the best of seasonal local produce in contemporary surroundings. That could mean Japanese-style chawanmushi savoury custard with local shellfish, or smoked and cured warehou, a popular Southern Hemisphere fish. The encyclopaedic wine selection features quite possibly the world's best selection of Marlborough wines, and craft beers from Renaissance and Boomtown also reflect a proud dedication to local provenance. *36 Godfrey Rd, Renwick; 03-572 7989; www.arbour.co.nz; 5-11pm Tue-Sat*

03 CLOUDY BAY

Established in 1985 as one of the first wineries in the Marlborough region, Cloudy Bay is world-renowned for its sauvignon blanc, a vibrant and fruit-forward expression of the wine varietal that made the region famous. The best place to try it is at the winery's Jack's Raw Bar open through the

Ask if the complex Sour Blanc, aged in oak barrels with wild yeast, is available at Moa Brewing.

summer months from December to April. Local aquaculture produce including Marlborough oysters and Cloudy Bay clams partner a Japanese-inspired menu by Auckland chef Sachie Nomura. With beautiful grounds and the opportunity to play croquet and pétanque, Cloudy Bay is an essential Marlborough diversion for a few hours. Also worth trying are Cloudy Bay's excellent Pelorus sparkling wines.
230 Jacksons Rd, Blenheim; 03-520 9147; www.cloudybay.co.nz; 10am-4pm

04 MOA BREWING COMPANY
In close proximity to some of the area's finest vineyards, Moa Brewing more than holds its own

in offering a refreshing and hoppy alternative. The leafy gardens are soundtracked by local birdlife, there's plenty of room for the kids to let off steam, and local food trucks are regular afternoon and early evening visitors from Wednesday to Sunday. Standout brews from Moa's year-round range include the Belgian-tinged Southern Alps White IPA, while the brewery's sour beers are also popular with New Zealand beer fans. Ask if the complex Sour Blanc aged in oak barrels with wild yeast is available.
258 Jacksons Rd, Blenheim; 03-572 5146; www.moabeer.com; 11am-6pm Mon-Thu, to 8pm Fri-Sat, to 7pm Sun

Past visitors usually rave about the sweet pork belly or steak and blue cheese pies, but the chicken, leek and mushroom one is also highly rated. Crunchy baguettes, local sausages and French cheeses are all for sale too, making The Burleigh an essential stop if you're planning a picnic or a barbecue. Try to avoid the lunchtime rush when queues out the door are commonplace. Yes, the pies are that good.
34 New Renwick Rd, Burleigh; 03-579 2531; www.facebook.com/ theburleighnz; 7.30am-3pm Mon-Fri, 9am-1pm Sat

05 WITHER HILLS

Named after the sparse and shadowed hills rising from behind the vineyard, Wither Hills' contemporary tasting room and restaurant complex is one of the most stylish in the region. The elegant Single Vineyard and Early Light ranges present excellent examples of chardonnay, pinot noir, pinot gris and sauvignon blanc – with premium prices to match – while the more affordable Wither Hills range is eminently quaffable on summer afternoons in the winery's arty gardens. Shared plates including South Island merino lamb with caramelised yoghurt and pomegranate are available in the classy restaurant.
211 New Renwick Rd, Burleigh; 03-520 8284; www.witherhills.co.nz; noon-3pm

06 MARLBOROUGH FARMERS' MARKET

It's not only grapes that grow well in Marlborough's warm, dry summers and crisp, cool winters, and the weekly Marlborough Farmers' Market offers everything from excellent dairy from Cranky Goat Cheese to kombucha from Banjo Brews. Check out the list of suppliers on the website for your own foodie hitlist, and kick start the day with a short black or flat white from the Ritual Coffee Cart.
Cnr Alabama & Maxwell Rds; 021 910 522; www. marlboroughfarmersmarket.org. nz; 9am-noon Sun

07 THE BURLEIGH

New Zealanders love a good savoury pie, and The Burleigh's busy corner location is renowned across the region for flaky pastry goodness.

08 SCOTCH WINE BAR

Most of the region's best eating and drinking experiences are in Blenheim's rural vineyard hinterland, but the Scotch Wine Bar is a standout option in the town's centre. Equal parts wine bar, wine shop – bottles of the region's finest are available for purchase – and shared plates restaurant, Scotch also partners craft beers from Wellington's Garage Project with a multi-course tasting menu costing just NZD45 per person. There's a good range of vegetarian dishes including beetroot with smoked yoghurt and sunflower seeds. Guilty pleasure fans shouldn't overlook the delicious fried chicken with aioli.
24-26 Maxwell Rd, Blenheim; 03-579 1176; www.scotchbar.co.nz; 4pm-late Mon-Fri

WHERE TO STAY
ST LEONARDS VINEYARD COTTAGES
Surrounded by the leafy grounds of an 1886 homestead, this collection of five rustic but stylish garden cottages is a fine place to return to after exploring the area's vineyards. All have self-contained kitchens – an ideal opportunity to take advantage of the region's farmers' markets and seasonal produce.
www.stleonards.co.nz

WHAT TO DO
OMAKA HERITAGE AVIATION CENTRE
This superb museum showcases the collection of original and replica WWI and WWII military aircraft owned by Sir Peter Jackson, director of the *Lord of the Rings* and *Hobbit* trilogies. Realistic 3D dioramas recreate dramatic wartime scenes, and it's also possible to take to the air in a vintage biplane. Adjacent to the aviation museum,

Omaka Classic Cars (www.omakaclassiccars. co.nz) has a very good collection of vehicles from the 1950s to the 1980s.
www.omaka.org.nz

WITHER HILLS FARM PARK
Providing balance to the sybaritic pleasures of food and wine on offer around this otherwise flat region, Wither Hill's rolling terrain combines spectacular views with rambling walks, gentle hikes and mountain biking trails.
www.marlboroughnz. com

CELEBRATIONS
MARLBOROUGH WINE & FOOD FESTIVAL
Vineyard, this hugely popular one-day festival combines wine, food and craft beer, as well as summertime music from NZ's most popular bands. Booking well ahead for accommodation is essential
www.wine-marlborough-festival. co.nz

GET THERE

Christchurch Airport is the most significant transport hub. Rent a car from the airport or jump aboard the TranzAlpine train service to Greymouth. Alternatively, Queenstown Airport receives flights from the North Island and from Australia. It's a long drive to the West Coast (almost seven hours), but a good excuse to stop at famous Fox and Franz Josef Glaciers en route.

01

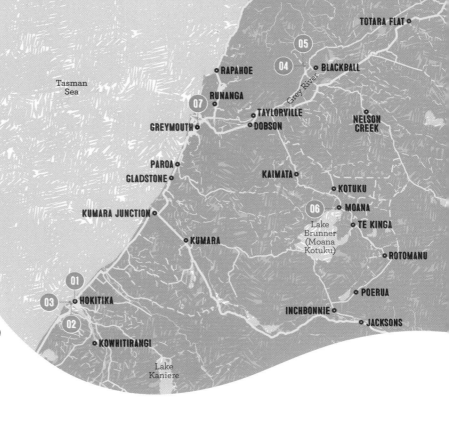

[West Coast]

GOURMET GRAZING ALONG NZ'S WEST COAST

Regional produce and homespun recipes define menus along the West Coast. This remote realm of New Zealand's South Island is a locavore's banquet...dig in!

On the South Island's windswept West Coast, the food pairs beautifully with the rugged setting. Seafood tastes smashing next to a wave-gouged stretch of coast, and sausages are even heartier when munched in the midst of fog-draped forests. As for whitebait fritters, patties of tiny fish fry bound together with egg, they're best consumed in a pub within earshot of local fisherfolk. Listen closely to their banter – they're almost certainly keeping the best fishing spots to themselves.

The West Coast, a region of glaciers, rocky coves and temperate rainforest, has long attracted hardy, enterprising characters. The original Māori inhabitants were drawn to the coast's teeming waters and abundant pounamu (greenstone). European settlers arrived in the mid-19th century to build fortunes from timber and coal. West Coasters are still tough types, only now they're farmers, pilots and small business operators – many of them making inventive use of local produce.

With abundant farmland, and lakes that flicker with trout and salmon, it's no surprise that lamb, dairy and fish take pride of place on West Coast menus. Some of the best produce is gobbled at takeaways or packed into picnics, while craft beers and ciders are gulped down in snug local pubs.

Start in cute-as-a-button Hokitika, a former gold-mining outpost that's now a surfy town with a sparkling food scene. Next drive north along the coast, taking the Taylorville Rd exit to Blackball for purveyors of salami and a curiously named gastropub. Backtrack southwest, then follow Arnold Valley Rd south to Moana for an uncommonly scenic train station cafe, before returning west to the coast and finishing in Greymouth's marvellous brewery. This road trip unlocks the flavours of a lesser-trodden part of New Zealand, accompanied by views that will linger long in the memory.

01 The windswept west coast near Greymouth

02 Monteith's Greymouth brewery was refurbished in 2012

03 Monteith's brewery

01 DULCIE'S

No trip to NZ would be complete without a warm, paper-wrapped parcel of deep-fried goodies. In Hokitika, Dulcie's is the local favourite for fish 'n' chips. Order crumbed hoki, blue cod, squid rings or even sweet fritters. A scoop of chips is the classic accompaniment though kumara (sweet potato) chips are very moreish. It's barely five minutes' walk from Dulcie's to Sunset Point, a scenic place to unwrap the precious package and scoff down its contents
Gibson Quay, Hokitika; 03-756 8018; www.facebook.com/ dulciestakeaways; 11am-8.30pm

02 SWEET ALICE'S FUDGE KITCHEN

Just 10 minutes' walk east of Sunset Point, Hokitika's own Willy Wonka is preparing fudge in a little confectioner's shop on Tancred St. On a whim, Peter and Andrea Bowden took over the shop in April 2018 and gave it a zesty green-and-white makeover. Front and centre are the ever-changing varieties of fudge. The owners' favourites? Ginger for Andrea, and after-dinner mint for Pete, but there's plenty to munch through: classics like chocolate flavour and rich Russian fudge, two dairy-free options, and seasonally changing variations such as strawberry and passionfruit. Local suggestions add to the menu: you can thank an imaginative

customer for the Caramilk fudge (caramelised white chocolate). Mix it up with hard candies, made on a 200-year-old drop-candy machine, or ice cream in a homemade waffle cone. Then sit back and enjoy the sugar high.
27 Tancred St, Hokitika; 027 858 0802; 10.30am-4.30pm

03 FAT PIPI PIZZA

Slightly north of Sweet Alice's lies Fat Pipi Pizza, legendary for its generous seafood toppings and uncommon flavour combos. Smoked salmon and heaps of mussels top the seafood pizzas, and the veggie options are equally substantial (opt for 'The Punk', piled with caramelised pumpkin, feta and cashews).

03

'Find old-fashioned, handmade fudge, hard candies, nut brittles and real fruit ice creams, all made in store, in our slice of paradise.'

Shannon Bowden, Sweet Alice's

During the West Coast's whitebait season (September to mid-November), tiny fish create a sensation among Hokitika's diners and fishing enthusiasts. The most popular delicacy is a whitebait fritter, in which fish fry are bound into an omelette. Fat Pipi's riffs on this classic by using an eggy whitebait mixture to coat a garlicky, butter-laced base, with added tang from capers and lemon.
89 Revell St, Hokitika; 03-755 6373; noon-2.30pm Thu-Sun & 5-8pm nightly, hrs vary seasonally

04 FORMERLY THE BLACKBALL HILTON

On the second day, drive north along the coast to Greymouth, turning southeast for the road to Blackball. This town of 300-odd people was established by coal miners who arrived after a short-lived wave of migration during the gold rush.

The main landmark is Formerly The Blackball Hilton. Originally named The Dominion when it opened in 1910, the hotel went into decline in the '60s after the closure of the mine. Later, a certain hotel chain caught whiff of its name-change to The Blackball Hilton; a payout eventually followed, and 'Formerly the Blackball Hilton' was born.

Chef Scotty Newcombe ensures that the menu ventures beyond the usual pub mainstays, with dishes such as grilled venison brightened by a blueberry jus.

04 Preparing Blackball Salami

05 Exotic eats at the Wildfoods Festival

Classic, comforting desserts, such as sticky date pudding, are turned out to perfection.

'We always have some retro, nostalgic dishes on the menu,' explains Cynthia Robins, who, together with Phil Lemmon, owns the hotel. 'I love our chef's signature dish of pan-fried fish with a passion fruit beurre blanc sauce,' says Cynthia. 'Light but satisfying.'
26 Hart St, Blackball; 03-732 4705 www.blackballhilton.co.nz; noon-2.30pm & dinner from 6pm

05 BLACKBALL SALAMI CO

Only a few steps northwest of Formerly the Blackball Hilton is an unmissable stop for picnic supplies: Blackball Salami Co. 'We smoke the salamis for a period of time, slowly on a cold smoke,' explains Phillip Russ, half of the husband-and-wife team behind Blackball Salami Co. 'It brings out the flavour and enhances it.' If you're self-catering, take

away their smoked bacon or black pudding, made from an old Scottish recipe, or their award-winning 'white pudding' (a blood-free version of the grainy meat pud). Blackball Salami Co also make some of the classiest snags around, in flavours from paprika-laced Hungarian style to pork and pineapple. 'The beef and lamb sausages are my favourite,' adds Phillip.
11 Hilton St, Blackball; 03-732 411 www.blackballsalami.co.nz; 8am-4pm Mon-Fri, 9am-2pm Sat

06 STATIONHOUSE CAFE

A half-hour drive south from Blackball, along the Taylorville–Blackball Rd and Arnold Valley Rd, reaches sleepy Moana. At the north shore of Lake Brunner, Moana is a stop along New Zealand's scenic TranzAlpine train route, and it's a top spot for family holidays. Enjoy the serenity with excellent cafe grub – toasted sandwiches, crispy battered

fish, whitebait fritters (in season), carrot cake – at Stationhouse Cafe, opposite the train station.
40 Koe St, Moana; 03-738 0158; www.lakebrunner.net; 9.30am-late

07 MONTEITH'S BREWERY

Return to Greymouth, a 35-minute drive northwest, to finish at sleek Monteith's. Brewing beers since 1868, Monteith's offers tours of the facilities, affording thirsty visitors a glimpse of its polished vats, along with lungfuls of hoppy air and tastings of the finished products. After learning about brewing techniques and working up a thirst, hang around in the lively bar. Snacks such as beer-battered fries and aioli, cider-spiked saucy ribs, and buttermilk chicken burgers are designed to pair beautifully with the award-winning craft beers.
60 Herbert St, Greymouth; 03-768 4149; www.thebrewery.co.nz; 11am-9pm

WHERE TO STAY

**DRIFTING SANDS,
HOKITIKA**

This friendly B&B has talk-your-ear-off hosts, elegantly weathered furniture and a restful lounge with fireplace. Mornings are spent enjoying jams and freshly baked bread, while evenings pass all too quickly in the seaside hammock.
www.driftingsands.nz

**GLOBAL VILLAGE,
GREYMOUTH**

A cheap and colourful hostel in Greymouth with eclectic decor (Persian-style rugs, zebra print bed spreads) and free-to-hire fishing rods and kayaks.
www.bbh.co.nz

WHAT TO DO

**THE OLD GHOST ROAD
TRAIL**

There's a pulse-racing range of activities on the West Coast, from rafting and sea kayaking to hikes and horse trekking. But The Old Ghost Road Trail combines gold-mining history with high-energy exertions. An 85km

Ø5

(53 miles) backcountry cycling adventure rated Grade 4 (read: thighs of steel), the rewards are spellbinding mountain panoramas and glimpses of 19th-century history.
*www.oldghostroad.
org.nz*

CELEBRATIONS

WILDFOODS FESTIVAL

Are those insect legs between your teeth? The region's wackiest food event is Hokitika's inimitable Wildfoods Festival. Daredevil gastronomy won it fame (beetle larvae, deep-

fried grasshoppers...) but Wildfoods is also adored for its feral fashions. If you prefer your food a little less, well, wriggly, there are also New Zealand classics such as whitebait patties, venison, and hokey pokey ice cream.
www.wildfoods.co.nz

GET THERE
Nelson's airport is located 5km (3 miles) outside of town, and is served by flights from New Zealand's major cities. It's also reached by long-distance bus and inter-island ferries linking the two major islands. If you don't have a car, hiring a bicycle is a great way to explore the region.

01

[Nelson]

HOP ON THE CRAFT BEER TRAIL IN NELSON

A must-visit for craft beer lovers, arty and attractive Nelson also offers some of NZ's best weather and coastal scenery to go with wineries and hip city diners.

At the top of New Zealand's South Island, overlooking Tasman Bay, is the laidback town of Nelson. It's one of NZ's most liveable cities, with a generally sunny climate to enjoy its outdoor attractions, along with a thriving arts scene and culinary offerings. Beyond the abundance of boutique wineries on its doorstep, Nelson is famous as New Zealand's craft-brewing capital. As the country's main hop growing region, here you'll find more independent, family-owned microbreweries per head than anywhere else in New Zealand. And that's not even taking the pubs and bars specialising in craft ales into account.

The first step for beer lovers is to check out Nelson Craft Brewing (www.craftbrewingcapital.co.nz), a super-helpful resource listing local breweries and craft beer bars. Here you can download a copy of the Nelson Craft Beer Trail map, a boozy treasure hunt that stretches 120km (75 miles) from the town of Nelson up along coastline as far as Motueka on

the Golden Bay. A good idea is to hire a bike to pedal and explore the region's dozen or so breweries, along with stops at pubs offering house-brewed ales. Nelson Cycle Hire & Tours (www.nelsoncyclehire. co.nz) are good for beer-themed tours or bike hire.

And while you've got that bike, the Great Taste Trail (www.heartofbiking.org.nz/tasmans-great-taste-trail) will lead along another wonderful route, this one past wineries, orchards, cafes and restaurants (as well as the breweries), in between passing Nelson's coastal and country landscapes. The most popular leg runs from Nelson to Kaiteriteri, via the Waimea Plains where you'll pass Nelson's wineries (www.winenelson. co.nz), with restaurants and cellar doors offering tastings of pinot noir and chardonnay.

In Nelson itself you'll find a good variation of places to eat, from sampling local produce at the farmers' markets and great coffee at lively cafes to enjoying fresh seafood and street food in its restaurants.

01 Downtown in easy-going Nelson

02 The Free House pub in Nelson

03 Nelson Lakes National Park, south of the town

04 Punchy flavours and a sleek interior at Harry's Hawker House

01 NELSONS FARMERS MARKET

Join the locals each Wednesday to wander Nelson's farmers' market, where food growers and artisanal producers set up stalls to sell seasonal, organic goods and street food. Grab a locally roasted coffee, and a croxinha (Brazilian croquettes) snack, before stocking up your picnic hamper with small-batch cheeses, freshly baked sourdough, organic fruit and nuts, and a stop at the vegan 'butcher' for meat-free bacon, steaks and snags.

Kirby Lane 105 Bridge St; 022 010 2776; www.nelsonfarmersmarket. org.nz; 8.30am-1.30pm Wed

02 FREE HOUSE PUB

Set in a beautiful converted city church, this temple for hop heads, offers 11 taps of an ever-changing selection of NZ craft beers. There's always something interesting to try, covering all palates and styles, along with three hand pulls for cask ales. Local ciders and wines are also well represented, and it has an enticing little beer garden with a caravan doing hand-cut hot chips – the perfect accompaniment for enjoying a cold frothie in the sun!

95 Collingwood St; 03-548 9391; www.freehouse.co.nz; 3-10.30pm Mon-Thu, to midnight Fri, noon-midnight Sat, noon-10.30pm Sun

03 SPRIG & FERN

Established by seasoned brewer Tracey Banner, known as the 'Mother of New Zealand Brewing', Sprig & Fern's craft brewery is a 15-minute drive from town in Richmond, but they've opened up a half dozen taverns across the Nelson-Tasman region to enjoy its ales. The city brewhouse here has an impressive 18 of its beers on tap, including one-off releases, to be enjoyed on the outdoor picnic table, along with $10 lunch specials, local wines and live music.

280 Hardy St; 03-548 1154; www.sprigandfern.co.nz; 11am-midnight

Take a coastal trip up to Motueka where you'll find a continuation of Nelson's love affair with hops and good food.

04 URBAN EATERY

Modern and vibrant, this fun-lovin' bistro is one of Nelson's most popular spots for a feed, with an appealing menu of kaimoana (seafood) starters and street food dishes that span the globe. Its fresh oysters are a must, either slurped down raw, toasted with wakame butter or a hard-to-resist tempura temptation. Next, order a few dishes such as five-spice wontons, sticky Korean lamb shoulder, Sichuan-spiced kung pao popcorn chicken, or maybe the smoked venison, all washed down with an excellent choice of NZ craft beers and local wines
278 Hardy St; 03-546 7861; www. urbaneatery.co.nz; 4pm-late Mon, 11am-late Tue-Sat

05 HARRYS HAWKER HOUSE

This modern, dark-lit diner, where it's all about shared plates of sublime Asian hawker cuisine, is one of the hottest seats in town. Treat yourself to a fragrant Southeast Asian–inspired cocktail while snacking on furikake-spiced edamame (boiled soybeans), before deciding between rendang beef cheek rolls, red-curry fish cakes or spiced pork momos. Move on to the more sizeable Massaman lamb shoulder, with a side of papaya salad, dousing that fire in your mouth with a cold pint of NZ craft beer or crisp local white. Bliss.
296 Trafalgar St; 03-539 0905; www.hawkerhouse.co.nz; 3pm-late Tue-Thu, from noon Fri-Sun

05 Sunset at on the Kumaras hike in Motueka

06 Hauling in Nelson's hop harvest

05 MAMA COD

An attractive heritage building is a classy space for this atmospheric reincarnation of the former Cod & Lobster Brasserie where – despite some tasty vegetarian options – seafood is the undisputed king. Its lobster roll is a hard one to pass up on, as is the blue cod fish and chips, but options of whole baked lemon sole or ginger-soy king salmon will make your choice difficult. Vegetarians may be tempted by jackfruit tacos and jerk-spiced halloumi. And the drinks list is something else, with a colossal choice of gins plus original cocktails, local wines and craft beers.
300 Trafalgar St; 03-546 4300; https://www.facebook.com/ mamacodnelson/; 11am-11pm Tue-Sun

06 MCCASHIN'S BREWERY

This family-owned microbrewery is a pioneer in New Zealand's craft beer scene and kicked things off way back in the 1980s, taking on the big boys at their own game. Its main brewery is in Stoke, a 15-minute drive south of Nelson's centre, where you can stop by the bar and restaurant to sample their beers and ciders as a tasting paddle or by the glass, pint or jug. They also do a non-alcoholic ginger beer, and offer craft spirits distilled by Nelson's Liquid Alchemy. The menu offers a pleasing beer-friendly choice from poutine and beef brisket cheeseburgers to fish and chips battered in McCashin beer. On Wednesday, Thursday and Friday they run 45-minutes tours ($25) of the brewery, which includes tastings of both its beer and ciders that are produced on-site.
660 Main Rd, Stoke; 03-547 0329; www.mkb.co.nz; 7am-4.30pm Mon-Wed, to 9.30pm Thu-Sat, 9am-4.30pm Sun

07 T.O.A.D HALL

Leave time for the 45km (28 mile) coastal trip up to Motueka where you'll find a continuation of Nelson's love affair with hops and good food. One fine example is T.O.A.D Hall, not only for its homemade pies and ice-creamery, but for its collaboration with Townshend Brewery who've moved in and brought along a taproom with them. All the beers are made using local ingredients, and there are eight taps to get through its range of ales – including an award-winning American amber ale.

In summer they open for dinner on weekends, when there are live bands and woodfired pizzas. All other times, T.O.A.D Hall does great breakfasts, seafood chowder and an ace slow-cooked roast lamb burger with mint jelly and tomato salsa
502 High St, Motueka; 03-528 6456; www.toadhallmotueka. co.nz; 8am-5pm Sun-Thu, to 10pm Fri & Sat

WHERE TO STAY

WARWICK HOUSE

One of Nelson's more unique places to stay is this monumental 1854 heritage hotel within a Victorian Gothic Revivalist–style mansion that resembles a castle. The suites and rooms are elegantly furnished, with high ceilings, claw–foot baths and views over the city and bay. Breakfast is served in its beautiful renovated grand ballroom, enjoyed to the accompaniment of classical music.
www.warwickhouse.co.nz

WHAT TO DO

HOP AND BEER MUSEUM

As the craft beer capital of New Zealand, it seems appropriate there would be a museum dedicated to Nelson's brewing history, which dates back to 1843. Located within a precinct of Victorian-era heritage buildings in Founders Heritage Park, the museum tells the story of beer making in Nelson, including its hop growing industry, beer production and a replica

of a hop kiln and early examples of brewing equipment.
www.founderspark.co.nz

CELEBRATIONS

MARCHFEST

The month of March is dedicated to Nelson's craft beer producers, most who brew one-off ales specifically for the occasion. Taking place in Founders Park, some 15 microbreweries are represented, giving you a good insight to the local beer scene. It's not just all hops, however, with wines and ciders from the Nelson Tasman area also featured, along with local food, a line-up of indie bands and plenty of festivities.
www.marchfest.com

INDEX

First Edition
Published in November 2020 by Lonely Planet Global Limited
CRN 54153
www.lonelyplanet.com
ISBN 978 1 8386 9102 8
© Lonely Planet 2020
Printed in China
10 9 8 7 6 5 4 3 2 1

Managing Director Piers Pickard
Associate Publisher Robin Barton
Commissioning Editor Kate Morgan
Art Direction Daniel Di Paolo
Layout design Daniel Di Paolo, Jo Dovey
Indexer Polly Thomas
Cartographer Wayne Murphy
Image Research Lauren Marchant, Ceri James
Print Production Nigel Longuet
Cover images: Courtesy of Sage at Paroa Bay; Jess Kearney / Harvest Newrybar; Mindil;
Yarri Restaurant & Bar; Man O' War; Grandvewe Cheese; Free To Feed

Authors: Anita Isalska, Trent Holden, Kate Morgan, Monique Perrin, Robin Barton, Sarah Reid,
Sofia Levin, Emily McAuliffe, Chris Zeiher, Brett Atkinson, George Dunford, Tasmin Waby, Andrew Bain,
Ben Groundwater, Lorna Parkes, Charles Rawlings-Way

Lonely Planet offices

IRELAND Digital Depot, Roe Lane (off Thomas St), Digital Hub, Dublin 8, D08 TCV4

USA 230 Franklin Road, Building 2B, Franklin, TN 37064 T: 615-988-9713

STAY IN TOUCH lonelyplanet.com/contact

Paper in this book is certified against the
Forest Stewardship Council™ standards.
FSC™ promotes environmentally responsible,
socially beneficial and economically viable
management of the world's forests.